Lacanian Psychoanalysis

Jacques Lacan's impact upon the theory and practice of psychoanalysis worldwide cannot be underestimated. *Lacanian Psychoanalysis* looks at current debates surrounding Lacanian practice and explores its place within historical, social and political contexts.

The book argues that Lacan's elaboration of psychoanalytic theory is grounded in clinical practice and needs to be defined in relation to four main traditions: psychiatry, psychology, psychotherapy and spirituality.

As such topics of discussion include:

- the intersection between psychoanalysis and social transformation
- a new way through deadlocks of current Lacanian debate
- a new approach to 'clinical structures' of neurosis, perversion and psychosis

Lacanian Psychoanalysis draws on Lacan's work to shed light on issues relevant to current therapeutic practice and as such it will be of great interest to students, trainees and practitioners of psychoanalysis, psychotherapy, counselling and other domains of personal and social change.

Ian Parker is Professor of Psychology in the Department of Psychology at Manchester Metropolitan University (MMU). He was co-founder in 1991, and is currently co-director of the Discourse Unit at MMU. He is also a practising psychoanalyst in Manchester.

Advancing Theory in Therapy
Series Editor: Keith Tudor

Most books covering individual therapeutic approaches are aimed at the trainee/student market. This series, however, is concerned with *advanced* and *advancing* theory, offering the reader comparative and comparable coverage of a number of therapeutic approaches.

Aimed at professionals and postgraduates, *Advancing Theory in Therapy* will cover an impressive range of theories. With full reference to case studies throughout, each title will

- present cutting-edge research findings
- locate each theory and its application within its cultural context
- develop a critical view of theory and practice.

Titles in the series

Body Psychotherapy
Edited by Tree Staunton

Transactional Analysis: A Relational Perspective
Helena Hargaden and Charlotte Sills

Adlerian Psychotherapy: An Advanced Approach to Individual Psychology
Ursula E. Oberst and Alan E. Stewart

Rational Emotive Behaviour Therapy: Theoretical Developments
Edited by Windy Dryden

Co-Counselling: The Theory and Practice of Re-evaluation Counselling
Katie Kauffman and Caroline New

Analytical Psychology
Edited by Joe Cambray and Linda Carter

Person-Centered Therapy: A Clinical Philosophy
Keith Tudor and Mike Worrall

Psychodrama: Advances in Theory and Practice
Edited by Clark Baim, Jorge Burmeister and Manuela Maciel

Neurolinguistic Psychotherapy: A Postmodern Perspective
Lisa Wake

Constructivist Psychotherapy: A Narrative Hermeneutic Approach
Gabriele Chiari and Maria Laura Nuzzo

Lacanian Psychoanalysis
Ian Parker

Lacanian Psychoanalysis

Revolutions in subjectivity

Ian Parker

LONDON AND NEW YORK

First published 2011 by Routledge
27 Church Road, Hove, East Sussex BN3 2FA

Simultaneously published in the USA and Canada
by Routledge
270 Madison Avenue, New York, NY 10016

Routledge is an imprint of the Taylor & Francis Group, an Informa business

© 2011 Ian Parker

Typeset in Times by Garfield Morgan, Swansea, West Glamorgan
Printed and bound in Great Britain by TJ International Ltd, Padstow, Cornwall
Paperback cover design by Sandra Heath

All rights reserved. No part of this book may be reprinted or reproduced or utilised in any form or by any electronic, mechanical, or other means, now known or hereafter invented, including photocopying and recording, or in any information storage or retrieval system, without permission in writing from the publishers.

This publication has been produced with paper manufactured to strict environmental standards and with pulp derived from sustainable forests.

British Library Cataloguing in Publication Data
A catalogue record for this book is available from the British Library

Library of Congress Cataloging in Publication Data
Parker, Ian, 1956–
   Lacanian psychoanalysis : revolutions in subjectivity / Ian Parker. – 1st ed.
     p. cm.
   Includes bibliographical references.
   ISBN: 978-0-415-45542-8 (hbk.) – ISBN: 978-0-415-45543-5 (pbk.)
1. Psychoanalysis. 2. Lacan, Jacques, 1901–1981. I. Title.
   BF173 .P28525
   150.19'5092–dc22
                                                                    2010008767

ISBN: 978-0-415-45542-8 (hbk)
ISBN: 978-0-415-45543-5 (pbk)

Contents

Series preface vii
Acknowledgements ix

Introduction 1

1 **Framing analysis** 15
   Reductions 15
   Transmission 30
   Replications 37

2 **Psychiatrising speech** 39
   Seductions 39
   Insemination 51
   Cuts 61

3 **Psychoanalytic psychology** 63
   Education 63
   Identity 74
   Mentalisation 82

4 **Distributed selves** 84
   Allocation 84
   Mindfulness 96
   Competition 105

5 **Psychotherapeutic capital** 107
   Representation 107
   Immediacy 115
   Conjunctions 127

6 Reflexive recuperation 128
Distance 128
Affect 137
Disjunctions 148

7 Mapping lack in the spirit 150
Alienation 150
Separation 166
Secularisation 173

8 A clinic in the real 176
Antagonisms 176
Relations 186
Conclusions 197

References 200
Author index 226
Subject index 231

Series preface

This series focuses on advanced and advancing theory in psychotherapy. Its aims are: to present theory and practice within a specific theoretical orientation or approach at an advanced, postgraduate level; to advance theory by presenting and evaluating new ideas and their relation to the particular approach; to locate the orientation and its psychotherapeutic applications within cultural contexts, both historically in terms of the origins of the approach, and contemporarily in terms of current debates about philosophy, theory, society and therapy; and, finally, to present and develop a critical view of theory and practice, especially in the context of debates about power, organisation and the increasing professionalisation of therapy.

Ian Parker is a well-known and well-respected author in the field of psychology and psychotherapy. He is an exponent of discursive analysis, discourse, Marxist psychology, and psychoanalysis, and, in particular, Lacanian psychoanalysis – and, as such, I am delighted to have engaged him to write a volume in this series. I met Ian some years ago at an Annual General Meeting of the United Kingdom Council of Psychotherapy at which, as a delegate from a person-centred education and training institute, I found myself voting along the same lines as Ian and a number of other psychoanalytic psychotherapists. When, a while later, I met Ian to discuss this project, we discovered that we may have met many years earlier on a demonstration or a picket line, and, albeit with different political analyses, again on the same side of the line. This history is no accident: Ian is highly political, and he combines this not only with a fine intellect, but also with the great virtue of being a clear and imaginative writer.

To this volume Ian brings not only his extensive knowledge of the subject but also, as we might expect from someone who is a critical thinker, a founder of a Discourse Unit (at Manchester Metropolitan University), and the author of a number of critical texts, a critical, discursive discourse, and a deconstructive analysis of psychoanalysis, psychotherapy, and, more broadly, the 'psy professions'. Of all the volumes in the series, this, to date, is the one that most articulates the aim of the series that is concerned with context, power, organisation, and professsionalisation – and I thank the author for his attention to this. Around a central question, or what Ian refers to in his Introduction as a riddle, that of the connection between change in the clinic and political change, he circles around the key elements of clinical practice, conceptual innovation, and their political implications and, in doing so weaves in the content of the book. This encompasses a theoretical articulation of the historical constitution of Lacanian clinical practice; psychoanalysis and psychiatry; ethics, diagnosis, and pathology; psychology and psychoanalysis; gender; psychoanalysis and psychotherapy; speech; training; cultural-spiritual contexts; the relationship – and disjunction – between clinical and political change; and much, much more. Ian's constant circling and revolving around the subject – and subjectivity – creates a complex tapestry of text which challenges not only linear thinking and reading, but also the reader, practitioner, and theoretician. Lacanian psychoanalysis has the reputation of being somewhat obscure, due at least in part to Lacan's own, sometimes deliberately, obscure prose. As a counterpoint to this, and without losing the complexity of Lacanian psychoanalysis and thinking, Ian brings great clarity to Lacan, Lacanian psychoanalysis and thinking, to his subject, and to this book.

Keith Tudor

Acknowledgements

I have bothered many people – Lacanians, non-Lacanians, anti-Lacanians – with the question that riddles this book: what is the connection between change in the clinic and political change? It is impossible to remember them all, but I would like to thank for many hours of fruitful conversation in our actual and virtual universes about these issues, and in some cases for reading manuscript drafts, Erica Burman, Christian Ingo Lenz Dunker, Nadir Lara Junior, Manuel Llorens, Ilana Mountian, David Pavón Cuéllar, Simona Revelli and Keith Tudor.

Introduction

This book is about the clinical practice of psychoanalysis as catalyst of personal change and its intersection with social change. Psychoanalysis contains resources aplenty to enable us to produce a theoretical articulation of the historical constitution of its own practice, and I seize the opportunity Jacques Lacan offers to examine the implications for the place of the clinic as such. This introduction sets out some of the ground for that theoretical articulation; it includes a brief account of what we might expect to find in a Lacanian psychoanalytic session, an extended metaphor for Lacan's divinely-comedic vision of the core of psychoanalysis, and then a review of some assumptions that we will need to make before we really get going on the journey into the book.

Lacan's elaboration of psychoanalytic theory was grounded in its practice and followed the revolutionary dynamic of Freudian analysis, clarifying and complicating it and also bringing alive the radical political ambitions of the early psychoanalytic movement. Each of the key elements – clinical practice, conceptual innovation, political implications – is worked through in this book. I circle around the same issues from different vantage points, the only way to elaborate an argument concerning a form of psychoanalysis so suspicious of linear thought. The book provides an explication and defence of Lacanian psychoanalysis through articulation of it with political-economic conditions in which it became possible, and through elaboration of a new way through some of the deadlocks of current Lacanian debate.

Lacanian psychoanalysis maintains a distinctive position in relation to other forms of therapeutic enquiry for it marks a 'return' to Freud which also enables an original development of psychoanalysis today. The designation 'Lacanian psychoanalysis' is one that is not favoured by many of its practitioners, even while they well know that they must answer to this understanding of them as a particular group among psychoanalysts. At the same time, the Lacanian corpus offers points of connection and dialogue with other forms of relational therapeutic enquiry, for Lacan's return to Freudian psychoanalysis was characterised by his use of conceptual and cultural resources that had developed alongside the psychoanalytic tradition.

Practical and theoretical aspects of Lacanian psychoanalysis are intertwined, but we need to conceptualise these aspects as being dialectically interrelated rather than smoothly meshed together. It would be tempting, but misleading, to treat the practice as direct application of theory, or to treat the theory as arising directly from its practice. Already we would thereby be trapped in some form of a correspondence between words and things, between representations of activity and the activity itself, a correspondence that Lacan rejects. Why?

Let us approach this question by starting with clinical practice as such, which is what this book about theoretical advances is concerned with. In this way we might arrive at one answer to the deceptively simple question, what is psychoanalysis?

The clinic of presence and absence

If one were to spy on a clinical session of Lacanian psychoanalysis, one might not immediately notice any difference between this form of psychoanalysis and much psychoanalytic therapy. We might easily guess which one is the analyst, the one sitting in a chair somewhere behind and out of sight of the 'analysand' who is gazing ahead into space, at the wall, out of the window, or into the backs of their eyelids as they ramble on in an attempt to follow what Freud called the 'fundamental technical rule' of psychoanalysis, free association. We will hear something of the tension between the analysand's attempt to provide a clear account and their attempt to follow a rule that gives to their speech a rather meandering disconnected quality. It might not be easy to make sense of what the analysand is saying, and the analyst does not appear to be trying very hard to clarify it.

The analyst is not necessarily lounging in a big leather chair smoking a cigar and idly scratching some notes as the other speaks to them, and another more important disconcerting feature, perhaps, is that the analysand may not be reclining on a heavily-draped be-cushioned couch. This apparatus has been sedimented in psychoanalytic culture. There have been attempts to define and regulate psychoanalysis in some parts of the world, and then what a 'couch' should be became an issue; in Brazil, for example, one of the evangelical churches noticed that there was a market niche for this kind of therapy and proposed legislation to regulate psychoanalysis which stipulated the size and dimensions of this equipment. In Britain there was once debate about how often cushion-covers should be changed, and suggestion that servants handle this hygienic concern.

Back to our session. The analysand may be sitting on a chair, perhaps a low chair, which faces away from the analyst. This does look odd, more so if the session takes place in a medical institution, with the patient – perhaps a more accurate term than analysand there – lying on a bare bed. In Japan there was an early debate in the history of psychoanalysis over the difference that might be engineered if the analysand were sitting in a chair faced away from the analyst, on a low sofa or on a couch as such, and much was made of the difference between these types of furniture. In India in the early days of the practice, analysands were seated in deckchairs, but not much was made of the difference between this and the couch, or rather cheap-looking bare foam blocks which seem to be à la mode in Scandinavia.

What is most important is that the analysand is speaking, but not speaking directly to another person, attempting, as in everyday conversation, to conform to the cues their audience gives about what is relevant. Psychoanalysis as a 'talking cure' is concerned with what happens when we put things into words or find it difficult to do so, and the search for a visible reaction on the face, non-verbal cues or tell-tale changes in posture of another serves as a convenient distraction from speech as such. The analysand's free association to whatever comes to mind, however irrelevant, ridiculous or unpleasant, will give to the apparent dialogue between analyst and analysand a rather strange quality, and all the more so because the analyst is not really engaging in the exchange. The analysand is producing a monologue which does appear, from time to time, to be directed to the analyst, and it is at these moments that there is the most earnest attempt to make sense; but the analyst does not say much in reply, indeed they do not often appear to be replying at all.

There are two distinctive features of Lacanian psychoanalysis we will notice now if we home in on the speech. The first is that the questions or comments made by the analyst are rather enigmatic. They seize on elements of the analysand's monologue, drawing attention to contradictions and slips – nothing so strange about that, but they do not spell out what the hidden meaning is. Most striking for those schooled to notice transference as repetition of childhood relationships, our Lacanian analyst does not spell out how the analysand is relating to them as if they are a significant other figure from the past. We cannot learn more here about the past of the analysand by attending to what the analyst says about it; it does not seem to be made present in the room as something excavated, turned over, redescribed.

In this we have a first crucial feature of Lacanian psychoanalysis: there does not seem to be interpretation of the transference; there is absence rather than the presence of something. A general analytic point is that what we see and hear in the session is organised around *absences* of one kind or another, not things that are immediately evident. There are important consequences for how we are to understand 'evidence' in psychoanalysis, and Lacanian psychoanalysis is not suited to an 'evidence-based' evaluation of how it operates. Psychoanalysis revolves around absences in speech, and Lacanian psychoanalysis is theoretically attuned to the importance of the analyst refusing to fill in those absences with stuff that is meaningful to an observer.

The second distinctive feature might come as a shock, and has been disturbing to other forms of psychotherapy concerned with the importance of 'boundaries' in analytic settings. We are unlikely to observe the analyst reaching across to the analysand and caressing them, for those kinds of boundary are as important to Lacanians as to any other kind of psychoanalyst. The rationale, however, is not that it is 'immoral' for the professional to have sex with someone they have taken into their charge *loco parentis* – and the danger with that moral frame is precisely that it tends to infantilise the patient – but rather that to engage in physical contact of such a kind breaks the psychoanalytic contract; it sabotages the possibility of psychoanalysis taking place. If the task is to find a way to speak, including to speak of fantasy, and to work out what the limits of that speech are – how and why there are some points where free association must fail and what this failure reveals about the nature of fantasy for a particular analysand – then to short-circuit the talking cure with a sensual touch is to destroy psychoanalysis.

The real boundary shock comes when the session ends, ends sooner than we expect or runs on longer than we anticipated, and it ends on an indeterminate note, one that might lead us to wonder what on earth is going on. Perhaps this ending does actually correspond to the beat of the clock, but it is more likely to strike at something less. The parameters for this Lacanian practice of 'variable length' sessions vary, and we describe them as 'variable' rather than 'short' because they are not necessarily shorter than any other therapy session. Again, we are confronted with an absence, something is ended without warning instead of something said to round the session off, to summarise and explain what might be meant by it. An absence of this kind poses a question for us, and for sure it poses a question to the analysand; it is a break, a 'cut' in the narrative which operates as a kind of interpretation and provokes a puzzling between sessions, perhaps even a resumption of issues that have been left open when the next session starts.

We will not easily detect some of the significant differences between Lacanian psychoanalysis and other varieties of analysis from this eavesdropping because we will not know from this session how the analysand arrived here on the couch. And we do not know from this little snapshot how it will end. I will have to tell you how it might have begun and what might happen next. You may have guessed already that the analysand has not been given a programme of work for the sessions, and because they have not been told what to do and exactly what to expect they have to make it up as they go along. That is what they are doing here, and that is how the particularity of each analysand as subject, appearing to themselves as incomplete subject in their speech, manifests itself in the session.

Had we observed an early session we would most likely have seen the two speaking face to face, and during that time the analyst would be anticipating how the analysand would take to speaking into thin air. It is difficult to speak to someone who is not directly present, who does not respond, and this thin air can be a little too insubstantial for some. Those who are invited to take that step to turn around upon themselves, to listen to themselves speak to an absence that they fill in and empty out and fill in again as they attempt to free associate, may do so in such a way as to turn in a little too much or to construct someone other against whom they rail in their speech.

The analyst has a name and a strategy for these different possibilities and 'directs the treatment' accordingly. Readers ahead of the game could conclude that those who find the couch too disturbing are called 'psychotic', while those who tend to turn in on themselves and blot out the other are 'obsessional neurotic', in contrast to those who insist on speaking directly to another they can identify and accuse, those who are 'hysteric'. (A fourth category of subject is assumed not to want analysis and causes the analyst anxiety when they do appear, and the shorthand and occasionally derogatory term for those characters bracketed out from psychoanalysis as such, defining its limits, is 'pervert', a hangover term from psychiatric classification systems.) The analytic judgement being made here we call 'diagnosis' of clinical structure, but the best practice of Lacanian psychoanalysis does not pretend that this 'structure' pertains to the mind of their analysand, and this book provides a theoretical elaboration of best practice in which diagnosis is seen as a function of historical and institutional processes. Anyway, as a first base starting point that all Lacanians will agree on, the cautious exploration in the 'preliminary sessions' does not ever lead to the diagnosis, if that is what it is, being handed to the analysand as a label which then educates them as to how they should speak or understand themselves.

Just as the pace of each session is rather unpredictable and unexpected – you were surprised when this session ended without warning and it turned out to be deliberately inconclusive – so is the pace of analysis. There are no targets or reviews of progress other than those covertly set by the analysand, and some analysands are more intent on this than others (and some analysts are more intent on classifying those analysands as obsessional than others), and there is usually no anticipation of breaks in the analysis that presume that the analysand should respond. They will respond in one way or another, of that we can be sure, but when they respond is a matter for them. And how the analysis itself will end is a matter for them too; the analysand will take that step, they will break from the analysis, and then perhaps the analyst will be nearly as surprised as they are.

Freud once remarked that there is no psychoanalytic 'cure', and every analysis ends badly, incomplete. This annoys those who assume that therapy should be based on 'evidence', and it frustrates those who want psychoanalysis to be scientific. It is not rocket science, all this; it is not science at all, though it does work upon the kind of subject who has bought into a scientific worldview, addressing what is cut out from that kind of subject for them to be able to imagine that they should be scientific. The unsatisfying ending of an analysis often annoys those who take part, but they get over it, and when they look back they may discover that it provoked a peculiar revelation, a revolution that opens up a new space for them as subjects. This is what the best therapy of any kind can hope for, and we cannot promise more than this. There are other practices of self-exploration and self-transformation that engage people in revolutionary change outside the clinic which I advert to in the course of this book – Marxism and feminism for instance – and Lacanian psychoanalysis in revolutionary key cannot substitute for those processes of social change. Lacanian psychoanalysis can facilitate a connection with those political processes, a connection that can only be maintained if we maintain a sharp theoretical and practical *disjunction* between what happens in the clinic and what happens in the outside world.

So, what we learn from this description of the session, a description which must flesh out what we cannot see with a theoretical elaboration of what is going on, is that the conceptual architecture of Lacanian psychoanalysis does not manifest itself directly in the practice, cannot be read off from it. The analyst does not inject their theory of what goes on into the analysis, but they need theory to map what might happen. It is when they try to abandon theory altogether that they end up applying some variety of commonsense that closes things down, and closes down the particular theoretical elaboration that the analysand engages in as they make each analysis into one which will take shape significant only for them.

One line to the core

One too-convenient way of marginalising psychoanalysis as a clinical practice is to consign it to the depths of introspective self-reflection. It is thereby turned into an essentially 'private' activity and sealed off from the 'public' sphere where cultural and political coordinates of our lives can be contested and transformed. This marginalisation of psychoanalysis operates in fields of academic research that appeal to the clinic as hidden core, guarantee for certain modes of interpretation. Defensive manoeuvres then serve to protect the supposed theoretical autonomy of psychoanalytic investigation outside the clinic, and lessons from actual psychoanalysis are reduced to being little moral narratives. Psychoanalytic case studies function as powerful anecdotes, the best thoroughly fictionalised to protect the identity of analysands while making theoretical points. But in such appeal to telling 'cases' we risk shifting gear from attending to the particularity of the subject – an ethical question in Lacanian psychoanalysis – to describing how people should talk. It is for this reason that I do not give 'examples' of how you should or should not speak as analyst or analysand in this book, and discussion of ethics as we go along will make clear why this is problematic, why it would turn psychoanalysis into something else.

This second section of the introduction is where you can locate yourself as reader of the book. I do not assume that you are Lacanian, quite possibly you are not, but if you do want some tendentious Lacanian guiderails for where we are going next you might find it helpful to think of the first section as a moment of our initial glance at psychoanalysis, this second section as the time for comprehending what psychoanalysis is, and the third section as the moment for concluding what you could make of the book.

One might think of our journey to the core of psychoanalysis as proceeding from an outer layer of pop psychology which includes psychoanalytic ideas: of the unconscious, the meaning of dreams and slips of the tongue, defence mechanisms and, for those who have bought into psychoanalytic versions of this pop psychology, 'transference', the idea that their relationships repeat patterns of relationships with significant others earlier in their lives. This notion of 'transference' is potent outside the clinic where those in thrall to psychoanalysis draw attention to it all the time. This outer layer of pervasive sticky ideology is a kind of limbo-land, idiotic everyday life bloated by media makeover and self-help nostrums with an insidious message that we should be content with our lot smuggled in along the way.

Here circulates a version of psychoanalysis purified of any radical critique, pure ideology hostile to theory, the accumulated dross of cultural memory of what life is under capitalism. Those who make a demand for analysis are pretty sick of this kind of life too, and they have just started to break from it. Lacanian psychoanalysts refuse to adapt people to society precisely because they are profoundly suspicious of the forms of happiness cultivated in this deceptive 'reality'.

Those who take a more active role in pop-psychological advice for accepting the world as it is and fitting in with it will perhaps also inhabit a second layer we must also travel through. This second layer is today informed by banalised versions of programmes of mental and moral improvement designed to get people back to work and ensure that they are docile. The first and second layer include in different measure doses of psychotherapy and psychology. Pop-spirituality, both that which demands conformity and that which incites discontent, is stirred in to offer consolation or the promise of escape. Pharmacological remedies are also increasingly at hand here as well, and old psychiatry even finds its place in these first two layers of our hellish world, but approaches pushed by an increasing number of governmental and non-governmental agencies take a more explicitly psychological approach to this endeavour to be 'happy'.

There are some historical peculiarities about this neat and tidy programme for adapting people. Although its practitioners studiously avoid sexuality, or reduce it to a set of techniques that elicit and contain sex, this programme has its roots in versions of psychoanalysis abbreviated and made compatible with a quasi-medical, instrumental agenda for encouraging emotional literacy in the world as it is now, not as it might be. In this, it is also compatible with the moral agenda of those who would like our limited questioning and affirmation of the world to also have a spiritual aspect to it. This is a hygienic world but with a little kick of enjoyment, a surreptitiously lustful second layer, comforting and pacifying us all the more efficiently.

Those who have signed up to psychological self-help programmes, tempted out from the second layer and gluttonous for something more, often conclude that 'cognitive behavioural' treatments are a little too shallow for them. This leads them closer, just a step closer, to a third layer we will be stepping carefully through, which comprises 'humanistic' and self-actualising varieties of counselling and psychotherapy. Here, it is not enough to borrow from pop-psychology, and those involved have usually been drawn into it through various pyramid-selling schemes in which they have become clients and then trained to become counsellors or psychotherapists or, why not, psychoanalysts peddling their ideas to others. This means that they are at one moment more deeply enmeshed in the ideological stuff of this taken-for-granted reality, but at the next questioning it; it bothers them and they do want to shake it up a bit. Dear reader, you are at least here, but you have probably already gone a little further on the journey down into the core because you thirst for more.

We are starting now to move into more hard-core territory of this upper-hell of pop-psychiatric, psychological, psychotherapeutic, spiritual and quasi-psychoanalytic ideology, encountering those who have a much tighter grip on the ideas and are keen to universalise them. This is the way of those who accumulate and hoard motifs condensed in descriptions of 'archetypes', perhaps, and imagine that there are deeper layers of the self that they must detect anywhere and everywhere. Acolytes who sign up to some kind of quasi-spiritual depth psychology are sometimes the worst of those spendthrift with psychological advice for others, but there are enough others who assume a quasi-psychoanalytic form in ideas about energies and auras and suchlike. We are here in the wackier realms of contemporary commonsense, on the edge of it while still recognisably part of it. Our journey takes us through these layers into the outer limits of pop-psychology, to those at the limits; still operating within the tracks of commonsense, albeit now just around the outside of it.

We are now moving out of the comfort zone of psychoanalysis as ideology and into the more disturbing form it takes as critical theory, the kind of theory that each analysand begins to elaborate for themselves as they disentangle themselves from their own peculiar version of commonsense. Theory in therapy takes us beyond the verities of the self, beyond psychiatrised, psychologised and psychotherapeutised images of who we are, and also beyond the most alluring way out of this mess that religion today promises. So, we now move into the realm of the heretics, those who inhabit the outer edges of the nether-hell of psychoanalysis, and what marks them out is that what they say does sound very strange even to those inducted into contemporary psychological, psychotherapeutic and psychoanalytic commonsense.

Here we meet those who challenge and disrupt taken-for-granted sensibilities but who the media still try to co-opt, still try to draw back into the first layers if not into the ideological limbo-land of pure ideology. Some names of the radical theorists working with Lacanian ideas outside the clinic may be familiar here and their ideas underpin some of the arguments in this book, perhaps even spiced up with some queerer feminist argument. You are not here already perhaps, and so you may be reassured by the at least recognisable political coordinates of feminism and Marxism that underwrite this work. Thrown off balance? Lost? You will be, and you need to go a little deeper to arrive at the worst, the best of Lacanian psychoanalysis.

We are trespassing now a little further into the heretic world, but closer to those breaking more violently from the outer reaches of commonsense, those who provide something quite different and who are inspiration for some 'social theorists' who are drawn like moths to the deeper hell of the clinic. Here we enter the inner circles of contemporary Lacanian psychoanalysis, in the guise of those who have built their own versions of organisations dedicated to the promulgation of a version of Lacan. They are those whose followers demand loyalty, those, who, it is sometimes said, do not operate as cults only because cults are easy to join and difficult to leave and these groups are difficult to join and easy to be cut loose from. The taint of heresy is in their blood, and perhaps that is also why those around them sometimes dabble in quasi-spiritual speculations about what an 'act' of revolt in psychoanalysis might be like.

We are nearly there, close to what looks to outsiders to be a realm of dangerous fraud, of the number one charlatan who pitted himself against Freud but pretended to return to him, the devil himself, or at least one aspect of him. Here is one face of Lacan, the Lacan of film and literary theory, mystifying and convoluted, and also giving us something that is very different now from pop-psychoanalysis. This is but the easiest, most acceptable version of Lacan, horrible enough for some but someone we take seriously, we have to take seriously if we are to arrive at the core. But here, so close to our anti-hero, we are at a critical boundary, between Lacanian social theory and Lacanian clinical treatment, into which we now step and from which we will interrogate the four elements of psy practice that organise subjectivity today in what we like to call reality. There is just one more last step.

At the core is the more complex character that is Lacan in the clinic, the devil himself and his courtiers and supplicants, those whose writing is so very useful and revolutionary. It is only when we come this far, when we have travelled into these deepest parts that we have access to something that will shake our symbolic coordinates, something that touches the real. The line we trace through these layers of hell bring us to something we can treat as the 'core'; the point is that it is the journey as such that is important, and when we arrive at the core we find theoretical and practical coordinates for a Lacanian psychoanalysis that operates as a permanent revolution in subjectivity. Here, at the end of this path is also what is sometimes called the 'end of analysis', for the most disturbing core of psychoanalysis only functions in the vortex of the clinic, perhaps for a moment and with only the littlest ripples out into everyday life, into the shallower waters of the limbo-land we started out from.

Suspensions of disbelief

Connections between the emergence of Lacanian psychoanalysis and radical political movements – particularly Marxism and feminism – are not accidental, though tensions between clinical and political perspectives on change are often left unexplored in accounts of Lacan's clinical interventions. The subtitle of this book, 'Revolutions in subjectivity' is designed to draw attention to those tensions; and the claim that attempts to change society will simply entail circular 'revolutions' between positions will be set against the claim that psychoanalysis itself links personal and social change in transformations, 'revolutions' in subjectivity. These transformations are often restricted to the space of the clinic, and may be hidden even to those close to the analysand – not much to write home about it would seem, so what is the big deal for politics, for real revolutions?

Here is a crucial place for theory in this kind of therapy, in this form of psychoanalysis that does have therapeutic effects. The theory operates not by directly moulding clinical practice – there are no specifications for how the analysis should be done – but in theorising the shape of it, its possibilities and limits. My elaboration of theory for Lacanian psychoanalysis sets itself against attempts either to make it conform to whatever particular political projects we subscribe to or to extrapolate from the clinic to the domain of Lacanian 'social theory'. That temptation, to conform or extrapolate, has been attempted many times by adjacent psy practices, with disastrous results, and so theoretical examination of disjunctions between individual and social change is vital if we are to actually trace the boundaries that define the 'personal' and the 'political'.

Lacanian psychoanalysis needs to be redefined as theory and practice in relation to four main traditions of work – psychiatry, psychology, psychotherapy and spirituality. These traditions are the source of controversial influences on psychoanalysis, particularly now in the Lacanian tradition, as medicalising, individualising, humanising and spiritualising influences. Each is freighted with political assumptions that are disentangled and questioned in the course of the book. The tense, antagonistic, sometimes dependent relationship Lacanian psychoanalysis has with these four traditions of work is a necessary condition for radical change at the level of the individual and the social.

The book traces the institutional and clinical context for the historical emergence of contemporary debates in the Lacanian tradition. The 'clinical structures' of neurosis, psychosis and perversion that Lacan adopted from Freud are reviewed, assessed and elaborated in relation to 'contemporary symptoms' that call for a questioning and re-elaboration of the diagnostic process; discussions of the 'end of analysis' are explored in relation to clinical structures and sub-categories of obsessional neurosis and hysteria in order to highlight the politically-charged background and opportunities for new representations of 'gender' in therapy. The emphasis here is upon the exploration of Lacanian psychoanalysis as contested terrain, not as a fixed correct line to be followed. It is in that sense too that Lacan's school is authentically psychoanalytic, for it revives the uncertain speculative character of early Freudian psychotherapy.

Lacanian psychoanalysis is not a set of techniques (not medical), complete system (not psychological), worldview (not therapeutic) or a guide to life (it is not spiritual). There is no immutable reading, but contradictory readings. We do not merely strip away misconceptions to arrive at the real thing; there is no real thing. I evoked something of the line I trace through to what I take to be the core of Lacanian psychoanalysis, and the extended metaphor of our journey from an ideological limbo-world to the devilish resources that Lacan and the Lacanians provide also indicates something of my own debt to Marxist and feminist politics. I want to spell out in a little more detail some assumptions I am making about the historical constitution of psychoanalysis now so that the political-economic analysis of the place of Lacanian psychoanalysis traced through in this book will make sense. There are two fundamental aspects of the construction of psychoanalysis that are at issue here; the first concerns the historical construction of psychoanalysis as a theory of the subject, the second concerns the construction of the clinic.

The historical construction of psychoanalysis as such is something that Lacan broaches many times. Let us briefly run through key elements of this historical character of psychoanalysis to make the point. We can note the impact in Lacan's writing, for example: of dispensing with Freud's prehistorical origin myths for the Oedipus complex; of locating clock-time as an organising principle in the context of industrialisation; of conceptualising psychoanalysis as a practice that operates on the subject of science; of characterising the unconscious as that which Freud 'invented' rather than discovered; of refusing attempts to turn analysis into adaptation of the ego to capitalist society; and of describing the decline of the paternal imago to rewrite the nature of the symptom. Lacan stripped out the particular contents of vulgarised Freudian theory, thereby blocking any attempt to extrapolate the 'meanings' elaborated by one subject to another, or to all others in what would amount to a false universal and moralising version of psychoanalysis.

Then we are left with formal elements that cannot be historicised, and I treat these as the barest elements we need to presuppose as defining the human material upon which different stages of class society have been built. These formal elements of the stuff of our 'first nature' are: necessarily mediated communication; a consequent forced choice between being and meaning; the loss of connection and traces of that loss as that mediation comes to operate; elements of language as the condition of our consciousness; the problematic nature of truth as we speak within a structured symbolic system; and difference between ourselves and others that is configured around what we imagine we have lost as we learn to speak. These barest formal elements do not yet have the status of any kind of 'second nature' that we construct to fill in the gaps, though we cannot but posit that nature retroactively, embedding it in an image of a human being as it is for us now (as, for example, 'homo sapiens'). Still less do they specify what content will be elaborated as something approaching a theory of the 'self'. It is not possible to strip away our 'second nature' in order to lay bare this subject, this human being, because without those contents we would not recognise this subject at all. This is already theoretical work, necessary if we are to be able to map how the false pretenders to a universal theory of the self – psychiatry, psychology, psychotherapy and spirituality – accumulate their power under capitalism.

The second aspect of the spatial, temporal and analytical specificity of psychoanalysis concerns the construction of clinical phenomena, and Lacan makes a number of comments about this. These comments again serve as a ground-clearing exercise to conceptualise the specific place and action of psychoanalysis. I will briefly note the import of these comments here, and you will have begun to grasp some of them from my description of a session of Lacanian psychoanalysis at the beginning of this introduction, for they include: that a demand for analysis is necessary for anything of the kind to take place; that defining characteristics of a particular analysis cannot be predicted in advance; that the focus must be on representations rather than feelings repressed and released; that we refuse intuitivist descriptions of the functioning of defence mechanisms; that the unconscious is produced in analysis rather than treated as interior to the subject; and that psychoanalytic effects, whether traumatic or curative, operate retroactively. (With respect to this last point, for example, I cannot tell you everything that is in the book in this introduction, and it is only after you have read the whole thing that even these grounding assumptions for the book will make sense.)

We are therefore left with some quite minimal conditions for there to be psychoanalysis, for us to say that something distinctively psychoanalytic is happening as a process of self-reflexive enquiry, and these conditions include: speech to another, about something, conceptualised perhaps as a symptom; a sense of something significant for the subject, operating beyond consciousness; some notion of personal meaning, appearing as if there is interiority and repression; attention to speech as marked by some traction, treated as itself meaningful; repetition of signifying processes revealed by blockages in the speech; and construction of a meta-position, a position for which responsibility can be taken.

This is not to say that these are the defining features of a complete analysis, whatever that is. Still less does this meet specifications of what are termed in high Lacanese 'subjective destitution', 'traversal of the fantasy' or 'identification with the symptom', let alone that idealised end of analysis through which the subject accepts, in some famous formulations, that there is no sexual relation, that there is no big Other, or that there is no Other of the Other. There are quite specific historical contexts for the elaboration of such desiderata for analysis, and I am concerned here with a minimal list of conditions which have not been, as we might say, 'imaginarised', not layered with additional arcane criteria that tend to operate in much the same way as the hierarchy of invisible degrees that structure quasi-spiritual sites of escape from our dismal reality.

Lacanian psychoanalysis *desubstantialises* theoretical concepts at the very moment it deploys them, and I try to remain true to this dynamic of the work in the 'ising' motif that will, no doubt sometimes rather repetitively and irritatingly, shift attention from reified things to processes. So, to anticipate some of these instances so they will not jar so much later on, you will encounter 'psychiatrising', 'psychologising', 'therapeutising' and 'spiritualising' conceptual capsules of the subject, as well as 'obsessionalising', 'hystericising', 'psychoticising' and 'perversionalising' processes by which clinical structures are named.

In sum, to follow the line of the book I want you to accept four arguments to begin with. The first is that psychoanalysis is not universally true (and analysands may also come to this conclusion, and so release themselves from its grip). Second, psychoanalysis is constructed as one of the various names of subjectivity, of what I call 'conceptual capsules of the subject' under capitalism (and it enables the analyst to comprehend those who would like to ignore psychoanalysis, for whom psychoanalysis sometimes gives the name psychotic or pervert, as well as those obsessed with it and those whose refusal of it is understood as some kind of hysterical protest). Third, Lacanian psychoanalysis is one of the names for the contradictory subjectivity of late capitalism, virtual, precarious, neoliberal, but this form of psychoanalysis introduces some new twists and turns and ways out of this state of affairs. Fourth, the contradictions that characterise psychoanalysis need to be connected with the other revolutionary emancipatory movements that were also formed under the rule of capital and as a response to capitalism – Marxism and feminism – but which have been more self-consciously attentive to the historical nature of the political-economic formations they pitted themselves against. Theoretical and practical articulation of clinical and political change therefore lies at the heart of the arguments that run through the next eight chapters.

Chapter 1
Framing analysis

In this chapter we focus on psychoanalysis as part of psychiatry, showing how Freud's work was grounded in German diagnostic categories and forms of treatment but also how psychoanalysis today begins to break from such assumptions about the relationship between analyst and patient. The limits of that break and the reproduction of psychiatric approaches in present-day psychoanalytic practice are explored. The chapter reviews the conceptual transformations in psychiatry and then psychoanalysis as a renewed emphasis on the talking cure took place, this to appreciate the repercussions of Lacan's training in French psychiatry. This is one way of approaching the historical context through which it is now possible to redefine and challenge diagnosis, adaptation and direction of patients in psychoanalysis, and to find new ways to articulate the enmeshment of the dimensions of the imaginary, symbolic and real with alienation in clinical practice.

Reductions
The collusive and competitive relationship between psychoanalysis as talking cure and psychiatry as medical treatment produces a peculiar condensation of regulative technologies in contemporary society, technologies revolving around a double reduction, to sex and to pathology. These reductive operations meet in the 'psy complex', the increasingly powerful meshwork of theories and practices concerned with the governance of the individual. This place, where sex and psychopathology are entwined in a complicated series of conceptual distinctions and definitions – of what is normal and what is not – has potentially lethal consequences for those caught in the psy complex and for modes of explanation that buy into the still-dominant assumptions clinicians make about distress (Ingleby 1981; Miller and Rose 1986).

Sex first. A popular accusation levelled against Freud is that he reduced everything to sex.

This claim is also replicated inside psychoanalysis by practitioners who are keen either to distance themselves from or to show their avid appreciation of received images of Freud. This replication of the claim, which has profound consequences for psychoanalytic theoretical debate and clinical practice, works in two ways, through two routes. One is that practitioners tempted to endorse the critics try to find a way of doing psychoanalysis without attending to the role of sexuality in the treatment. The second route is to accept the terms of the claim, revel in outrage and thereby confirm a caricature of psychoanalytic argument. However, pious appeals to sweet reason, dissolving sex into attachment in 'relationships' or suchlike, or righteous adherence to cardinal truths formulated by the founding fathers, anchoring everything into sex as such, both fail (Forrester 1997).

It is the task of psychoanalysis to show how 'everything' that pretends to be nothing to do with sex thereby sticks to it, becomes entangled with it, comes to point to sex as if it were the source of all joys and ills. Overtly or covertly, the things we try to cleanse of sex are then haunted by it, and it comes to inhabit those things and cling to them all the more so because it is so unwelcome. The question therefore is twofold, a quite different double-question that repeats the complaint about Freud in reverse, while refusing to subscribe to what those hostile to psychoanalysis say about it. On the one side we track in analysis how sex comes to attach itself to our representations of other things. Not so that sex appears as the bare ground on which the rest of our life is played out, but how sex comes to influence, by turns to enliven or ruin, that ground, the ground of being. On the other side is attention to the production of sex in life, how it comes to figure as if it were the centre or is kept away from what we imagine to be the centre of who we are. Not so that sex is discovered as hidden underneath our everyday activities, but how it derives its disruptive force by insinuating itself into our thoughts as if it were the core of our being. For Lacan (1964/1973: 257), 'the coming into play of the signifier in the life of man enables him to bring out the meaning of sex'; and indeed, chains of signifiers now seem to compel man and woman to search for sexual meaning (Foucault 1975/1979, 1976/1981; cf. Miller 1989; Hook 2007).

Pathology next. A powerful ideological claim is that distress should be reduced to individual pathology.

This claim enforces the very social relations that constitute disturbance as if it were individual mental or emotional distress to begin with. It has a 'performative' quality – enacting the operations that it describes, entailing that certain sexed individuals be marked out for attention – and obscures other explanations (Butler 1990). It thereby reinforces the most malign sectors of the psy complex where psychiatry has pride of place and where psychiatrists define in medical terms what appears to have gone wrong. Again, this claim is also often replicated, taken up or turned down in such a way as to give it substance in psychoanalysis. Here, those who have had psychiatric training still in awe of their masters locate psychopathology within a medical frame, and psychoanalysis becomes another dialect of dominant descriptions and treatments of psychopathology. Or there is evasion of the process of pathologisation, evasion of it on principle in line with attempts to affirm creative refusal of everyday rationality (Laing 1959/1965; Szasz 1961).

Psychoanalysis can be elaborated as a conceptual critique and practical alternative to the knot of errors that structure psychiatry and bewitch its enemies. Neither seizing the levers of psychiatric power, repeating the categories that keep it in place, nor simply romanticising resistance to it will do. We need to elaborate an account of pathology as irreducible to the individual, an account in which there is refusal of the reduction of forms of submission and protest to psychopathology, to the claim that submission and protest are underpinned by pathology that can be treated. This necessarily embroils us, once again, in the question of sex, for this is one thing that psychiatry has played its part in pathologising. Definitions of psychopathology have become focused on sex, in psychiatric institutions that pretend to cure it and for the individual who is incited to circulate around it as something fearful and tantalising; psychoanalysis, part of the problem, can then also provide a way out.

Medicine

Psychoanalysis emerged from within, and as an alternative to, psychiatry. The trajectories of Freud and Lacan, who marked out their own distinctive positions in and against psychiatric knowledge, defining themselves in relation to it, have left traces, contour lines that we now have to work our way across. We need to grasp, first, how psychiatric knowledge functions, then how Freud was able to speak with his own voice inside it, and then how Lacanian psychoanalysis subverts it. Psychiatry is a domain of medicine, and the medical framing of what is understood to be 'mental illness' thus gives to its practice three key characteristics.

First, there is a concern with *diagnosis*. Psychiatry in the late nineteenth century and through the twentieth saw a flourishing of diagnostic categories through which symptoms could be grouped into syndromes – patterns of abnormality for which an organic dysfunction had yet to be detected – and underlying disease entities. Unfortunately for the psychiatrist, the discovery of direct causes for distress which would anchor the discrete clusters of abnormal behaviour they described seemed forever just out of reach, and such a 'positive' grounding for the illnesses they described eluded them. This has also been the case through to the twenty-first century, and the process of diagnosis has therefore revolved around deficits that can only be defined against a shimmering ideal of mental health.

Psychiatry at the time Freud developed psychoanalysis was a flourishing industry devoted to naming the abnormal mind, and his intervention in the field was marked by some remarkable successes. Freud may have failed in some minor skirmishes – failing to replace the term 'schizophrenia' with 'paraphrenia', for example – but psychoanalysis still seemed to win the day as the German tradition of psychiatric knowledge took root in the United States. There was success insofar as psychoanalysis came to shape the formation of the Diagnostic and Statistical Manual of Mental Disorders (DSM) as mainstay of the American Psychiatric Association, an ever-expanding system of classification (Kirk and Kutchins 1992; Spiegel 2005).

However, even before psychoanalytic conceptual reference points were extinguished from the DSM, and so also from the International Classification of Diseases that ran in parallel to it outside the US as a handbook for the rest of the medical profession, those reference points had been, as it were, 'psychiatrised'. Freud's polite rebellion against medical psychiatry was quashed, and psychoanalytic energies were harnessed to mainstream psychiatric practice. The making of diagnoses using Freud's preferred terminology – 'neurosis', 'psychosis' and 'perversion' – was a triumph for his followers. But it soon became clear that these diagnostic categories were being defined by medical psychiatrists, already a pyrrhic victory for the analysts. And this was before that terminology was systematically eradicated and replaced with forms of diagnosis more compatible with the agenda of the pharmaceutical companies, at which point psychoanalytic alternatives inside psychiatry in the English-speaking world were all but finished (Healy 2002, 2004, 2009).

Lacan's interventions in terminology were made later on, when psychiatric classifications were already systematised and there was even less room for manoeuvre. The tradition of 'French' as opposed to 'German' psychiatric traditions provided some space for alternative notions, for a different account of what the basis was for a diagnosis, but while this alternative tradition is much-vaunted by Lacanians today, it is still rather a promise than a full-blown alternative to medical psychiatry (Macey 1995). Nevertheless, Freud had elaborated psychoanalytic diagnostic categories that challenged psychiatric images of healthy bodies and healthy minds as the measure of what patients lacked, and Lacan articulated a quite different way of describing the relationship between the human subject and 'Freudian structures' that Lacanians today refer to as 'clinical structures' (Lacan 1981/1993; Fink 1997).

The second characteristic of medical psychiatry, *adaptation*, is a function of its double-project of normalising certain kinds of behaviour and pathologising others. In this, psychiatry traces a rigorous logic through which it proves itself to be part of the onward march of reason, an ally and advance guard of the scientific edge of the Western Enlightenment. Adaptation is warranted by a series of duplications of the motif of 'health', reiterative processes that produce a certain image of health in different domains and confirm what the psychiatrist understands by 'mental health' and the 'mental illness' in which they specialise. The motif of adaptation is guaranteed when mind and body are treated as two aspects of the self-same organic matter, and the puzzle about how and where exactly the mental and the material meet is left to those in other disciplines, philosophers perhaps, and, all the more indicative of how the status of such puzzling is viewed by the doctors, even theologians. Here a fateful opposition is installed between treating and curing; hence Freud's (1912: 115) lament, borrowed from Ambroise Paré, 'I dressed the wounds, God cured him'.

Adaptation as a moral goal becomes all the more pressing when the body of the individual subject becomes a model for and is then also based upon representations of the body politic, society as pulsing organism which functions at its best in a state of balance but is convulsed from time to time by ailments internal to it. To adapt an individual to society is then to beg a question about the nature of society itself that is usually answered by those who enjoy a comfortable enough position within it, that all should be well. The answer is provided first by dominant theological traditions and then reinforced by a version of naturalist explanation that some adherents imagine is anti-theological, often the ideological fate of arguments for natural selection. In this, the Enlightenment itself is torn into competing traditions operating in the popular imagination and in professional institutions. In the German intellectual tradition, in which Freud first develops an alternative mode of reasoning, there is a division between the natural sciences and the human sciences. The temptation here is to follow one track or the other, or to fall in step with one path simply because one is fleeing the other.

On one track runs medical psychiatry and Freud makes a case for psychoanalysis as a natural science, as one of the *Naturwissenschaften* in an argument that we will need to follow carefully in order to understand how its logic unfolds in keeping with what is usually taken to be 'human nature' (Hardt 2006; Gómez 2009). Here also, despite Freud's (1926) own argument for 'lay analysis' and against psychoanalysis being in the hands of the doctors, is the medical profession which domesticated psychoanalysis as it passed into the English language. On the other track run humanist interpreters of Freud, those seeking to recover from the American mind-doctors the deeper meaning of psychoanalysis and an attention to the meaning that inheres in the story of each individual patient. Here is an insistence that Freud really, most-times secretly, meant psychoanalysis to be a human science, one of the *Geisteswissenschaften* (Bettelheim 1986). This might account for some telling amendments Freud made to his own texts: of a 'mental life' rather than 'nervous system' restored to health in editions of *Studies on Hysteria* after 1925, for example (Breuer and Freud 1895: 305).

It was a nice try, but it evaded deeper questions about the actual function of psychiatry and its role in the adaptation of the individual to an image of what is normal. So, as humanism often does, it collapsed into its own version of adaptation, adapting those who fail to measure up to what the humanist imagines a human being should be to the good of society, even to the good society itself. Lacan, in contrast, departs from both these paths – the human being is, in Hyppolite's Hegelian formulation during Lacan's (1975/1991) seminar, 'disadapted'; psychoanalysis then breaks from reduction to either medical or humanist precepts, and refuses to adapt the subject to a social order organised around them (Van Haute 2002; Chiesa 2007).

The third defining characteristic of psychiatry as a medical practice is that it concerns itself with *direction*, with directing the patient; this is a function of diagnosis informed by motifs of adaptation. Attempts to mark out a specific disciplinary domain inside and implicitly at times against medicine make this concern with adaptation quite explicit. The emergence of hypnotism in the nineteenth century, a practice that provides the setting for Freud's own early work, is precisely concerned with the role of suggestion; it obtains in the peculiar state in which the subject might be placed in order that some suggestion or other might be made in order to illustrate how ostensibly organic illnesses could be conjured into existence or dispelled (Ellenberger 1970; Beloff 2008).

In this, however, the psychiatrist himself – he is a figure who often directs the behaviour of women patients – is more an accomplice of existing systems of meaning than one who actually masters them. Psychiatry towards the end of the nineteenth century is still something of a handmaiden to medicine, and its domain of work is also already fairly feminised. It is a lower-status calling, and in Freud's early career it becomes a medical speciality that gives him professional standing as a doctor to which he can realistically aspire, and only this far because he is a Jew. The intersection between status, to be lesser than real medicine, and feminisation, being lesser than real men, already creates psychiatry in German culture at the end of the nineteenth century as a kind of disciplinary space that is homologous with the place of middle-class Jews in cities like Vienna, perhaps most typically in Vienna (Mitchell 1974; Frosh 2008). And then the diagnostic and adaptation-oriented practices of psychiatry require the practitioner to submit to certain stereotypical categories of sexed, raced subject, to conform to certain social mores (Gilman 1991, 1993).

When Freud takes the lead from hypnotism – from outside German culture, in the work of Jean-Martin Charcot in Paris and Hippolyte Bernheim in Nancy – he also gives a further twist to our understanding of what might be suggested to the patients, to our understanding of the forms of suggestion that are at work well before the patient becomes such. The hypnotists showed Freud that underlying biological categories cannot be the bedrock of explanation for mental disorders, for even hysteria which was once assumed to be a malady peculiar to women is now evidently something that also afflicts men. Sex is crucial to this particular form of neurosis – hysteria necessarily entails the eroticisation of distress through the way it organises the bodies of those who suffer – and sex is a meaningful symbolic construction rather than a name for the brute nature of women and men (Laqueur 1990; Showalter 1997).

Lacan's psychiatric training is one in which he is to some extent marginal as a function of his class background rather than racialised position (Roudinesco 1997). His training is significantly later than Freud's but the spectre of mental automatism and the role of suggestion is still a powerful influence even if hypnotism as such has faded out of psychiatry. Freud showed that hysteria is a representational practice well before Lacan drew attention to the role of language in the formation and treatment of distress. What Lacan then shows us is not that psychoanalysis should focus on language instead of sex, but that we are faced in psychoanalysis with the language *of* sex. The necessary additional ingredient, power, which will ensure that there is a link between certain forms of language and certain forms of sex, is still also at work in the attempt by psychiatrists and then many psychoanalysts to direct the patient (Freud 1912; Lacan 1958). In this, the psychiatrist and psychoanalyst maintain the illusion that they are not simply confirming dominant representations of distress, knowledge that also subjects practitioners themselves to it. The practitioners address this knowledge and, in attempting to complete or reform it, they imagine that they are thereby able to assert some distinctive position, some agency inside it.

Feudalism

Psychiatric knowledge operates as a particular kind of symbolic universe, an evolving expanding hermetic system in which symptoms are treated as signs. It has undergone a series of mutations, but its underlying structure, and the model that it provides for the symbolic as such, is still present in contemporary psychiatric practice and has a bearing on how psychoanalysts define their own activity. We need to grasp how particular features of this universe of signs, of what are taken to be signs, interlock and provide conditions of possibility for speakers to address it, and locate who they are within it. In this way it will be possible to appreciate how psychiatry developed and how it survived as a historical constellation, as a system of social relationships as well as a symbolic system. Lacan provides some coordinates for mapping what Freud was up against, and how psychoanalysis comes to be caught in the grip of dominant systems of knowledge. Then we can see how Lacanian psychoanalysis may also release itself from that grip.

We have been describing a universe of knowledge that confronts each speaking subjects that subsists through the articulation of a language system, a system of what are ostensibly complete and well-formed signs that relays and sustains a network of social relations. Lacan made good tactical use of a theory of language borrowed from structural linguistics, Saussure's (1915/1974) writings grounded in anthropological studies (Lévi-Strauss 1958/1972). The question now is how we might reflexively turn that theoretical apparatus, which gives us a historical and systemic perspective on how the psychiatric universe of knowledge functions, against itself, to also give our account of the emergence of psychoanalysis a further psychoanalytic turn (Wilden 1972).

The term 'structure' in second-hand accounts of Saussure's foundational lectures on semiology has had unfortunate resonances, first with 'social structure' – as if language comprised a series of interlocking components that enabled it to function – and then, secondly, with 'clinical structure' so that a form of language might be assumed to replicate itself inside each speaking subject. To refer to the semiological concept 'system' is slightly better, and to thereby introduce a terminological dispute into this theory of language is itself a smart psychoanalytic move for those who want to emphasise the instability of language, to disturb taken-for-granted ways of understanding the world. This 'system', a language system that encompasses all of the meaningful elements of human activity – words and gestures and pictures of every form of everyday reality and envisaged worlds beyond it – is composed of the barest of theoretical building blocks, the *signifier*. Lacan's innovative reading of Saussure extracts the signifier from what has come to be called 'structural linguistics', and produces something quite different. Lacan (1981/1993: 184) comments that 'to be interested in structure is to be unable to neglect the signifier', and his reference to Saussure cued in by Lévi-Strauss's recently published writing proves to be a more fruitful linguistic frame to warrant the return to Freud than other studies of language to which Lacan also had recourse (e.g. Jakobson 1975).

While Saussure described the signifier as a 'sound image' combined with what that image signified as a 'concept' to which it had become attached by linguistic convention, Lacan followed through the logic of the argument to show how our access to concepts is itself structured by a system of signifiers. Saussure (1915/1974: 16) treated signifier and signified as two sides of the 'sign', and conceived of semiology as a 'science of signs'; Lacan showed that the system of signifiers itself constructs a universe of meaning operating in such a way as to give us knowledge about reality and also, it seems, things that lie beyond it. To stay with the signifier and to track the connections between signifiers therefore entails, among other things, a conceptual break from psychiatry as a system of knowledge that treats symptoms as 'signs', signs of underlying mental disturbances and organic malfunctions.

A signifier is defined not by its arbitrary connection with a signified, the concept to which it corresponds by historical circumstance, but by its relation with other signifiers, and so a founding claim of Lacanian psychoanalysis is in line with Saussure's (1915/1974: 120) comment that in a language system there are only 'differences, without positive terms' that exist in their own right, as such, independent of the others. A discrete signifier is thus dependent on a series of signifiers, and stands out against that series as but one mark that serves to confirm the pre-eminence of the rest. It is where a signifier stands out as one mark against the rest, one that is distinctive but conjunctural rather than universal, that we start to have a conception of structure that is historical rather than natural. This also serves to ground claims by structural anthropologists that they can thereby trace the conditions by which human nature is necessarily also a form of human culture (Haraway 1989; Young 1992). This peculiarly human predicament is grounded in a 'second nature' which we mistakenly assume is itself the bedrock for who we come to be in a particular culture; we see emerge a Lacanian approach to the history of the subject that has repercussions for how we understand human history as such (Brennan 1993).

This unravelling of the status of the signifier has profound consequences for how we should view the attempt by individual speakers to pit themselves against a reigning system of knowledge. It throws into relief how 'agency' may come to operate as a comforting illusion when this abstraction is actually embedded in a necessary relation to an other, a relation that serves to define how the agent understands themselves. To return to psychiatry and the place of psychoanalysis within a medical frame of reference, we can see how Lacan's theoretical work can be put to work on particular sets of social formations. This lays the basis for later claims by Lacanian psychoanalysts to be able to address the subject's symptom, form of enjoyment and their place in social links, cues to a revival of lost connections between individual analysis and political critique; that interpretation produces effects on suffering, jouissance and 'the subject's position in the social link' (Guéguen 2008: 65).

Psychiatric knowledge operates first as a system of signifiers functioning as something 'other' to the practitioner that he, occasionally she, is drawn into and invited to master, but that promise of mastery is never fulfilled. The psychiatrist, and then also the psychoanalyst who buys into that promise, is an agent who fails, repeatedly fails, to be a master in this system. Rather schematically for the moment, drawing on another theoretical system – Hegelian phenomenology – influential on Lacan's early work, we might say that the psychiatrist becomes a master who discovers that he is dependent on the slave he commands to work, who discovers that he himself relies on the other he imagined he would dominate, for without that domination his activity would amount to nothing. This master–slave dialectic is actually rooted by Hegel (1807/1977) in the feudal relationship between what he preferred to term 'lord' and 'bondsman', and it only then starts to have retroactive hermeneutic effects on the way longer past historical relations between masters and slaves might be understood (Kojève 1969; Bisson 2009). We will return to Hegel in due course, but we can already see the spectre of a totalising system of knowledge – very much of the kind he is accused of unrolling and celebrating on the stage of history – haunting psychiatry.

Medical science, which takes form as a positivist accumulation of facts about the body and observations of behavioural regularities after the

Enlightenment, still operates in psychiatry as a kind of cosmology, a harmonic worldview that Lacan explicitly rejects (Mazin 2007). Positivist conceptions and empirical study combine in an ideological grid to direct and justify the dominant diagnostic systems, but first diagnosis, adaptation and direction are framed by a conception of health and illness that is borrowed from physical illness and applied to the mind. The disjunction between body and mind is sealed over, 'sutured' we might say, and at that very moment when one system of knowledge is applied to another domain it becomes a system as such (Miller 1977). Systems of physical medicine, medicinal systems concerned with bodily functions, are themselves embedded in particular worldviews, and there has been a constant struggle to disconnect scientific enquiry from such often idealised structured belief systems (Turner 1987). But here, as it loses what moorings it had in the material from which it was first elaborated, psychiatric knowledge can only maintain itself by meshing itself together as a circuit of assumptions about the mind and 'mental illness'. This much was noticed by some psychoanalysts who broke from psychiatry and then, as a consequence, became positioned by their former colleagues as well as by those who were victims of the psychiatric system as if they were 'anti-psychiatrists' (Burston 1996; Szasz 2004, 2009).

This cosmological system feeds on images of the body and operates as if it were an organic form of knowledge; the organicism of psychiatry locks the patient into a particular ideological representation of their body – of their own mind as if it should be modelled on the body – and into an ideological representation of society. It is against that ostensible organic grounding of psychiatry as a cosmology that debates over 'madness' and 'badness' come to operate as different versions of an underlying moral system. An organicist cosmology, a quasi-scientific system that remains within the frame of a pre-Enlightenment worldview, is structurally and institutionally hierarchical, and still replicates feudal power relations and forms of social link now within capitalist society.

Psychiatry has become one of the most powerful forms of social control under capitalism, but it operates so efficiently in this respect precisely because it is double-edged. This double-edged character of psychiatry cuts against itself, tears it into competing tendencies. On the one side it is a technical instrumental apparatus now at one with the pharmaceutical companies and enrolled into the delirious search for neurological certainties; it is expressed in the claim that we were recently living in the decade of the brain or that we are on the edge of the discovery of a gene for schizophrenia. This underwrites bourgeois ideology, the most malign side of the Western Enlightenment at work in the illusion of scientific progress through technology (Adorno and Horkheimer 1944/1979). On the other side it is a system of patronage and disdain for any kind of dissent, all the more dangerous when it senses that its power is precarious. Here it betrays its aristocratic lineage and loyalties, even if it must play a marginal and often demeaned role, lesser than its other masters in medicine proper (Young 1999; Kirsner 2000).

The bourgeois-democratic revolutions that ushered in new forms of the state in Western Europe to guarantee capitalist interests never completely eradicated feudal power relations, and the remnants of feudalism were recruited into and re-energised in specific ideological projects that served class society well. Psychiatry was thus incorporated into the psy complex, the meshwork of practices that individualise subjectivity and regulate the activities of bourgeois subjects (Ingleby 1985; Rose 1985). Each individual subject is modelled on the apparently autonomous decisions made by entrepreneurs, and incited to believe that they each – subjects as agents – were really free to sell their labour power in contract with their masters. The illusion that each signifier is distinct and complete, independent of the series of signifiers that structure its existence as a series, is in this way of a piece with bourgeois ideology that depicts each individual as if they began life as Robinson Crusoe and only then entered into relations with others. This replication and recuperation of feudal social links under capitalism has consequences for political-economic analysis of the development of psychoanalysis.

Unconscious

The peculiar dependent relation that the signifier, and agent that identifies with it, has with the series of other signifiers forming a system of knowledge maintaining itself as a dominant hermetically-sealed universe of meaning is theoretically elaborated by Lacan (1991/2007; Clemens and Grigg 2006). Here, the closest that Lacan comes to social theory, there is an opportunity for rethinking the place of 'structuralism' in Lacanian psychoanalysis. It is necessary, first, to insist on the disjunction between psychoanalysis as such – a clinical practice that deals with individuals or collections of individuals in defined social groups – and the level of political economy. Conceptions of the individual are condensed from the ideological operations necessary to capitalism, and so to model society on that individual is to endorse the very kind of subject that psychoanalysis aims to dismantle (or at least that psychoanalysis provides the conditions for the individual to dismantle itself).

When Lacan extracted the signifier as a conceptual device from Saussurean linguistics and embedded that signifier in a distinctive theory of discourse, he also paved the way for the repayment of a debt to structuralism as such, but repaid it in order that the ideological currency of structuralism could now be dispensed with (Pavón Cuéllar 2010). That antiquated ideological currency of structuralism is crystallised in the claim that forms of language are underpinned by binary operations, and even that those binary operations are wired into the brain (Lévi-Strauss 1958/1972). Now, instead, we have a theory of discourse that attends to a certain kind of binary operation in the structure of this discourse – the opposition between a signifier and a dominant system of knowledge upon which it depends – but we need to embed that binary opposition in a historical process instead of an underlying structure of the human mind. There are ramifications for how we conceptualise what appears to lie under the surface of the chain of signifiers as truth, truth for the subject.

Psychoanalysis repeats and refines a series of binary operations psychiatry worked on as its conceptual ground, which include, in a historical accumulation of notions through the Western Enlightenment, oppositions between civilisation and madness, reason and unreason, and health and illness (Foucault 1961/2009). Freud (1930) reorganised these oppositions into an overarching distinction between consciousness and the unconscious, and then set psychoanalysts the interminable task of exploring without necessarily endorsing how that distinction restructures the rest. Here we are faced with what we are now able to see as an ideological double-reduction, the reification of the conscious and unconscious mind. In the hands of psychiatrists, particularly those influenced by psychoanalysis, consciousness is treated as coterminous with civilisation, reason and mental health. Truth, which is assumed here to correspond with reality, is then threatened by what lies outside consciousness, and so to enlarge the domain of the ego is necessarily to drain the reservoirs of irrationality that swill around under the surface; 'Where id was, there ego shall be. It is the work of culture – not unlike the draining of the Zuider Zee' (Freud 1933: 80).

The unconscious then becomes 'another place', perhaps even inhabited by something that would correspond to self-centred conscious awareness, and to characterise it as 'id' too-neatly maps this other place from where we view it, very much like while so unlike us (Freud 1915a: 175). Then, when the unconscious speaks it seems as if there is indeed someone knocking on the other side of the door, so that we are then led to 'the impropriety of trying to turn it [the unconscious] into an inside' (Lacan 1966a: 711). If we were to simply reverse our picture of the relationship between consciousness and the unconscious – as did the surrealists, in an anticipation of some versions of anti-psychiatry – it would be possible to find the true subject not on this side of the door but on the other. Surrealists were interested in Freud for this very reason, and rather disappointed when they travelled to Vienna and found a staid, conservative figure behind that apartment door, suspicious of their romanticising of the unconscious (Rosemont 1978). Lacan (1933), on the other hand, actively participated in surrealist debates over the nature of paranoiac rebellious crimes, and was more sympathetic to attempts to dissolve the sharp boundaries between reason and unreason, to access what is positive about hysterical rebellion and to celebrate 'convulsive beauty' that grounded truth, deeper truth, in sex (Macey 1988).

Lacan's engagement with surrealist anti-psychiatry also enabled him to develop a more reasoned approach to the separation between conscious and unconscious. It was rationalist, still psychiatric, but a reflexive rationality that also concerns itself with what divides reason from what is other to it. Lacanian psychoanalysis now enables us to avoid the double-reduction which reifies either side of the separation, and this is where Freud's account of why the talking cure requires a theory of language is taken a significant step forward. Freud (1915a) described how different forms of representation – word presentations and thing presentations – structure consciousness and the unconscious. While the unconscious is structured by thing presentations – images, impressions, sensations – consciousness combines the two kinds of representation, and so the process of speaking of something brings it into language and into consciousness. There is therefore an intimation of the 'truth' of the subject before it is put into words, but it is not nearly fully-formed enough and available for the subject to articulate as such.

Lacan draws on a theory of language not immediately available to Freud, and we now have a quite different account of what consciousness is. It is now what appears to be present and centred on a single point of awareness because it is organised around a signifier, 'I'. But that signifier, which is treated as the 'ego' in psychoanalytic jargon – itself a translation of Freud's everyday term for I, '*Ich*' in the German language – crystallises and comes to stand in for a number of signifiers, and other signifiers replace it moment-by-moment as we speak (cf. Bettelheim 1986; Timms and Segal 1988). A further disturbing conceptual displacement occurs as psychoanalysis is decanted through the French distinction between this ego as 'me' ('*moi*') and another more personal and numinous 'I' ('*je*') that marks the place of subjects who speak of themselves as if from their ego. There is thus a split in the ego that riddles the subject as they speak of who they are, a split that goes well beyond that described by Freud (1940) in his late comments on splitting as a mode of defence. Lacan's particular reading of Saussure is crucial, for in the place of the signified as 'concept' that Saussure describes as corresponding to the signifier as 'sound image' – as if they together comprised one full sign – there is, for Lacan, a chain of signifiers, some of which are repressed as we learn to speak a language and which constitutes the unconscious as the other of what we are conscious of.

Language is now seen as the condition for the unconscious, and a subject is given shape by that constitutive division of consciousness from unconscious that turns it into something other to us. A signifier, which is dependent on a chain of signifiers as we speak, might give us some access to truth but it must at the very same time necessarily misrepresent what it signifies. And, on the other side of the wall of language, is a subject locked in and locked out, a subject simultaneously revealed by and masked by language, divided. Something of the 'truth' of the subject therefore lies in the very nature of its division, and reappears in a process of speaking of what has come to be lost. As Lacan (1953: 214) puts it, 'The unconscious is that part of concrete discourse qua transindividual, which is not at the subject's disposal in reestablishing the continuity of his conscious discourse.'

Loss

Division of who we are from what we are not, of what we have from what we have lost, gives to the speaking subject concerned with mastering himself, in command of the signifier that defines him, an only illusory certainty. There is a set of distinctive ideological operations here that invite individuals who are masculine enough to be masters, to desire to occupy the place of a master signifier as they speak. It is not simply that these are bourgeois individuals, for something also remains of the architecture of the self given by feudalism, another pre-capitalist world that is also lost as if there were once a golden age, even as if it were equivalent to an idealised childhood of those subject to it. Just as childhood itself becomes marked off as a separate realm – a time of creativity and spontaneity – in late feudal society and only retrospectively acquires its allure of freedom, an image of bourgeois freedom, so our possession of objects of enjoyment is constructed as if that was the way things once were, constructed after the event (Ariès 1962; Burman 2007, 2008).

Again, an attention to the signifier in Lacan's work gives more force to Freud's (1925: 239) argument that we search in vain for the object that will once again bring us a sense of wholesome happiness, in vain because we never possessed such an object in the first place; such 'recognition of the unconscious by the ego' as 'expressed in a negative formula' is then refracted through a Hegelian reading (from Hyppolite 1956: 751) of the object in psychoanalysis as also requiring the genesis 'of the outside and of the inside'. It is an argument picked up and endorsed by Lacan (1975/1991) in *Seminar I* – the occasion of that Hegelian reading – and repeated throughout his work. The allure of the object is a function of its status as always already lost, and we circulate around the places where we hope to find it; its template is given in the formula for fantasy in which there is a non-existent subject, what Lacan calls the barred subject, in relation to a non-existent object, the '*object a*'. This little object has the status of a fantasised connection with a first other who would complete and satisfy us (marked in 'a' for '*autre*', other, in the object a). This fantasy itself relies on a cosmological conception of the world, one rooted in organic naturalised relationships between infant and mother and in a more pleasant caricature of feudal relations between lord and bondsman. This gives the frame – a psychiatric frame – for conceptualising trauma, otherness, language and alienation, and it anchors us in a particular kind of relation with what we have lost.

In this now ideological frame what is lost is actualised in some other form, rendered into a product of our activity and in principle available to us, if not actually ever possessed. Trauma is thus transformed into an event that hit us directly once upon a time and which can be identified as the cause of distress. It is even sometimes seen as a function of modern life, given emblematic status as something connected with industrialisation and tracked as cause in the flurry of early reports of 'railway spine' (Harrington 2003). Such accidental injuries, traumata as breaches of the body and by implication also of the mind, provided one model for understanding how other shocks to the system might operate. One might say that trauma here is formatted into the life experience of the subject and also into psychiatry as something 'imaginary', organised around the register of perception, representation and communication and what has failed yet to be integrated into that register.

Failure of representation as such, however, is governed by our use of language, our grasp of the symbolic, or at least of one dimension of it. It is here that a constellation of commonsensical symbolic forms – civilisation, reason and health – cluster together with categories of gender, class and race, and particular forms of otherness are thereby constituted. In the psychiatric system at the end of the nineteenth and beginning of the twentieth century the otherness of femininity is thereby captured by the descriptive category of hysteria, and the ability of mad women to symbolise their distress is refracted through their class position and so also with a particular, limited it is assumed, relation to language. And civilisation is increasingly racialised, with motifs of barbarism assuming some importance as the other of civilised reason such that otherness becomes rendered into something opposed to the realm of the dominant language system as a dimension of the 'symbolic' (Fanon 1967; Said 2003).

At the same time, however, language itself is a material force – a system of descriptive labels, grammatical rules and symbolic resources – that hooks our representations of the world onto the world itself. The conception psychiatry has of symptoms, as signs to be interpreted in order to reveal another level of functional arrangements and forms of dysfunction, requires a particular, if implicit, theory of language. Here there is something more than a simple assumption that language gives us access to reality, though that notion of reality and realistic appraisal of things in the world is important enough as an index of rationality. The concern with language disturbances as the observable manifestations of mental disorder makes of language itself a symbolic system that should facilitate communication between subjects – there is therefore something necessarily 'symbolic' and 'imaginary' to it – but it seems now to also have its own independent existence as something resistant to representation, 'real'.

It is not possible to separate these three registers – imaginary, symbolic and real – and to attempt to disentangle them is to court disaster, but they are knotted together by something that is itself a malaise of modern life, something that appears to be a function of the disintegration of clearly ordered social relationships under feudalism. This something is alienation, and it is no accident that the psychiatrists in those early years were known as 'alienists' (Littlewood and Lipsedge 1993).

Transmission

We now have a frame in place, a psychiatric frame, within which and against which psychoanalysis emerged at a particular historical moment, with the birth of capitalism still dependent on pre-capitalist modes of production and corresponding social relations. This frame provided an institutional context for a distinctive kind of reduction to sex and pathology, and this is a reduction which also serves to combine the two, exemplified in the gaze of the male psychiatrist on the female hysteric. One of the first key differences that opened up between psychiatry and psychoanalysis was articulated by this gaze, a difference between the attempt to render pathology visible, putting patients on display so that the hysterical complaint could be observed, and an attention to language so that the process of speaking about distress could also become a talking cure (Copjec 1993; Gilman 1996). This turn to language, with the patient speaking to the doctor in the consulting room, shifts the space of the cure from public into private space. In addition there is a significant shift in the way psychoanalytic practice is transmitted through a training that comes to rely on apprenticeship devoted to speech and reported speech (Bakan 1958/1990).

The late-feudal character of the psychiatric frame also draws attention to another form of reduction intertwined with those of sex and pathology which still has a bearing on the training of psychoanalysts today. This form of reduction, expressed in the class character of psychoanalysis, operates by way of the silent presuppositions that are made about who may and may not access treatment and who may or may not train as analysts. We can lay out some coordinates for mapping the class character of psychoanalysis, coordinates concerned with received wisdom about class as a link between identity and position, class assumed to be relayed through fixed status and marked by attributes given by breeding and comportment (Gibson-Graham *et al.* 2001; Chakrabarti and Dhar 2010). One should note here that psychiatry takes shape as a normalising practice precisely at the moment when feudalism is disintegrating, but it then relays feudal relations into the encounter between doctor and patient that define the early years of psychiatric treatment in nascent bourgeois society. It is possible for psychiatry to flower as a late-feudal apparatus only when Enlightenment preoccupations with rationality take hold in a triumphant capitalist economy. The class character of psychoanalysis is thus marked by social relations in a state of decay, out of kilter with the emergence of a 'democratic' ethos in the West. These feudal, and classically psychiatric, notions of class are rather different from those of the more meritocratic ideology that comes to the fore under capitalism, but they still operate inside psychoanalysis today.

First, there is the class composition of the body of psychoanalysts constituted as a professional group determined either directly by medical training, which filters out working-class applicants, or by a trajectory through university education (Greenhalgh *et al.* 2004). Second, there is the response by this group to issues brought to analysis, which is indicative not only of the practitioner's own class position but also of their unwillingness to acknowledge and transcend it (Layton *et al.* 2006). Third, there is the class composition of those who become analysands, who have the inclination and time to devote to self-exploration (Danto 2005). Fourth, there is the way that particular things are spoken about, and how particular concerns – sex and pathology – are focused upon and other questions are interpreted in relation to those concerns (Kumar 2009).

Psychoanalytic training usually succeeds in bracketing out these questions, and it is the very abstraction of the clinical encounter from social relations that makes it possible for class to be treated as extraneous, as a disturbing factor when it is raised as an issue. It is then that the taboo on class in psychoanalysis becomes evident and those who touch it are pathologised for speaking beyond the taken-for-granted parameters of the conceptual order that organises its practice (Samuels 1993).

Representation

The distinctive set of human relations that structure the core theoretical principles of psychoanalysis, described in Freud's (1913) historical account of the Oedipus complex, are *class* relations. They are many other things besides of course, and critical attention has tended to focus on the patriarchal assumptions built into what is sometimes taken to be a purely logical triangular relation, a relation between infant and its first love object and with the 'third term' that separates the first two and so introduces the infant into the domain of other people in human society (Muller 1996). It derives its patriarchal character from the ideological-affective valence that is given to the father as the one who intervenes between infant and (what is usually assumed to be) the mother. Then there is a political assessment of what this means, whether on the one hand this describes particular historically-specific patriarchal conditions of the relation between child-rearing and the public sphere or whether it does actually describe universal conditions by which a child of whatever sex is necessarily of a woman born. Disentangling the formal triangle from social context has been one of the tasks of feminist analysis, which has taken place both inside and against psychoanalysis (Mitchell 1974).

These critical analyses then intersect with conceptual debates inside psychoanalysis over the importance that should be accorded to the third term – the 'father' perhaps, or some other logical operator – as facilitating the mediation of the human subject with others. The theoretical questions for psychoanalysis then concern the perils that befall those that have experienced no mediation at all – in which case it is assumed that they risk being trapped in a variety of narcissistic disorders or subject to the ravages of the maternal super-ego – or they concern how we should understand the nature of mediation itself, as function of castration of some kind or as the construction of a different form of relation to others that goes beyond what is conceivable under patriarchy (Ettinger 2004; Pollock 2004; cf. Neill 2008). There are clearly political issues here concerning how little boys and girls are borne into human culture as beings separate and distinct from one another. What these debates also draw attention to, however, is the way that relations of class become sexualised and distribute gender roles and affective qualities to different kinds of being.

Oedipal relations are refracted through feudal class relations when individual development becomes part of the interpretative matrix of psychoanalysis formed at a time when those feudal class relations operate as archaic residues within nascent capitalist society. These relations then come to function as a relay through which the compact between lord and bondsman provides an underlying structure of recognition (Benjamin 1988; Butler 1997). The boy infant is only able to accede to rights of property and status by attempting to seize what is rightfully his – the body of the mother – and accepting that he must wait for his appointed time and place in the chain of being. The girl, in this patriarchal system, is herself a form of property, and eventually gives up her hope of ever gaining mastery over it.

This division between human subjects around property ownership and rights to it given by a direct lineage governed by the figure of the father also lays down the still hegemonic ground-rules for notions of social structure assumed by psychoanalysis. Sex and class are thus meshed together so that a particular set of class relations comes to structure psychoanalytic theory and practice, and it also underpins the institutional arrangements that govern psychoanalytic training. These institutional arrangements are also necessarily meshed in with the division between nation states through which psychoanalysis is complicit with forms of colonialism. Psychoanalysis in each part of the world has been torn between affiliation to a centre and an acknowledgement of cultural particularities, and the distribution of the sites in which psychoanalysis is recognised as existing by those who assume the position of the master in such matters always separates a place of origin, perhaps even marked by displacement through migration and exile, from what the English-speaking psychoanalytic organisations once called 'the rest of the world' (Derrida 1988: 75). One significant way that class relations are manifested and reproduced is therefore through where in the world the training and clinical practice take place.

Demonstration

Lacanian psychoanalysis was inaugurated at a moment when feudal class relations decayed to the point where it was doubtful whether they could actually sustain the normative child development and distribution of the sexes that the oedipal paradigm demands. Lacan (1991/2007) declared fairly late in his teaching that conceptions of the Oedipus complex rooted in appeals to anthropological studies of a primal horde and overthrow of the leader of the horde are but elements of 'Freud's dream', and this dream should, he says, be interpreted as a fantasy about human relations that has a retroactive structuring effect on the way we have come to make sense of our history and identity. But it is very early in his writing that a key motif in his work appears, that of the 'decline of the paternal imago' in Western culture (Lacan 1938). Then the question that comes to haunt Lacanian theory is whether that decline is a traumatic moment at which human civilisation itself starts to collapse or whether it opens up the space for quite different kinds of mediated social relations (Dufour 2008).

Nevertheless, those forms are still reproduced in a teaching in which the master displays himself, displays his knowledge and sometimes even his patients to the class. There are even more grotesque remainders of this practice in the public 'case presentations', popular pedagogic forums in German and French psychiatry in which those labelled with different categories of disorder are paraded in the auditorium. Freud was able to see how hysteria could be induced through hypnosis by Charcot, and kept a picture of one of Charcot's case presentations on his study wall, then over his couch in his consulting room. Lacan (1980), and some of his followers today, repeat this pedagogical practice, and one can see in the records of such presentations how one patient, who evidently knows who Lacan is, refers to the imaginary, symbolic and real, sending back to Lacan a message about the character of 'imposed speech' in a 'Lacanian psychosis'.

Such spectacles are not only public events that operate in the register of the gaze, but they provide the setting for an operation of 'interpretation' of the classical type. That is, they call for the psychiatrist to display his powers of diagnosis and to take that further, into something approaching psychoanalysis, which claims to change as well as describe distress. Then there must be an interpretation that will have an impact on the patient, indeed an interpretation dramatic enough to itself produce a public demonstration that it has an impact on the patient (Strachey 1934).

Lacanian psychoanalysis has since undergone a significant shift away from the gaze to the voice, and this has taken different forms in versions of the practice. In one version, for example, there is a shift away from interpretation conventionally understood to the 'cut'. The argument here is that the unconscious feeds on interpretation; it does already in fact operate by continually interpreting, and so psychoanalytic intervention needs to work in a different way, finding different techniques by which this interpretation can be questioned and the subject shifted into a different relation to their interpretative activity (Miller 1999a). There is thus a shift to the voice here, voice as object a (Miller 2007a) – but in another version the shift is also away from the cut as something that keeps psychoanalysis within a 'phallic' paradigm toward a different way of working with the subject around motifs of 'borderlinking' and 'metramorphosis' (Ettinger 2004; Pollock 2004), though there are concerns that this slides back from Lacan to some version of object relations (Chiesa 2007).

There is, in both practices – both, it should be noted, elaborated from within but one of the many Lacanian organisations founded since Lacan's death – an attempt to go beyond the rule of a 'master signifier' and the activity of an individual agent modelling themselves upon it as independent of the rest of language and of social networks that constitute it. Such variations on standard treatment demonstrate that a field of clinical activity has opened up that is capable of replacing psychiatric appeals to reality and the reordering of those who have slipped its net.

Reality

Psychoanalysis usually refuses to fall in line with one of the most powerful ideological forms bequeathed by late feudalism, that of 'experience', and it replaces experience as a space of meaningful activity with 'structure' as a phenomenon that needs to be theoretically mapped. Experience, which provides a warrant for an agent to immerse themselves in a system of knowledge and thereby become an accomplished practitioner in the arts of interpretation and management of others, accumulates a series of connotations under capitalism by which it becomes both more scientific and commonsensical. Experience still has resonances with experimentation; through this semiotic link it maintains itself as a category that can be accommodated by psychiatry, and it chimes with a more humanistic sentiment that guarantees the integrity of each individual's perception of the world. Here it becomes sedimented in the democratic rights of the bourgeois subject, and so it is possible for psychiatry to both free the mad from their chains and to circumscribe their freedom of movement among other free-thinking individuals (Foucault 1961/2009).

It is here that the false promise of 'anti-psychiatry' breaks from psychiatric terminology but then, in its very appeal to experience, risks functioning as an all the more seductive ante-room to the psychiatric clinic. So then, some Lacanians argue, the very care that an anti-psychiatrist shows for their patients will serve to intensify their 'psychiatrisation'; they dream of therapeutic communities that are not only compatible with liberal-democratic ideology but which are still always organised around one strong personality (Spandler 2006); in this vein Jacques-Alain Miller (1980: 46) argues that when anti-psychiatrists speak of rendering society 'psychotic', 'they are preparing it for "psychiatrization"' (cf. Sedgwick 1982). It was indeed the fate of the anti-psychiatry movement that it was led by maverick psychiatrists, and it is a significant complexly-layered irony that many of these strong personalities were trained first as psychoanalysts, some even as Lacanians (e.g. Guattari 1984).

The relationship between the psychiatrist as the strong personality and the fragile divided self that he experiences himself to be as he practises and then fails needs to be opened up in a different way. The late-feudal structure of psychiatric discourse – the figure of the master embedded in a system of knowledge that they are dependent upon, and prey to doubts about their power – is subverted and rearticulated by Lacan. The direction of the patient in psychiatry is subverted and rearticulated already by Freud (1904) who notices that the fundamental technical rule of psychoanalysis throws into question the tyranny of the doctor who intends to give moral guidance. Free association opens up a dimension of speech in which the subject who analyses as they speak to the analyst realises that there is something beyond their experience which blocks, diverts and distorts what it is they think they want to say. The blockages, diversions and distortions are themselves meaningful, and the lesson of the dream-work that Freud (1900/1999) outlines as a principle that can be applied to every form of self-censorship is that this is the very stuff of desire. Desire is encoded in the distortions, and can be unlocked as it is interpreted or cut to shape, rather than being excavated from another realm of experience that bubbles away under the surface as if it is actually in another place.

In psychoanalysis an appeal to reality will not do the trick, and neither will an appeal to yet another reality behind commonsensical everyday reality. One of the lessons of analysis is precisely that there is 'no Other of the Other'; there is a significant shift to Lacan's position that 'there is no Other of the Other' in *Seminar VI* from his claim a year earlier that 'the universe of language could not articulate itself' without the existence of an Other (Chiesa 2007: 107; Roper 2009). And so the task of the analyst, Lacan (1958) insists, is to direct the treatment instead of directing the patient. In fact, the figure of the patient as such as the one who should be directed has been replaced by the figure of the 'analysand', the one who analyses. Uncertainty is not now a sign of failure on the part of the doctor, but is viewed as a necessary activity of questioning, even of challenge to the doctor, on the part of the analysand. A pathological condition – 'hysteria' – is thus transformed into a positive condition for psychoanalysis, in the 'hystericisation' of the analysand. Here we also have a necessary challenge to adaptation, for if the reality that psychiatry subscribes to is thrown into question then any adaptation to it becomes undesirable, even impossible. There are still residues of an adaptationist ethos in Freud's practice, but we have seen that Lacan argues that the human being is always already 'disadapted' to the culture that makes it human – as a subject who speaks – and that forms of psychoanalysis that do aim to adapt this subject to society have betrayed the questioning that the practice is predicated upon.

Structure

Lacan breaks almost entirely from adaptationist tendencies in psychoanalysis, tendencies given by the feudal character of psychiatry and then assimilated to the operations of the psy complex under capitalism, and he breaks almost entirely from the temptation to direct the patient. There is a limit to the break, however, and this is expressed in the incomplete reformulation of psychiatric diagnostic categories by most Lacanians even when they tackle the emergence of 'contemporary symptoms' said to include 'addiction', 'eating disorders' and 'depression' (Britton 2004; Klotz 2009).

There is, first, a tension between German and French psychiatric traditions, a difference that is mined extensively by Lacanian psychoanalysts. French psychiatric conceptions of 'structure' do provide a fruitful alternative to the tabulation of symptomatology derived from German psychiatry that then provides the basis of the diagnostic systems now dominant in the English-speaking world. However, to invoke 'structure' as an absent cause of forms of speech is still to remain trapped in those categories, and the limits of the break can be seen in the reference by Lacan (1966b: 65) to certain psychiatrists as respected antecedents who are treated as masters in such matters (cf. Stavrakakis 2007a: 135, for the suggestion that this display of deference was sarcastic).

There is, second, a tension between the use of psychiatric terminology to categorise those who are not normal (which presupposes that there is still a healthy subject position from which the others may be described), and the use of this terminology to describe each and every subject. Freud usually opted for the first approach, and so the psychoanalyst would either be recruited from the ranks of the normal subjects or would become normal through their own analysis. This is a motif that recurs in claims that there are certain kinds of person who are more suited to being psychoanalysts than others, those defined by the character of their very being rather than their training (cf. Lacan 1958). Lacan (1961–1962), opting for the second approach, makes the point toward the end of *Seminar IX* that 'the neurotic like the pervert, like the psychotic himself, are only faces of the normal structure' (13 June 1962: 11) (Vanheule 2009). There is no absolutely normal subject position outside these categories, no position from which it would be possible for the psychoanalyst to be able to adopt a 'metalanguage' to describe the others; there is a general point here that 'there is no metalanguage that can be spoken, or, more aphoristically, that there is no Other of the Other' (Lacan 1960: 688).

This second approach raises a question about the nature of diagnosis as formulated from within the other structures. This question is often resolved too quickly, stitched over in Lacanian psychoanalysis, and the 'desire of the analyst' comes to operate as a filler term that comes to stand in for something like 'normal' (Libbrecht 1998). This limit, and the solution that reiterates it, is recapitulated in the way the position of the analyst is described in Lacanian psychoanalysis. Lacan pits himself against traditions of psychoanalysis that direct the patient and that aim to adapt the patient to reality – against traditions of psychoanalysis that function in an uneasy alliance with psychiatry – and identification of the ego of the patient with the ego of the analyst is scorned and refused (Hartmann 1939/1958). There is, however, a surreptitious form of identification still at work in Lacan's attempt to escape the reduction of psychoanalysis to 'ego psychology', surreptitious because it operates by way of the very structure of the treatment and the institutional context in which it operates rather than through the direct intentions of the analyst.

Within the psychiatric frame the patient is treated as an object, and the nature of this object is reformatted in psychoanalytic discourse that simply defines itself against psychiatry. It is now the psychoanalyst who aims to take the position of an object, and the analysand defines themselves as subject against that position, defines themselves through a series of reflections concerning who they are in relation to that object. The series of relations to the analyst as object takes place through signifying operations we call 'transference' (Lacan 2006). There is then a transformation through which the analysand comes to drop the analyst as prized object, to 'desuppose' them as a subject supposed to know, which defines, provides one definition for, the end of analysis.

However, this transformation does not lead to a fullness of being, an expansion of subjectivity, still less to the strengthening of the ego. Instead it leads the analysand to their lack, to a different relation to language, to the clinical structure that defines the parameters of their relation to language, precisely to being able to drop not only the analyst as object but their attachment to object a such that they come to terms with what it is to be an object themselves. At which point they may become an analyst, and so some form of institutional identification is installed (Lacan 1967–1968). That identificatory structure risks replicating diagnostic categories that become embedded in the experience of the analysand whose treatment is directed in a manner that is tailored to their own particular clinical structure. It may even serve to adapt them to a system of clinical structures that they will repeat as a master-code if they go on to become analysts themselves.

Replications

Psychiatry, a late-feudal medical apparatus for the diagnosis, adaptation and direction of those viewed as eccentric to society, provides some distinctive conceptual capsules of the subject that are still current and poses some particular problems for progressive politics. Psychoanalysis that shows fealty to psychiatry is then hamstrung, and risks replicating oppressive social relations, the most archaic reactionary social forms that are no longer even functional in contemporary capitalism. Lacan's work also replicates some of those archaic social forms, and we will need to work through reinterpretations of this work in order to shake them off. Such reinterpretations are already present in Lacan's own writing, and we will elaborate how these bear on different facets of psychoanalysis.

There are, first, questions of epistemology – conceptions of knowledge and the process by which it is possible to know about oneself and the world – which are, as we have seen, organised in Lacanian psychoanalysis through reference to 'structure' and to 'recognition'. Linked with the appeal to these contradictory conceptual frameworks, there are, second, institutional questions that concern the sites in which psychoanalysis is practised, and the way the position of the analyst gives to the treatment a direction that is shadowed by silent assumptions about the nature of class and sex and other axes of exploitation and oppression. There are, third, ontological questions concerning the way the being of the analyst is formed through their own analysis, and how the trajectory of the analysand through the analysis as they speak to another is traced and how it is thought to end. Bound up with these questions of being and becoming, there are, fourth, political questions concerning the nature of social categories and identities, and how ideological and moralising conceptions of the world in psychoanalysis seep into the clinic and then, equally problematically, out of it again.

The limited space for self-transformation that a psychiatric conception of the subject bequeaths psychoanalysis is, however, challenged by the more radical elements of Lacanian clinical work. I explore in more detail how it may be possible to shift emphasis from limits to possibilities for change in the next chapter.

Chapter 2

Psychiatrising speech

This chapter examines psychiatric conceptions of ethics and implications for clinical practice. It reviews the assumption that there is some good to which we should aspire as a state of mind or form of behaviour, and it shows how Lacanian psychoanalysis breaks from that assumption. The importance of ethical questions in the analytic process is explored, to include discussion of how Lacanian psychoanalysts make 'diagnoses', including some problematic resonances with the pathologisation of those who dissent from current social norms. There is a focus on specific forms of pathology here; on obsessional concerns with compliance, on psychosis in relation to certainty, on hysteria as productive challenge, and on perversion as transgression of a bond with others. Against this backdrop of psychiatrised forms of analytic work it is possible to discern how sexual difference, jouissance, naming of the subject, the phallus and transference are played out, inside and outside the clinic.

Seductions

Psychiatry chains ethics to a version of life organised around an image of what it takes to be the good, and that 'good life' is then pitted against madness, badness and, of course, death. It is sometimes said that psychoanalysis, when it is not busy reducing what we are to sex, reduces life to death, detects in the trajectory of our lives a drive toward the inorganic state from whence we came. But if '*the aim of all life is death*', as Freud (1920: 38) averred, it is a kind of death as emptiness that precedes, haunts and awaits us (Sulloway 1980); it gives rise to an ethics in Lacanian psychoanalysis that is very different from mere moralising in favour of a full good life.

This is why psychoanalysis is a scandal in psychiatry, unfolding a new logic that questions the late-feudal phenomenological bedrock of positivist medical practice applied to maladies of the mind. Psychiatry subscribes to an opposition between life and death that is enclosed and informed by a struggle for recognition that constitutes lord and bondsman, 'master and slave' (Hegel 1807/1977; Kojève 1969). An old European model of ethics and the good life also comes to be inscribed within this battleground, an ethics of the ideal standard, accessible perhaps only to those who can assume the status of dead masters, experts on the moral worth of the living (Rajchman 1991). The problem with this ethical position, a problem disclosed by psychoanalysis, is that such an ideal is based on a particular experience of what is alluring to us, whoever 'we' imagine we are. It is an ideal that is now suffused with fantasy such that objects of delight for some are liable to mutate into objects of horror for others, even for us too. The emergence of a new form of 'biopolitics' with the birth and decay of capitalism, one concerned with the management of the self and forms of 'bare life' at the margins of normal civilised institutions, is warning enough of how perceptions of delight and horror are distributed now between masters and slaves (Agamben 1998).

Just as the lord needs the bondsman and so despises and fears him all the more for that, so this version of life needs death as its other, another twist in this dialectic, and psychiatrists have depended upon an ever-expanding corpus of sick material in which signs of peculiar life conditions and the risk of death will be discovered. And just as psychoanalysis finds the death drive buried deep inside every life-affirming activity – Lacan transforms this vision with the claim that every drive is a death drive – it shows us now that psychiatry is but a deathly life, an empty shell. Lacan (1964/1973: 257) contends that 'the sexual drives' are 'articulated at the level of significations in the unconscious' and this 'in as much as what they bring out is death – death as signifier and nothing but signifier'.

Psychiatry as such is a parasitic enterprise that absorbs and represents in its own specific rhetoric alchemical, mystical and then scientific investigations into pathologies of the human subject. Its status and location in the madhouses, asylums, hospitals and then university clinics gave to it some substance. Now, as psychoanalysis and other radical approaches to distress disentangle themselves from psychiatric discourse, we are able to treat this medical substance as a *process*, a reiterative process by which knowledge from adjacent disciplines is 'psychiatrised'. There is then a series of consequences for diagnosis, for how psychoanalysis might tackle 'obsessionalising', 'psychoticising', 'hystericising' and 'perversionalising' strategies in the clinic. Our task is to trace how these categories are historically constituted and to engage with them as lived positions in relation to structures of power in contemporary capitalist society, structures of power that now enforce closure around forms of sexualised identity and community just as efficiently as psychiatry enforced closure against the 'non-European' as something other to reason (Said 2003, 2004; Fernando 2003).

Such a kind of nationalist closure was already at work in French psychiatry, and is manifested in responses to psychoanalysis as 'German', differentiated from but accompanied by alien nosological systems of classification, those that were eventually to triumph internationally in the DSM

(Macey 1995). And it is present in Lacan's own predilection for nationalist writers in different intellectual fields of work adjacent to psychoanalysis, even at the same time as he absorbed German philosophical systems of thought through which to read Freud and to engage with organicist currents in French psychiatry (Lacan 1946a).

Psychoanalysis breaks from psychiatry in two significant steps, ethical steps that entwine the life of the doctor with that of the patient. The first step is taken by Freud, and this has the analyst listen to and intervene in the speech of the analysand. There are paradoxical effects here concerning diagnosis. The position of psychiatry as a form of medicine for 'cretins' is refused and replaced with an engagement with its objects of knowledge, an exchange of speech that treats the other as a subject to whom the analyst is accountable as they listen and speak (Moscovici 1976/2008: 73). Psychiatrists displaying exemplary cases to students in the medical theatres at the end of the nineteenth century or diagnosing and prescribing medication at the end of the twentieth can avoid an intersubjective engagement with those they diagnose; psychoanalysts cannot. However, psychoanalysts do not as a rule disclose the diagnosis they make concerning Freudian 'clinical structures' to the analysand, and, as we shall see, Lacanian psychoanalysts should not do so.

The second ethical step is taken by Lacan, and this has the analyst take responsibility for the forms of 'resistance' that kick in as they listen and intervene. Lacan (1958: 235) is with Freud in tracking and addressing resistance in speech in analysis, but insists that 'there is no other resistance to analysis than that of the analyst'. Now let us follow this ethical position in the forms of resistance we encounter as a function of the relation between doctor and patient and expressed in forms of diagnosis.

Obsessionalising

A psychoanalyst working in the shadow of the psychiatric frame which presumes to know the good of the patient has a name for those who are difficult to engage with, those who appear to resist the progress of the analytic work precisely because they are so compliant with the analyst, 'obsessional neurotic'. Compliance is a telling characteristic of this kind of patient, but their resistance may be covert and efficient enough to provoke the analyst to assume – 'almost surreptitiously' Lacan (1979: 407) says – the position of master, a 'moral master'. It is precisely that dialectical interrelationship between positions of master and slave, one constituting and inciting the other to resist what they are being pulled into, that we need to keep focused on here to grasp how psychoanalysis itself participates in an obsessionalising practice.

Freud (1894) noted that there is often to be detected, in the mind of the analytic patient charged with the impossible task of free association, a protected private space of thinking, an obsessional secretive enclosure which sabotages the work. The analysand in these cases holds close to themselves some thoughts, and derives some satisfaction from being able to keep the analyst out. When Freud first grouped together a series of symptoms into the category of 'obsessional neurosis', he was identifying a system of rituals that inhabit and imprison the mind of a particular kind of individual.

If we decompose this diagnostic category into its constituent elements we can start to see how this image of the individual, usually a stereotypically male individual, functions ideologically. By 'ideological' here I mean the way in which a system of beliefs corresponds with and warrants a set of political-economic arrangements, specifically those of bourgeois democracy emerging from the cocoon of feudal relations that psychiatry replicates under capitalism (Kovel 1981). Here these beliefs are about the individual, beliefs the individual has about themselves, two aspects of belief that are mutually implicative in the field of mental health. The representation of 'false consciousness' as some kind of mistaken view of reality on the part of individuals caught in the grip of ideology can then itself also come to function ideologically. Under capitalism we are necessarily falsely-conscious about the world and our place in it precisely because that consciousness of the world is actually a fairly accurate way of mapping and moving about the symbolic now (Sohn-Rethel 1978; Žižek 1989).

Those who suffer in obsessional mode under capitalism are subjects who buy into the separation of intellectual and manual labour, the separation of thinking from being, and live out the predicament of a puzzle about the nature of being as if false consciousness really did operate only at the level of the individual. Lacan argues that the question that haunts the obsessional neurotic concerns being, existence, their right to exist and whether they are alive or dead (Lacan 1981/1993: 178–180). The 'obsessions' are repetitive ideas manifested in a series of actions from which the subject seems unable to escape. Even though this eventually may result in suffering that is too much to bear, enough to bring someone to ask for help, it is still stubbornly tied to personal administrative strategies that contain an unbearable surplus of satisfaction – 'jouissance' is our name for this excess – within the domain of the 'pleasure principle' (Miller 2000a; Corti 2004). The obsessional neurotic, then, seems able most of the time to rein in the drives and to stop them taking him over onto the 'other shore of enjoyment' (as one early Japanese translation of 'beyond the pleasure principle' had it) where they spill over from the realm of life to death (Sato 2002: 11).

That Freud (1907) should see obsessional neurotic activities as homologous to religious rituals indicates the way he positions psychoanalysis in the Western Enlightenment tradition and against feudal-mystical residues. Lacan (1979) also homes in on this connection between the individual and the social, but from a different angle, when he explores the 'individual myth' of the neurotic in a discussion of the young Goethe, for whom there are elaborate disguises affected during courting his love and an alienation from himself that reproduces a series of impasses. This exploration leads Lacan (ibid.: 422) to shift our attention to the 'quaternary' nature of oedipal relations and to characterise what he calls 'the early experience of the modern subject' as one in which 'the father is the representative, the incarnation, of a symbolic function'. This brings us to the predicament of the obsessional modern subject, or rather the obsessional mode in which the subject lives under capitalism, and a form of necessary false consciousness that is itself misapprehended as if it comprises individual cognitive errors; there is 'an extremely obvious discrepancy between the symbolic function and what is perceived by the subject in the sphere of experience' (ibid.: 423).

Why is the oedipal relation 'quaternary' rather than triangular? Here the answer Lacan (1979: 424) gives is that there is a fourth element at work, which is death. The answer is different later in his work when the father appears as a fourth element to supplement and structure the relation between child, mother and phallus (Lacan 1981/1993: 319). In the case of the obsessional neurotic this death appears not only in their own enclosed self-questioning about their right to exist. It also reappears in their relation to the figure of the master and the idea that it will not be possible for them to really live until their master dies. It is here that the subject also locks themselves into a temporal structure in which they procrastinate, and it is the moment when Hamlet – hesitating over an act that will define his right to exist – is reconfigured as a modern subject, subject to what it is only now – after psychoanalysis – right to call the Oedipus complex (Lacan 1959/1977).

It is of course possible to trace the obsessional neurotic enclosure of thought, hesitation over the question of being and the futile wait for the master to die, to the way an individual is formed within a particular kind of nuclear family, engendered in the little feudal kingdoms of child-rearing crystallised under capitalism. The figure of the master is reinstituted in the analytic relationship and the individual patient is configured as a kind of mirror-image of their analyst, an analyst who may be tempted to imagine that they are a master. The appearance of psychoanalysis on the world stage is predicated on a split between mind and body, a split that it also attempts to resolve. Freud's invention of the subject of psychoanalysis takes seriously René Descartes' (1641/1996: 68) dictum that the doubting subject is certain only insofar as it is thinking – 'I am thinking, therefore I am, or I exist' – and Lacan then buries the Cartesian cogito in the unconscious (Dolar 1998).

The modern subject divided between consciousness and the unconscious is therefore always already obsessional, and this is why we can describe the very structure of capitalism in this way. The stereotypically masculine second nature of psychiatrically-framed psychoanalytic practice is structured by the feudal preoccupation with mastery, replicated in the patriarchal nuclear family structure, and then in the encounter with the analysand who complies with the demands of the master to the point where they may sabotage the analysis. This second nature constitutes the too-patient patient as a problem to be solved and tangles the analyst in a practice that is itself 'obsessionalising' of those they aim to treat. To name this process is a first step to disentangling ourselves from individualising strategies that are a necessary part of a political-economic system that triumphed over feudalism and its avatars in psychiatry.

Psychoticising

Those who assume the position of master in the analytic process – as psychiatrist or as simulacrum of this figure – meet their match in a certain kind of patient who refuses to assume the position of analysand. And, Lacan notes, it is certainty that is the defining feature of what he, and his masters before him, call the 'psychotic'. This is the patient who both replicates and subverts the certainty that the analyst may enjoy when they conclude that the patient speaking or refusing to speak is really psychotic, and then this enjoyment is quickly followed by a glimmer of doubt. This replication and subversion of certainty is the source of the oscillation between sureness and tentativeness of diagnosis that has come to mark contemporary psychoanalytic clinical case presentations, including those by Lacanians. (One hears the analyst declare that the patient they are describing is without doubt psychotic, and then in the next breath there is justification for this decision which revolves around the claim that it is wise to err on the side of caution.) This, because the unravelling of a belief system that may in fact be delusional and protective of the subject – the belief system that is itself the attempt at recovery – may 'trigger' psychosis.

There has been an incremental rise in the number of diagnoses of psychotic structure by Lacanian psychoanalysts in recent years, a function of two theoretical shifts. First there was a significant shift in Lacan's own writing – from a description of psychosis rooted in 'foreclosure' of – refusal to acknowledge, let alone recognise as legitimate – the 'Name-of-the-Father' to an account of a particular form of knotting together of the symbolic, imaginary and real (Thurston 1998, 2002). The second shift took place after Lacan's death, particularly in the work of Miller (2009), from psychosis seen as a discrete clinical structure to a theoretical elaboration of 'generalised foreclosure' in the human subject and of 'ordinary psychosis' (Grigg 1998; Klotz 2009). The second shift has sought warrant in the first, in the appeal to a 'late Lacan' who rearticulated the notion of 'clinical structure' as such through the conceptual device of the Borromean knot in which the three registers of the symbolic, imaginary and real are linked together, depicted by the interlinked circles of a knot in which each circle holds the other two in place (Voruz and Wolf 2007). These theoretical developments take forward the progressive revolutionary dynamic of the Lacanian return to Freud, to the possibility of repeating Freud now in a new key that is more in tune with radical political questioning of the normal and the pathological. But before those alternatives can be pursued we need to ask how it is that 'early' Lacanian diagnosis deals with certainty – including its own certainty – by 'psychoticising' it.

First, the patient unwittingly replicates an institutional assumption about agency and knowledge. The analyst whose work is still informed by psychiatric reasoning then receives their own message about the nature of pathology back from the patient who seems very certain about the nature of reality, who does not seem troubled by the doubts that characterise a properly Cartesian subject, the neurotic suffering of a potential analysand. In the face of this certainty the analyst is thrown into a state of perpetual hesitation which they mask by way of careful deliberation, and their status as an obsessional master becomes more evident. This analyst is structurally positioned as a master who is subject to division, who is marked by the effects of an unconscious that they have come to invent for themselves and live with as a consequence of their training and their own analysis.

Second, the patient subverts the relationship between agency, knowledge and the unconscious. Lacan (1959) comments that the psychotic knows something about the nature of language and the relation of the subject to language, knows something more than a neurotic subject, something that an ordinary ('neurotic') subject precisely must not know in order to obtain access to and function in the symbolic. Even the neurotic model subject also has to employ a mechanism as drastic as 'foreclosure' in order not to know how language constitutes the perceiving subject, a mechanism which will enable what Lacan (1959: 447) terms 'subjective "synthesis"' (and recognition of this aspect of foreclosure opens the way to later Lacanian debates over the role of 'generalised foreclosure' as the condition for becoming any kind of subject whatsoever). The analyst is thus faced with a subject who knows something about the unconscious that they, the analyst, must *not* know.

A subject deemed retroactively to be properly neurotic will come face-to-face with the nature of language and their relationship to the signifiers that bear them at the end of analysis when they meet the analyst's desire as one 'that tends in a direction that is the exact opposite of identification', as Lacan (1964/1973: 274) puts it, as 'a desire to obtain absolute difference' (ibid.: 276). This means acknowledging the differential work of language, the 'absolute difference' between signifiers and the cuts into the field of signification which produce meaning, which produce a place for the subject itself to speak. This absolute difference also entails lack, for it is at this point in analysis that we could say that the analysand becomes a pure Saussurean, recognising that in language there are only differences without positive terms and without a positive fullness of intention underneath which produces the meaning; 'It is at the point of lack that the subject has to recognise himself' (ibid.: 270). The psychotic subject, however, already knows about absolute difference – they suffer the void of being and cuts in language – and that is precisely why their rendezvous with the analyst is seen as so very different from that of a neurotic subject. The direction of the treatment for this kind of subject is therefore designed to recreate symbolic systems, a stable order out of nothing, rather than to dissolve them into nothing.

Lacan makes an intriguing move here concerning sexual difference in his discussion of 'psychosis', one which perpetuates the defining if covert role of masculinity in feudal-patriarchal varieties of psychoanalytic work. In place of Freud's (1911) dubious essentialising claim that paranoia is a defence against homosexuality, Lacan at one moment shows us that such a sexual motif is constructed as part of a delusional system but at the next reconstructs an account of psychosis around what has been described as the 'push to the woman' (Brousse 2003). The 'psychoticising' of certain kinds of patient who appear to live their relation to reality in a way that is delusional because it is so certain is thereby infused with a series of assumptions about how 'woman' is constituted; she is that which erupts against those who would be the agents of psychiatric knowledge, 'men' (cf. Rosemont 1978; Macey 1988).

Hystericising

There was already in Freud's writing acknowledgement that the peculiar relationship between analyst and analysand provides the setting for 'transference neuroses', and Lacanians have then drawn the conclusion that this is where psychoanalysis departs from psychiatry, for transference provides the means by which clinical structures can be differentiated (Soler 1996a). In the case of hysteria – the quintessential neurotic condition identified and displayed in late nineteenth-century psychiatric training – transference provides the occasion not only for psychoanalysts to diagnose hysteria but even to incite it as that which will question, challenge and dismantle the symptom when the subject speaks to another in the clinic. In this, hysteria anticipates the trajectory of transference itself first as a hindrance and then as a tool in psychoanalysis, for it is first specified as a problem to be solved and then treated as a necessary obstacle, a double-function for which the German term '*Anstoss*' to simultaneously signify obstacle and condition is so useful (Žižek 2006: 223). Here is resistance to analysis that is productive, but the place of the analyst in this form of resistance still has to be teased out, together with the distribution of representations of femininity and masculinity in the cure.

Unlike the motif of 'suggestion' in the quasi-medical traditions of mesmerism and hypnotism, traditions which psychoanalysis had to distance itself from in order to distil a theory of transference, hysteria was absorbed ready-made from psychiatry into psychoanalysis. The category of hysteria therefore carries with it a history concerning sexual difference, a history not so easily dispelled when we see psychoanalysis as entailing a process of 'hystericisation'. Freud took a first step against the characterisation of hysteria as a female malady when he saw displays of it while visiting Charcot and Bernheim, and they showed him not only that suggestion could conjure up and dissolve hysterical symptomatology but that 'conversion symptoms' could occur in men as well as women (recognition of which was actually fairly commonplace in nineteenth-century psychiatry). Hysteria, in which psychical conflict was expressed in the body, was governed by forms of representation, representation of the body rather than the expression in the mind of underlying organic dysfunction. Among other things this raised a question about the representation that patients labelled hysterics had of female and male bodies. A shift of emphasis in psychoanalysis from the body and 'affect' to representations now enables us to trace how such representations are historically constituted (Showalter 1997).

In contrast with the obsessionalising of analysands who seal themselves off from the relationship with the analyst, those who seem to annul the Other's desire, the process of hystericising forms a subject who questions the analyst as master, rebels against the relationship but by attempting to redefine it. In place of obsessional guilt, in which the internalising of real or fantasised encounters with jouissance is re-enacted in a private space which also then tries to shut out the analyst, hysterical accusation is turned outwards and even messages from the unconscious that have been trapped in the body are designed to be noticed by others. 'Hysteric' was the name for those women who dramatised their distress, opened it to the gaze of others including psychiatrists and embarrassed those subjected to such a spectacle. That this caused embarrassment for those who watched, as much if not more so than for those who acted out their distress, is crucial to the way what is sometimes referred to as the analyst's 'countertransference' comes to define what they see and hear (Heimann 1950). Psychiatric description of their patients' lack of decorum, description that marked them as 'unfeminine' at the very same moment as it reduced them to their sex, then comes to suffuse psychoanalytic concern with those who affect others and appear to have designs on the desire of others.

'Hysterical identification' which is supposed to underwrite mass psychology is conceptually modelled by Freud (1921) on the ostensibly feminine predisposition to form alliances between those subject to the figure of a leader, perhaps to a 'leading idea' but even so an idea which is derived from a representation of a father for all others. Hysterical identification is already now at work in psychoanalysis to explain how the desire of another could be lived out in a dream, even (or especially, perhaps) in a dream which aims to block the satisfaction of the dreamer and the analyst to whom she tells it. The dream of the 'clever patient' who wants to disprove Freud's (1900/1999: 147) theory that dreams represent the fulfilment of a wish, for example, is traced to the hysterical identification with the desire of another woman, represented in the dream by the appearance of smoked salmon. This example appears early in Freud's work and is then retrieved by Lacan (1958) – who renames it the dream of the 'witty butcher's wife' and finds in the smoked salmon the 'phallus' – to show how the desire of the hysteric is for an unsatisfied desire, and so also to show how that desire is kept alive as desire as such (Chase 1987; Fink 2004). If the condition of the labouring subject under capitalism is obsessional, this is now also layered upon a deeper condition of the subject as such, retroactively posited as always already hysteric.

To 'hystericise' the analysand is therefore to bring to life the analytic subject, to produce a subject of analysis who will question desire and their relationship with the Other, an other who in the transference is present in the figure of the analyst. From Freud on, and up to the present day in Lacanian psychoanalysis, the engagement of women with psychoanalysis is contrasted with the reserved distance that obsessionals, 'men' let us say, tend to strike against it; 'Psychoanalysis suits women, because, as Freud says, they incarnate in culture the subjects who are preoccupied by the question of sexuality, love, desire and *jouissance*' (Miller 1999b: 21). It is not surprising, in this light, that the hysteric becomes a model subject for Lacanians not only in the analytic process which revolves around strategies of hystericisation but also as a conceptual template for what the human subject, subject to language and speaking out in and against it, might be like. The enduring question which drives this subject, and many a psychoanalyst, is what a woman is and what she wants (André 1999). Obsessional neurosis is but a 'dialect', Freud (1909a: 157) says, of hysteria which is the form of neurotic disorder that expresses what is most painful about being human (see also Žižek 1989: 191); it is neurotic disorder bearable perhaps as the 'common unhappiness' which is the most we can hope for at the end of analysis (Breuer and Freud 1895: 305).

A temptation in analysis is that the hystericising process that incites and makes use of a particular category of subject – women more often, men if possible – also invites a form of identification. The hysteric is the ideal partner of the psychoanalyst. They could be other and guide to the analyst who is thereby, whatever their sex, positioned as man. Alternatively, they could be identified with at the very moment they identify with the analyst, and the analyst is thereby, whatever their sex, positioned as woman and so, even more alluring this option, as true subject of psychoanalysis. Lacanians try to circumvent identification between analysand and analyst, but even though there is a sharp critique of such identification as the desired end of analysis in the 'ego psychology' (e.g. Hartmann 1939/1958) and other normative dyadic forms of analysis – Sándor Ferenczi (1909), James

Strachey (1934), Michael Balint (1950) – that Lacan (1958) pitted himself against, there is still a series of lures that are structured into theories of desire and of the subject in Lacanian psychoanalysis (Solano-Suárez 2007).

Perversionalising

The relationship between analyst and analysand – whether that described by the early Lacan's appeals to 'intersubjectivity' or the later Lacan's alternative 'non-relation' more explicitly indexed to lack of sexual rapport – defines psychoanalysis as a practice pitted against psychiatry. While psychiatry is often content to slot manifestations of distress into diagnostic categories, psychoanalysis provides the setting in which interpretations which describe the nature of a symptom accurately also change it. The analytic relationship calls upon a mutual understanding of the goal of psychoanalysis – albeit also as a misunderstanding which itself is of significance during the treatment – which some are unwilling to make use of, and it is these subjects that psychoanalysts have tended to 'perversionalise'. Lacan argues that perverts are those who make themselves the object of another, into an instrument of the jouissance of the Other; in this bare definition we find a source of unease for the psychoanalyst whose position is still structured by psychiatry and who then encounters others who disrupt the relationship that defines their practice (Lacan 1964/1973: 185).

Freud (1927) late in his work saw perversion as a consequence of the 'disavowal' of castration in which, in place of the mother's missing phallus, a fetish is installed. The presence of the phallus – actually in Freud's account it is the absence of the penis as such which is disavowed (a very different matter) – would have provided a guarantee that there was no difference between mother and father, and so also that there was no difference between the lack-less male child (who is the template for perverse subject) and mother. The fetish takes the place of that phallus, and provides just such a guarantee that there are no differences, and no lack in any subject. This view of perversion neatly buttresses psychiatric lists of perverse activities, and provides yet another warrant for pathologising those who flout generational or sexual differences; incest and homosexuality are seen as of a piece, and psychoanalysis continues in the grand tradition of psychiatry in knowing what is good and bad about human behaviour and in knowing the meaning each subject gives to it. Freud (1910: 100) argues that the homosexual 'loves in the way in which his mother loved him when he was a child' for example, and this has fuelled an industry of homophobic analytic accounts of infantile narcissism (e.g. Chasseguet-Smirgel 1985).

It is the breaking of oedipal mediatory structures, those structures that under capitalism define what a human subject should be, that also unfortunately leads Lacan (1960–1961) to oppose Freud's attempt to define homosexuality entirely in relation to cultural norms. We all, Freud (1905:

145) says, make a homosexual object-choice in our unconscious, and fantasy is itself, of necessity, perverse. While normal neuroses of various kinds come to organise suffering in consciousness – to some degree conscious, and in a relationship between consciousness and the unconscious marked by repression – the perversions organise a relationship to sexuality that is not necessarily ever conscious at all. The 'pervert', he – usually, stereotypically – who is 'perversionalised' by psychiatric practice because he sees no use for it and no way by which he can be of use to it, is defined negatively, and this, for example, is one meaning of Freud's (ibid.: 165) comment that the neuroses are the 'negative of the perversions'. Lacan (1960–1961) also fills the oedipal structure with a particular content, insisting that homosexuality was as perverse in ancient Greece as it is in modern France, if marked by a different 'quality of objects' in the two cultures. Lacan was not against homosexuals coming to psychoanalysis and he did not aim to 'cure' them, but even so his position on perverse clinical structure resulted in claims by some analysts that those with such a structure ruled themselves out of analysis whether they liked it or not (Roudinesco 2002; cf. Sauvagnat 2007).

The four subject positions I have outlined so far, those that psychoanalysis names and through which it repeats, even as it tries to distance itself from, the psychiatric categories of obsessional neurosis, psychosis, hysteria and perversion, map the field of human distress as it comes to be organised in Western culture. This is a field of human distress that is then populated by subjects outside the West when they speak within the terms that mental health professionals are able to understand. There are moments when Lacan sets himself against this colonial imposition of structural positions, and here there are openings to conceptualise psychoanalysis as a historical phenomenon and so also as a questionable if not also sometimes enlightening European one. Lacan (1991/2007: 92) comments, for example, that for some of his analysands, colonial subjects in psychoanalysis, 'their childhood was retroactively lived out in our *famil-ial* categories'. To rename these positions as functions of a process that signify the encounters between analyst and analysand – as obsessionalising, psychoticising, hystericising and perversionalising – is also to mark different kinds of relationship of the subject with language. Taking forms of clinical practice as our reference point enables us to avoid essentialising those kinds of relationship as if they were graspable outside language, even outside the language of the clinic.

Once diagnostic categories have been elaborated to capture in a quasi-psychiatric grid the various positions of subjects who suffer in their relation to others, positions that are actualised and reiterated in their relation with the psy professionals they turn to for help, it is possible to allocate other particular forms of pathology to places in that grid. Debates over whether a phobic object might be related to a fetish, whether there may be some connection between phobia as another discrete clinical structure and perversion, provide one example. These questions tend to be settled by way of a description of how those who are outside analysis manage their anxiety about a father who fails to set limits and so how they traverse the Oedipus complex themselves (Machado 1993).

Lacanian psychoanalysts have often resisted the temptation to expand their own diagnostic system beyond hysterical and obsessional neurosis, psychosis and perversion. Lacan's account of the three clinical structures as defined by three specific forms of defence – neurotic 'repression', psychotic 'foreclosure' and perverse 'disavowal' – has laid down the bedrock of a classification which forestalled the proliferation of names for mental disorders that has characterised psychiatry in the last century. At the same time, Lacanian psychoanalysts have been chained to this bedrock, and it will take a good deal of theoretical work inside psychoanalysis to transform these three clinical structures from being seen as underlying pathological formations in each and every human subject to being treated as a function of the spread of psychoanalysis itself.

Insemination

Psychiatry as an apparatus enforcing mental hygiene has come to operate as one of the names of politics in contemporary culture, but the medical model applied to diverse behaviours and modes of experience in order to bring them into line is now also prone to break down under pressure. Political movements that challenge psychiatric definitions of normality and abnormality, particularly those focused on questions of sexual difference and sexual orientation, have brought bourgeois-democratic demands for equality and respect to bear on a discipline that attempted to drag in late-feudal conceptions of the good into life under capitalism. Psychoanalysis has been a sometimes unlikely ally in this struggle, and there has even been, we could say, some kind of 'disavowal' among activists concerning the disjunction between the sphere of civil rights and the domain of the clinic. At the very same moment as psychiatric power was challenged – over the inclusion of 'homosexuality' in the DSM, for example – there has been a bizarre turn to psychoanalytic modes of explanation to account for the grip of prejudice and 'internalised homophobia' (e.g. APA Task Force on Appropriate Therapeutic Responses to Sexual Orientation 2009: viii).

There was once hope that social critique might infuse psychoanalytic clinical work, change at the level of the individual that would really render the personal political. However, the reference points for a practical alternative to ideological normalisation and pathologisation have more often than not been in traditions of work other than Lacanian (e.g. Kovel 1988; Layton *et al.* 2006). This is not accidental, for the Lacanian tradition is a hard-core version of psychoanalysis; it insists on the role of sexual difference in the meaning the subject gives to their life and death, on the way a subject constructs themselves and their ambivalent relation to their objects of love and hate. This means that there is no seamless connection between the struggle of analysand and analyst on the one hand and the struggle for social revolution on the other. The relationship between politics and the clinic is *impossible*, and so instead of skirting around the disjunction between the two domains we need to tackle it head on.

The 'Freudian clinical structures' that Lacanians condense from the position they adopt as masters in relation to their subjects – a psychiatrically-sourced position that still inflects the work of the most enlightened analyst – entail a constellation of theoretical elements. Among the most salient are jouissance, the Name-of-the-Father, the phallus and transference, and even though those four elements are embedded in a hermetic interrelationship with a host of other defining features of Lacan's work, we can approach the crucial question of the disjunction between politics and the clinic by focusing on those elements first.

Psychoanalysis sexualises social relations, and Lacanian description of the subject appears to dissolve boundaries between what is interior to it and what lies in the outside world. Fantasy is not, for Lacan, contrasted with reality such that a moral position or political demand in the 'real world' could be treated as independent of what the subject wants, or does not want even though they say they want it. However, even though the boundary between self and others is not drawn around the 'individual' – as if that were an undivided and discrete entity thinking and choosing between good and bad – a boundary is constructed, questioned, and reconstructed by Lacanians at another level, the level of the subject (Fink 1995; Chiesa 2007).

This kind of subject can make use of psychoanalysis as a particular kind of space to question itself only if there is a *disjunction* between that space and space outside the clinic. It is at the point of connection between the two that there is a double-insemination, an injection of contents from one space into the other. Cultural representations of psychoanalysis – of the clinic as a sexualised closed space – intersect with the fantasies of the inhabitants of that space, analyst and analysand, about the nature of 'reality', of the outside world. Theoretical elaboration of the disjunction between these spaces, the disjunction as it operates in different elements of Lacanian psychoanalysis, is therefore a clinical concern and a political one.

Excess

Lacan 'formalises' Freud. That is, he recasts psychoanalytic concepts in terms derived (as we have seen in Chapter 1) from structural linguistics – the 'signifier' here formalises the nature of speech in the talking cure – and phenomenology, in which our theoretical account of the 'subject' re-elaborates what it is that speaks and is spoken by language. That formalisation also almost completely empties out the ideological contents of Freud's writing, anthropologically-grounded universalised descriptions of human nature that refracted available representations of the individual and society in the late nineteenth and early twentieth century. This revolutionary re-reading of psychoanalysis – formalisation of a theoretical practice that interprets and changes the relation of the subject to language – opens the way to three conceptual moves by which this revolution can be reiterated, repeated and extended.

The first move is specification of structural elements that constitute the condition of possibility for one human subject to speak to another. This move also calls for a specification of the management of enjoyment. Lacan distances himself from nineteenth-century psychiatric notions of animal magnetism, instinctual forces and Freud's (1920) own bio-energetic account of a 'death drive' that complements and competes with a life drive. This also, needless to say, pulls us back from a conception of ethics that is organised around a notion of the good, because something always seems to take the human being beyond that good, to throw that good into question. Once one takes the position of the good, there are names aplenty for the malign causes of wickedness that refuse it, but psychoanalysis shows us that there is something fantastically excessive about an attachment to the good that itself can transform that good into evil (Badiou 1998/2001).

This something beyond, beyond pleasure and at the edge of an enjoyment that is painful, too much for the human subject to bear, is what Lacan calls 'jouissance', and the master-stroke in his formulation of this concept is that it is not susceptible to capture as something mystical, instinctual or energetic. It is, instead, something constituted by the very human activity that keeps it at bay, constituted as a something beyond, something that drives the subject as they speak, and drives them beyond speech. This is why Lacan (1964/1973: 257), while wanting to be loyal to Freud most of the time, does break from him quite sharply in this respect, arguing that every drive is a death drive, that the distinction between life drive and death drive 'manifests two aspects of the drive', and sex impels the subject to somewhere deadly beyond it. Jouissance is a 'path towards death' (Lacan 1991/2007: 18), and castration brought about by the rule of the signifier as we become subject to language is factored into a fantasy of what we once had as a loss of jouissance; jouissance 'is prohibited to whoever speaks' (Lacan 2006: 696). Note that 'castration' as a cut into power is a motif Lacan borrows from an image of a drastic restriction of sexual potency, but that motif is used metaphorically in Lacanian psychoanalysis, and it is then that this metaphorical cut into power comes to haunt a masculine experience of sex, with masculinity as template for active libido in heteropatriarchal society at least (Freud 1933: 131; cf. Frosh 1994).

The second conceptual move takes place when Lacan homes in on how this excess is localised as a product of human activity that is simultaneously a loss of jouissance, and how the human subject circles around it while driven by it as cause of desire. This point is condensed at the lost object that

Freud (1925: 236) describes as the object which never actually existed as such – a fantasised first object of love which we attempt to 'refind' – and which Lacan (1964/1973) redefines as the object a. This object a, to which the subject divided by language is attached in fantasy, assumes particular form as capitalism triumphs over the feudal political-economic system that preceded it in Europe (and over cognate forms elsewhere as colonialism and imperialism displaced local systems of power and remade the rest of the world in the image of Western capitalism). The theoretical question this then poses is whether it is the localisation of excess as such that is a product of capitalism, rather than simply the formation of particular products – commodities that promise and then fail to satisfy desire – that embody the object a, as what appears to be allowed of jouissance.

Now we are in the world of profit and loss, overproduction and underproduction, of surplus value around which capitalism revolves and in which there is incitement and control of expenditure. Perhaps, Lacan suggests, this surplus value is now also a kind of surplus enjoyment which is condensed in commodities as the promise of complete satisfaction and lost from the creative labour of the worker, localised as cause of their alienation. The spectre of jouissance does seem then to intimate something beyond in an economic system in which it seems that every traditional form which circumscribed and deferred excessive human activity is dissolving into the market-place, a world in which everything 'melts into air' (Marx and Engels 1848/1965: 36). At this point all manner of ideological contents are sucked into images of excess, representations of jouissance that are both alluring and frightful. The phenomenon of 'class' is itself a representation of substantive social categories that are ideologically distilled from a particular organisation of surplus labour under capitalism (Marx 1863; Mandel 1990); the 'surplus value' that Marx describes is, Lacan (1991/2007: 20) argues, 'surplus *jouissance*' (see also Declercq 2006). Apart from the ideological configuration of class around motifs of decorous good taste and base concupiscence, there is a self-representation of the civilised West defending itself against various orientalised others.

The localisation of excess is then also, in Lacan's later writing, organised around sexual difference; there is a differentiation between 'phallic jouissance' – a stereotypically masculine pursuit which is doomed to fail – and the 'jouissance of the Other' which the woman aims at in a search for something more transcendent (Lacan 1975/1998). This difference is condensed in the figures of 'man' and 'woman' – figures that do not necessarily correspond to those of biological males and females – and in the figure of the obsessional neurotic for whom thought is a vehicle of jouissance, and of the hysteric for whom desire is always unsatisfied (Soler 1996a). Obsessional features of capitalism, faithfully reiterated by some subjects, are thus complemented and contradicted by hysterical features lived out by others. Frugality and excess are grounded in the sexual division of labour that capitalism inherits from feudalism and transforms as that division is harnessed to commodity production.

The third conceptual move through which we can now repeat and extend the Lacanian revolution in subjectivity is to map this particular organisation of jouissance, to map representations of excess and its ideological character as the psychoanalytic clinic develops in and against psychiatry. Psychoanalysis requires closed institutional sites in which fantasy is elaborated, this in alienating political-economic conditions of production and consumption which also incite a search for something beyond that may be more meaningful and satisfying. Lacan's account of alienation in the signifier provides one theoretical framework fruitful for working with those conditions in one institutional site, the clinic. The hope that this might be the setting for an 'intersubjective' relation and 'full speech' is an expression in Lacan's early work of fantasies that came to be attached to this site as the clinic became a place in which it would be possible to elicit and work through the nature of fantasy.

The analyst is faced with the demand to reveal what they know and then with the attempt on the part of those who come for help to keep knowledge at bay. There is a 'passion for ignorance' on the part of the analysand that is at one with the idea that there is jouissance to be had and that psychoanalysis is betraying its claim to provide access to it (Lacan 1958: 524). It is then from within this site that psychoanalysis also encounters the fantasies of those outside psychoanalysis, and too often defends itself by reproducing itself as a closed hermetic system. The clinic then becomes a site for the localisation and containment of jouissance, and this site is structured not only by the distribution of fantasies of excessive enjoyment among the different categories of patient but also by the desire of the analyst (Libbrecht 1998).

Names

Capitalism inaugurates a ceaseless transformation of commodity production and of forms of subjectivity, but even as every social relation and ethical norm is dissolved in the market-place, as they seem to melt into air, this political-economic system is ordered, organised by private property. Ownership of the means of production mutates under capitalism, but the enclosure of space and resources is governed by the imperative to maximise profit, to channel surplus value and condense it into sites from where it can be reinvested. One of the ideological motifs of capitalism is the belief that money and power are siphoned into the hands of a few who then conspire to exploit the rest. The circuit of commodities confronts the individual subject as an 'Other', and then, so such ideological modes of reasoning go, manipulation of the system can be explained with reference to an 'Other of the Other'. This is the setting for a neat ideological trick in which each poor individual seems to be deprived of their jouissance by other individuals who pull the strings. Ideological belief, manifestly absurd and so operating often only at an unconscious level, glues the barred subject to an object which localises jouissance – object a – and now we can say that under capitalism such beliefs are configured for the subject as fantasies (Žižek 1989).

This revolution in modes of production is accompanied by a revolution in forms of reproduction, the reproduction of domestic labour power in the family and correlative fantasies about the rights of individuals borne by the nuclear family into the world as well as about the rights of those who govern it (Zaretsky 1976). However, there is a paradox at work in this contained space, for the reorganisation of the nuclear family under capitalism installs the father as the master in the house at the very same time as he is stripped of his power. The figure of the father that the subject of psychoanalysis imagines is the agent of castration – castration as a threat to the boy and accomplished fact in the case of the girl – is himself castrated, and the identification that takes place with this figure is with someone who is always already alienated, able to do little more than prepare his little subjects for an alienated existence in the outside world.

Freud already suspected that familial forms of authority were empty – most of his patients suffered at the hands of weak, not strong fathers – and Lacan (1938) locates the emergence of psychoanalysis precisely at this moment of failure in the family, in the 'decline of the paternal imago'. This moment is then repeated, reiterated in Lacanian psychoanalysis as suffering in the clinic, and is located in the context of the decline of the father. The ravaging power of the mother then seems to fill that power-vacuum in the family, also disastrously to fill the lack that is a precondition for desire in the subject (Lacan 1956–1957; Chiesa 2007).

We have noted that Lacan accomplishes a formalisation of relations in which the human subject is constituted and describes the role of a theoretical element – the signifier – that will anchor the subject in the structure. The signifier provides a point of identification for the subject around which the elements of the structure are organised, a distinctive point which serves to mark the subject as subject to the structure but with an idiosyncratic trajectory through it. The signifier in the family, then, is a name, one which names the child as such and names it as a child who will become an adult able to assume another position in the structure in another family. (The suffering psychoanalysis addresses is not the result of the analysand's unhappy childhood but of the fact that they did once have a childhood as such.)

Now we need to embed this formal articulation of structure and signifier – an articulation by which it is then possible for the signifier to represent the subject for another signifier – in ideological representations of the family and in a particular ideological representation of the place of the subject in the clinic. The bourgeois nuclear family is itself organised around a romanticised image of pre-capitalist society, an image that forms the basis of the 'family romance' described by Freud (1909b), the idea that one's real parents might be kings and queens for example. The position of the 'father' as the one who names, gives his name to his son and heirs, is thereby only retroactively guaranteed, and it is in this sense, only in this sense, that we should read Lacan's (2006: 230) comment that the name of the father (which is often capitalised in Lacanese as 'Name-of-the-Father') goes back to the 'dawn of historical time'.

This patriarchal lineage of the family provides a vision and warning for what lies inside and outside the structure, and it also structures a relation between what can be accommodated by the psychiatric system, the inside of the individual as a logically-ordered mental process, and what cannot, madness beyond reason. Lacan described how the refusal, 'foreclosure' of the Name-of-the-Father, operates as a drastic form of defence such that the psychotic subject is then shut out of the symbolic; they shut themselves out. This process is one that concerns not only the particular kind of refusal that occurs inside the family – the subject refuses the rule of the signifier that names them in that structure – but also the consequent inability of the subject to move around a symbolic system in the world outside a family that is organised around the names of fathers, structured by particular kinds of signifiers and relations between them. That very same symbolic system is replicated in and crystallised as the rule of the master diagnosing forms of pathology in the psychiatric system. The psychiatrist names pathology, those that refuse their names are psychoticised, and we should treat this naming and refusal of naming as one of the sites from which psychoanalysis derived its understanding of psychosis as clinical structure.

However, as we have seen, Lacan himself unravels this naming with a diagnosis of the decline of the paternal imago, and there is a shift to conceptualising new forms of subjectivity when that Name-of-the-Father is pluralised, fragmented into 'names of the father' (Lacan 1987b). The shift from the 'name' as signifier to a constellation of 'names' then also throws into question what the father has that the mother does not have, and what value should be placed on it.

Failure

Lacan takes up the well-known Freudian claim that 'anatomy is destiny', but 'anatomy' is treated as a historically-constituted practice of cutting up the body (Zwart 1998). Marking and dividing flesh has consequences for how the body is represented and experienced, just as hysterical conversion operates on how the subject conceives of their body. However, shifting focus from the biological organ to that which is narcissistically cathected and charged with signification, from the penis to the 'phallus', does not immediately solve the problem of accounting for why it is that the penis is so charged. In this respect Lacan follows Freud, commenting that it is the 'turgidity' of the phallus that makes it 'the image of the vital flow as it is transmitted in generation', and that it is 'the most salient of what can be grasped in sexual intercourse as real' (Lacan 2006: 581). A sexual relation of a particular kind – heterosexual intercourse – is still taken as the bodily ground of the signifier that defines that sexual relation as impossible. Nevertheless, Lacan's terminological shift does give us an opening onto a conceptualization of the phallus as not necessarily equivalent to a biological organ. The penis is an anchor point of patriarchy, that which pertained at the point in history at which the feudal rulers really were men, and the shift to the phallus is a different kind of symbolic anchoring point that marks a reconfiguration of power as something less certain, even as point of failure (Fink 2004).

Lacan's reformulation of sexual difference as governed by symbolic laws rather than biological processes actually began long before his employment of structuralism and attention to the work of the signifier. His article on 'family complexes' in the 1930s, for example, makes it clear that he viewed the similarity between 'normal components of the family as they are seen in our contemporary western world' and those of 'the biological family' as 'completely contingent'. This also meant that symbolic forms that determine the location and internal shape of the family became all the more important for Lacan (1938: iii): 'From the beginning there exist prohibitions and laws', he says, and in this statement we can start to see why structural anthropology will be of use to him later to explore the nature of the symbolic law in which the lack of the mother and her child are constituted. The intimate relationship between the orders of the symbolic, imaginary and real thus locates what we have come to call 'gender' as itself a signifier that operates as an imaginary effect of a real difference, a tangle or knotting of the three orders historically constituted (Klein 2003: 52). Lacan's insistence on the contingent and necessary signification of the phallus as penis in the contemporary Western world ensures that psychoanalysis describes the contours of patriarchal society without prescribing it for all. Hence Mitchell's (1974: xv) argument that 'psychoanalysis is not a recommendation *for* a patriarchal society, but an analysis *of* one'.

Speaking within this system of signifiers is sexualised, as is the condition of possibility of speaking itself. When Lacan (2006: 579) refers to the phallus as the signifier of signification as such, this necessarily entails an analysis of the way that signification is suffused with what we imagine the erotic to pertain to, that it must be to do with the relation between men and women (Muller 1996: 148). Three aspects are thus knotted together – the function of signification, the eroticised nature of signification, and the organisation of this eroticised signification around the problematic of 'gender', three aspects that cannot be disentangled empirically to the satisfaction of a subject. They can only be disentangled conceptually, or in psychoanalysis, and then only transiently as a subject speaks and fades within that very eroticised signifying stuff that makes them man or woman (Soler 1994).

The end of analysis entails incompleteness and an acceptance of castration as cut into power. The phallus is never actually possessed by men, marks a point of failure, with masculinity and femininity both forms of 'masquerade' that tears the subject between obsessional maintenance of their gender 'identity' and hysterical refusal of it (cf. Riviere 1929). This provides a crucial link with political analysis of the history that has formed us as beings that imagine that they must revolve around the phallus. We can then accept the role of the phallus itself as a historically-structured symbolic function.

Repetition

Lacanian psychoanalysis is concerned with the signifying operations through which human beings come to be positioned in relation to each other and through which they struggle to position themselves (Dunker 2005a, 2010). Here, the phenomenon of transference is crucial, and works because the analysand supposes that there is another subject who knows something more about their symptom than they do, supposes that this subject is listening to them in analysis, is incarnated in the figure of the analyst. For Lacan (1964/1973: 232), 'As soon as the subject who is supposed to know exists somewhere . . . there is transference', but he does not specify that this will necessarily be located in the analyst for there are also institutional effects of the place of the subject in the clinic as a site of knowledge that need to be taken into account. However, this aspect of transference – defined by the operation of a 'subject supposed to know' or a 'supposed subject of knowing' – is made present to the analyst (and analysand as they hear themselves speak) in a distinctive repetition of signifiers. The analyst is addressed at points in the analysis by signifiers that repeat those used by the analysand to refer to other significant figures in their life.

The repetition may be explicit and obvious to the analyst, or be allusive – working through metonymy and metaphor – requiring some measure of interpretation, but not usually interpretation voiced to the analysand because that aspect of the interpretative work in analysis may then serve to suggest to the analysand that they carry on speaking as if to one particular figure, may serve to close down the transference, may even be incorrect (Cottet 1993). The Lacanian analyst thus works *in* the transference, and is attending to it all the time, but they are not turning what they make of it into a kind of knowledge to be given to the analysand in order to educate them, still less to bring them in line with good knowledge operating as a moral ideal.

Lacan (1991/2007), like Freud, was a materialist (if not a 'believer' in materialism), and the practice of analysis is set against any form of idealism, including that form which idealises knowledge. We meet the opposition between materialism and idealism time and again in the history of psychoanalysis, and so we need to be clear how psychoanalytic materialism differs from psychiatric materialism, and then how psychoanalytic materialism pits itself against a return to idealist conceptions of the subject. Psychiatric materialism (and cognate forms in biologically-reductionist psychology) attempts to explain away psychic processes with reference to physical or neuro-physiological deformations, sometimes also with reference to genetic abnormalities in the history of the individual; as has been pointed out in polemics against the recent neuro-biological turn inside the International Psychoanalytical Association (IPA), the 'biologistic perspective that underlies neuropsychoanalysis runs counter to the essence of a psychoanalytic worldview' (Blass and Carmeli 2007: 36), though we should also be wary of psychoanalysis as a 'worldview' itself (Freud 1933: 181–182). In contrast, psychoanalysis works on the materiality of representation, representations of the body and distress that Freud noticed in his earliest studies of hysteria. Lacan then embeds the Freudian focus on representation in the work of the signifier.

Lacan's attention to the productive role of the signifier treats language as a material force, and it thus maintains the materialist character of Freud's psychoanalysis while elaborating it at a higher conceptual level. It has then been possible in recent years to turn back to questions of biology and to reinterpret neurological research in light of the signifier as a peculiar kind of matter (Soler 1995; Miller 2001; Ansermet and Magistretti 2007). This attention to the materiality of the signifier leads the Lacanian psychoanalyst to avoid appeal to a domain of feelings hidden beneath the signifiers (or inside the analyst as if in a separate domain of their 'countertransference' that they intuit through their feelings about it) or recourse to a 'metalanguage' that would provide a point of escape from the effects of the signifier (or a place from which the transference could be interpreted to the analysand who remains trapped within it).

Once we treat the repetition of the signifier as the stuff of transference in psychoanalysis we have to ask how that signifier comes to appear, what the precise material conditions are for a particular kind of representation to be formed in a relationship between the analysand and analyst. Here we come to the crucial claim that psychoanalytic phenomena are *constituted* in the space of the clinic (cf. Lichtman 1982). They do not pre-exist the clinic in some numinous realm independent of the speech that takes place there – this would be the idealist option, and it would lead to a host of interpretations of anything and everything in the world using psychoanalytic categories to unlock things hidden under the surface – but they are produced there. So, Lacan (2006: 707) argues that 'psychoanalysts are part and parcel of the concept of the unconscious, as they constitute that to which the unconscious is addressed'.

We have already pointed out that the Lacanian psychoanalyst does not interpret the transference with reference to what they think they 'feel' (as their 'countertransference') or with reference to what they think they know (as from a 'metalanguage'). Now we are in a position to grasp the implications of that materialist account of psychoanalysis: 'The analyst does not interpret the analysand's unconscious from the "outside"; on the contrary, the patient's unconscious is *produced* in the analytic relation' (Voruz 2007: 177).

The symptom itself is produced, 'constituted by its capture in the analyst's discourse, whereby, having become demand, it finds itself hooked onto the Other' (Miller 2008: 11). Analytic speech requires address to, and response from, another that is mediated by the terms of a defined social space. Psychoanalytic interpretations are made to another subject for whom they function more by way of the response to the interpretation being made than with reference to its content. And, in many cases, the interpretations are made not by the analyst but by the analysand themselves, or they are interventions that come to take the form of interpretations as the analysand refuses or reconfigures what was said by the analyst, sometimes quite a while after the event (Soler 1996c).

Cuts

Lacanian psychoanalysis developed from within a particular local version of medical practice in the 1930s, a French psychiatric tradition that was already marginalised come mid-century by the German and the US nosological systems that are now globally hegemonic. It was marginal, and perhaps more nationalist and patrician for that, and it provided a good breeding ground and breathing space for Lacan to work. And from that psychiatric shell psychoanalysis took on a new form, able to pose a series of challenges to conceptions of the subject borne from late feudalism.

There were then, first, openings to a different view of the relationship between the clinic as site of treatment and the culture which encircled it, and this has implications for how we should specify the disjunction between the inside and outside of that site so that we better understand how crucial psychoanalytic concepts leak from one domain to the other and become banalised in that process.

There were, second, openings to re-conceptualising the way pleasure is balanced by the individual subject and by ethical systems concerned with the good life, a shift to examining how surplus enjoyment spills over into something less manageable and how traditional psychoanalytic descriptions of such phenomena as 'castration' can be reconfigured as a cut into power.

There is, third, an opening to how it may be possible to rethink categories that were reified, turned into substantive entities by early psychoanalysis that too-closely followed in the path of psychiatry, and here we take seriously the existence of social categories – 'infants', 'races' and 'clinical structures', for example – but re-elaborate these as interlocking sets of social relations, as processes of, say, infantilisation, racialisation, and psychiatrisation.

And, fourth, there is an opening to a re-examination of what is taken to be 'good', with a first step to this re-examination proceeding by way of desubstantialising psychoanalytic reference points like 'phallus' and then even the 'name' of the subject as 'Name-of-the-Father' so that such entities can be explored and demystified by each subject in their own analysis.

Lacanian psychoanalysis subverts psychiatrised conceptions of 'the good' and opens the way to an ethics of the subject that also breaks from biological definitions of sexual difference. The question now is how far it can shake itself free from feudal remainders in the realm of ideology, forms of knowledge that still inhabit and structure our attempts to connect ethics with politics; to connect ethics with clinical practice, and to hold true to that ethics of the subject by refusing to confuse quite different spaces for revolutionary change.

Chapter 3

Psychoanalytic psychology

Now we move on to explore the role of psychology as an ostensible alternative to psychiatry in the development of the Lacanian tradition, with a focus on the political limitations this places on progressive therapeutic work. I discuss the historical context for the development of the psy professions and the place of psychology today as an observational practice concerned with operationalised measurement of self-efficacy, a disciplinary approach that rests on conceptions of cognition abstracted from the subject. The relationship between psychological and psychoanalytic methodology is explored in clinical practice, and quite different conceptions of training and supervision, of psychologists and psychoanalysts, are described to draw out the problems that Lacanian psychoanalysts face when we are expected to adhere to an educational process defined by psychological assumptions.

Education

The complementary pathological relationship between psychiatry and psychoanalysis was disturbed and recast by the growth of academic and professional psychology through the course of the twentieth century. That relationship was both complementary and pathological for it was marked by resentment and distortion that locked the partners together. There was analytic resentment at the power of the psychiatrist and also, on the part of those still wedded to their medical training, at the psychoanalytic unravelling of organic disease categories. And there was distortion of alternative conceptions of distress as they became rendered into a language understandable enough to each partner to enable them to work together. In some cases, and all the more so inside institutions and organisations more closely tied to the old dispensation through familial and personal links to the aristocracy, psychiatry still tended to assume pride of place in what was in some contexts known as 'medical psychology' (Hinshelwood 1995). Medical psychiatric practice which had adapted itself to psychoanalytic ideas thereby managed to insulate itself from the potentially unsettling effects of psychology.

Psychoanalysts, who were usually medically trained, especially after Freud's (1926) failure to safeguard the role of 'lay analysis' from the US American medics in the 1920s, still had to operate within the frame of treatment regimes tainted by late-feudal assumptions about the quite different rights and responsibilities of doctors and patients (Jacoby 1983).

There are far-reaching demographic and geographical disputes at play here through which psychology was refracted as a new discipline that pretended to provide progressive resources for psychoanalysis. Psychoanalytic ideas were starting to spread throughout the world in the early years of the twentieth century in a series of networks organised by way of letters, publications and visits, networks at which Freud was the nominal centre. For these networks to function as reference points, and also as the clinical anchor points for psychoanalysis as a globalising ideological force, there would need to be a re-composition of populations and engagement with new economic conditions.

Psychoanalysis is an urban phenomenon. That is, it only becomes feasible when there is a concentration of professional adherents and the emergence of a layer of the population alienated enough and with sufficient financial and temporal resources to spend time and money on self-exploration and, perhaps, even training. Psychoanalysis was all but destroyed in continental Europe when the fascists targeted it as a degenerate Jewish science (Frosh 2005). This led to a shift of the centre of gravity of the International Psychoanalytical Association to the US and to the construction of psychoanalysis, its reconstruction, in three different contexts.

There were, first, the old feudal, old colonial centres in which the legacy of medical psychiatry was bound up with archaic institutions. London, for example, was the site from which Freud, his daughter Anna and other *émigrés* formulated new versions of psychoanalysis around the ego's relation with its objects (Richards 2000; Frosh 2003). There were, second, parts of the world where burgeoning capitalism could pretend to itself that it was making a new beginning, as if free from the weight of the past. The US East coast, for example, became a centre of attraction for those willing to start afresh and called upon theories of the adaptable ego (Feher-Gurewich et al. 1999; Rabaté 2000). And, third, there was the 'rest of the world', in which new professional associations, sometimes including analysts fleeing Europe, were dependent on recognition granted to their work by the old centres. In Latin America and South Africa, for example, and in Israel, new directions in psychoanalysis had to take second place to professions of loyalty to institutions in the old world or the new world or both (Kutter 1991, 1995).

Psychoanalysis is a democratic phenomenon. The democratising impulse of psychology, at work long before the injunction by 'positive psychologists', to make it available to the greatest possible number of people as a knowledge shared about the nature of individual mental functioning, corrodes feudal power relations and threatens to isolate psychiatry as a rather antique medical speciality (Seligman 1998). On the one hand, psychology becomes powerful in the psy complex as an apparatus of surveillance and normalisation of populations and each individual member of them. When it generously invites each person to speak about their ills to another it serves to bind the individual all the more tightly to the professional apparatus, and it then does seem as if that spiral of confession confirms the operations of disciplinary power (Foucault 1975/1979, 1976/1981). On the other hand, psychology brings the knowledge of the psy-practitioners out well beyond the domain of moral improvement aimed at by the more enlightened nineteenth-century alienists. Psychology as the quintessential subjectivising discipline of bourgeois democracy requires the education of its actual and potential clientele; psychology aspired to be 'the meta-theory of all the sciences, taking care of the breaches subjectivity causes in the constructions of science' (De Vos 2009a: 234).

Psychology functions whether or not people are actually consciously aware of the principles that underlie it. Time and motion studies and behavioural conditioning procedures, for example, trace the physical movements of workers in different occupations in urban centres and then the preferences of consumers inducted into the activity of making choices between arrays of commodities available to them. In this sense, much early psychology merely reiterates in miniature the social forms in which it is embedded and reinforces the taken-for-granted second nature of those forms. However, more sophisticated versions of academic psychology require reflexive activity on the part of those who make use of it (Giddens 1992). This is an aspect of psychology in which psychoanalysis comes to play an important role, and which Lacanian psychoanalysis has had to confront (Malone and Friedlander 1999; Owens 2009); each element of contemporary psychology – cognitive, behavioural and even 'discursive psychology' – is antithetical to Lacanian psychoanalysis (Pavón Cuéllar 2009).

Psychologisation

We are now faced with an increasing psychologisation of individual subjectivity, and of the way that social processes are understood using that psychologised individual experience as a theoretical template. Psychologisation commences with the birth of capitalism, and is a necessary condition for capitalism based on commodity exchange to work. Not only does each worker enter into a contract to exchange their labour time for money as if of their own free will, but the entrepreneurial activities of the capitalist provide a model for thriving competitive individualism that seeks to maximise profit. Psychologisation is necessary through the development of capitalism as the material ideological texture of everyday life through which economic mechanisms appear to be grounded in the survival of the fittest, and it has become all the more important in times of neoliberal deregulation of welfare services and intensification of precarious competitive labour conditions in which the worker is now also a kind of entrepreneur. An indication of the early popularisation of psychology can be seen in the spread of 'practical psychology' as a self-help movement in Britain and beyond between the two world wars; by 1948 there were more than 200 'clubs', including in Palestine, Nigeria, Gold Coast, Australia, India, South Africa, Malaysia and Burma, and 'practical psychology handbooks' in the 1930s and 1940s were on topics ranging from making friends to beating shyness, and included one on the inferiority complex (Thomson 2006; Benjamin 2009).

Despite the difference between psychology and psychoanalysis, and with the popular conflation of psychology and psychoanalysis as symptomatic of the problem, the circulation of psychoanalytic representations of the self is part and parcel of this process of psychologisation. Whatever the subversive potential of psychoanalysis in the clinic or in social theory, psychoanalytic vocabulary has seeped into psychologised accounts of individual and social activity in everyday life.

There is, in a psychologised culture that corresponds to the needs of contemporary capitalism, a process of recuperation of psychoanalysis into a particular model of clinical practice. This then also provides a particular model of social change, and of the place of an individual who is trying to understand and participate in it. Psychoanalysis is, on the one hand, often reduced to being focused upon a form of psychology – a description of childhood development, personality differences, pathological interpersonal relationships, and so on – but this betrays the radical potential of a psychoanalytic deconstruction of subjectivity under capitalism. Lacanian psychoanalysts do not render treatment into a process that can be made susceptible to prediction as part of 'evidence-based' practice, nor do they promote rationality as the touchstone of conscious understanding. Lacanian psychoanalysis goes beyond psychology, but we need to embed its alternative account of subjectivity in political-economic processes in order to connect the clinic with society.

Under conditions of 'psychologisation' social processes are turned into something that seems to operate as if it were independent of those processes, even as if that something was the cause of them. Psychologisation was essential for psychology to be able to borrow material from adjacent disciplines such as philosophy, biology and sociology, and to rework that material as if it were psychological. This is the context in which cognitive behavioural approaches have emerged as a therapeutic approach – developed from within a particular tradition in psychoanalysis – that renders complex emotional responses into formal procedures into what is popularised as Cognitive Behavioural Therapy (CBT) (House and Loewenthal 2008; Loewenthal and House 2010).

CBT has become popular in clinical psychology, but 'it is essentially a form of psychiatric treatment, the roots of which are not in cognitive science' (Pilgrim 2008: 252). One only has to look at the history of the DSM to see how 'the standardization and transformation of qualitative categories into quantitative scales' then managed 'to eliminate the psychiatrist's subjectivity', a first step to eliminating the subjectivity of the patient (Guéguen 2005: 133). The rise of CBT from within US ego psychological psychoanalysis, and its popularity now as an alternative to psychoanalysis, highlights the importance of psychology as an emergent ideological system competing with psychiatry. Key figures in the development of cognitive psychological treatments – Aaron Beck, a medical doctor who developed Cognitive Behavioural Therapy, Albert Ellis, a clinical psychologist who came up with his own brand of Rational Emotive Behavioural Therapy – trained as psychoanalysts and then shifted direction; Beck still claiming very late on that he was a 'closet psychoanalyst' and Ellis that Freud was not 'sexy enough' (Beck and Ellis 2000).

CBT is popular because its model of thinking chimes with bureaucratic modes of organisation, and it fits well with the work of time-pressured clinicians working in organisations reducing self-discovery to efficient and transparent outcomes. This reduction defines our age of happiness, in which becoming 'a countable and comparable unit is the effective translation of the contemporary domination of the master-signifier in its purest, most stupid form: the number 1' (Miller 2007b: 9). This is above and beyond the cynical calculations that might be made about economic investment, in the programme paying for itself as it blocks access to welfare entitlement for those who have been rendered willing and able, cognitively and behaviourally prepared, for work. The assumption is that 'a symptom will respond to CBT to the satisfaction of the evaluation systems and return to productive happiness' (Evans 2007: 145). Cognitive behavioural approaches function well in an administered world, and they need compliant individuals who will administer their own activities. We are encouraged to work on solutions that promise quick fixes, and now CBT embeds that mistake even in the way we think about ourselves. The rise of CBT therefore exemplifies contemporary psychologisation. Psychologisation operates through an experiential commitment to psychological explanations, not only of what happens to each individual but also what happens to society. Then the language of psychology comes to replace political explanations, and this language limits the room for manoeuvre and, even more so, for social change, and even for the way that those who facilitate change are monitored in 'supervision'.

Observing supervision

Key texts on supervision in recent years have been quite clear about what is expected of analysts and trainees as they account for their practice.

Descriptions and recommendations for 'supervision' in the 'British tradition' of psychoanalysis, for example, typically reframe the analytic process in cognitive psychological terms. This psychological account is clearly tied in the literature used in psychotherapy training to developmental models. It is said, for example, that there are three 'stages of training' in which the trainee therapist develops an 'internal supervisor' (Casement 1985: 31–32). This formulation repeats and extends accounts of the relationship between analyst and analysand by Balint (1950) against which Lacan (1958) pitted himself half a century ago. This literature warns against the supervisor 'offering too strong a model' which will encourage identification with the supervisor, but this warning only serves to highlight the ground-rules against which correct practice is to be measured. In stage one of that model, 'the supervisor provides a form of control'; in stage two, the trainee acquires 'a capacity for spontaneous reflection within the session alongside the internalised supervisor'; and in stage three they are expected to develop 'more autonomous functioning' (Casement 1985: 32).

Notice here the way that 'internalisation' is viewed as a mental process, one that should take place as if it were independent of language. Recommendations for the analyst 'monitoring the patient through trial identification' similarly rest upon a separation of the 'observing ego' from the 'experiencing ego', a separation that is conceived of as if it were outside language (Casement 1985: 35). It then makes sense to refer to the presentation of material in supervision sessions as 'abstracting the themes' (ibid.: 41), and this leads the account of the analysis away from the actual words, away from the play of the signifier. The perception the analysand has of the analyst is thus viewed as something that is subject to distortion, and so 'transference' comes to describe their misperception of the potentially real relationship between the two of them. The understanding the analyst has of internal mental operations of the analysand is seen as being beset by 'countertransference', which it is the work of supervision to identify and clear up.

The attention to 'parallel processing' of different levels of meaning compounds this image of the analysis in the supervision, and it encourages the analyst to search for underlying psychological processes (Clarkson and Gilbert 1991). It is then said that there is a 'parallel process' as a 'mirroring in the supervision session of the process between therapist and client' (Gilbert and Evans 2000: 105). Supervision is conceived of as patterned upon analysis, and there is sometimes also evoked a notion of 'supertransference' to describe the supervisor's own unresolved conflicts (Teitelbaum 1990). This gives rise to descriptions of cases in which there may be a 'supervisee whose development is arrested and stunted by the narcissistic needs and demands of the supervisor' (Gilbert and Evans 2000: 109).

These processes are described as if they are obscured by what is actually said, and transference is then understood as something happening inside the mind of the analysand, to be detected by the analyst. It then makes sense for the trainee to look for what is described as an 'island of intellectual contemplation as the mental space within which the internal supervisor can begin to operate' (Casement 1985: 32). The role of language is conveniently sidestepped but there are certain assumptions about language at work in these accounts. First, we are presented with a model of language that reduces it to 'communication'. These psychologised traditions of work endorse, for example, 'clear and direct feedback' in supervision (Gilbert and Evans 2000), and rest upon a model of 'effective feedback' that has the characteristics of being 'systematic, objective and accurate', 'timely', 'clearly understood' and 'reciprocal' (Freeman 1985). Second, these accounts assume that it is possible to step back from language into a meta-position that is in principle independent of its effects. We are invited to pursue 'the attainment of a meta-perspective on the relationship that will provide the psychotherapist and the client with an overall view of the interactional field' (Gilbert and Evans 2000: 24).

Change is then understood as the meeting of two individuals, the analyst and the analysand, who may communicate directly with each other ego-to-ego and who may together take a meta-perspective on what goes on between them. These recommendations for supervision, for the way feedback and internalisation of the supervisor may proceed, thus reproduce and inform a certain image of the analysis that reduces it to a kind of psychology.

Evidence of development

Psychotherapy training organisations have often searched for evidence that they were attracting the right kind of person, teaching them what they needed to know and producing someone who would practise without doing too much damage to their analysands. Evidence is sought of the development of the psychoanalyst, perhaps through their training analysis with someone who could be trusted to impart the right sort of knowledge in the right measure to the candidates. The application of criteria is as a grid to determine who should be allowed to call themselves an analyst.

With intensification of interest in the self-governance of individuals, 'accountability' has become the trademark term used by those keen on ensuring training standards in the professions, and there has been accretion of additional layers of professional and governmental bodies charged with quality control (Litten 2008). The idea that there should be another superordinate system by which evidence of development of the psychoanalyst in the course of their training should be accumulated and assessed – the pretence at a 'metalanguage' which would subsume psychoanalysis – has gained currency, and the clamour for recognition by the state has led many psychoanalytic trainings across the world to conform to this kind of surveillance and specification of learning which is antithetical to psychoanalysis as such (Parker and Revelli 2008).

Lacanian psychoanalysis has always been chary of external administrative procedures that would determine how long it should take to train analysts, and of the forms of knowledge and the relation to knowledge that these procedures produce. Notwithstanding the actual participation of Lacanians in university departments, there has been a suspicion of an academic framing of knowledge, of the idea that psychoanalysis should be given authority by virtue of its appeals to fixed truth underneath the surface. Lacan (1967/1995: 1) declared that 'the psychoanalyst derives his authorization only from himself', not from an accrediting body or even from the school in which they were trained (see Wolf 2007). This is not to say that one individual decides all on their own that they are an analyst, and we have already noted that 'analyst' is not an identity of a kind to be assumed once and for all. Rather, the school functions as a space, even as a guaranteed space, in which the analysts who authorise themselves can assume their position without looking to others to tell them whether or not they have 'developed' enough (Miller 2000b; Vanheule and Verhaeghe 2009).

We are drawn here into a complex theoretical argument that grounds an anti-psychological notion of the 'formation' of analysts in two notions, notions of recognition and retroactivity in the formation of subjectivity that have far-reaching consequences not only for the place of psychoanalysis in relation to the regulation of psychotherapy training but also for its place in relation to adjacent human sciences.

The first notion, of recognition, is originally Hegelian in nature and it brings us to the deconstruction of the opposition between exteriority and interiority accomplished by Lacan in coining the term 'extimacy'. Miller (1986) deploys this concept, alluded to briefly by Lacan, to capture how the distinction between interior and exterior of the subject is blurred in analysis and what is most intimate to the subject is treated as exterior to them. This enables a specification of the object a, for example, as something that is not 'psychological'. The elaboration of 'extimacy' is of a piece with the unravelling of the relation between inside and outside of the subject through the topological device of the Moebius strip (in which one flat surface is twisted around so that as we trace our way around it in one continuous movement what is at one moment on the outside of the strip becomes at the next moment inside). The place of the analyst in the school is that of any other human subject in a human community, formed by and existing in relation to networks of relationships through which recognition is granted or withheld. Hegel's (1807/1977) anthropological fairy-tale of the intimate self-perpetuating relationship between master and slave is designed to mark the commencement of human history as such but pertains, as we have already seen, to conditions of feudalism, of the dialectical relation between Lord and his Bondsman. The lesson, however, goes far beyond those particular social conditions, and serves to emphasise the interdependence of the fate of those constituted as master with those assuming the position of slave, including in psychoanalysis (Regnault 1999).

The second notion, of retroactivity, is one that is already at work in Hegel's own account, in the way that the slave comes to recognise what they have been only after the event, for it is when they recognise that they are a slave and the master recognises that he is dependent on the slave for recognition that the master–slave dialectic really begins (Kojève 1969). Such recognition of that state of things, the nature of the dialectical interrelationship between subjects seeking recognition, operates not as a knowledge that confirms relationships but as an interpretation that simultaneously changes what it describes at the very moment that description is offered; as does psychoanalytic interpretation described at moments, in traditions of work albeit very different from Lacan's, as 'mutative interpretation' (Strachey 1934).

Freud's first published case studies at the birth of psychoanalysis are structured around retroactive effects, to the point that it would seem that 'trauma' is never, psychoanalytically speaking, an enclosed discrete event but is turned into something traumatic, turned into the 'trauma' by another event (Breuer and Freud 1895). This retroactive effect can be summarised by the Lacanian observation that it takes two traumas to make a trauma (Laplanche 1989; Van Haute 1995). Here Lacan is justified in claiming that he 'returned' to Freud, for retroactivity – *Nachträglichkeit, après coup* – is a key psychoanalytic notion that has indeed been retrieved by Lacanian psychoanalysis from early psychoanalytic writing and made a centrepiece of its theoretical contribution to clinical practice.

Now we can see how a reduction to 'psychology' cuts both ways; how it ties a psychoanalytic organisation into regulatory procedures that are external to it which then distort it, and how it reproduces non-psychoanalytic visions of development based on observation in order to come up with 'evidence' to those outside psychoanalysis (Stern 1985; cf. Cushman 1991). One of the reasons why Lacanian psychoanalytic organisations have refused to base their training on empirical and experiential 'child observation' is precisely because they do not subscribe to the story of 'development' that such an observation presupposes; if 'every truth has the structure of fiction' (Lacan 1986/1992: 12), then the truth of child development presupposed by adults also needs to be treated as structured in this way (Dunker 2005b). The dictum that it takes two traumas to make a trauma draws our attention to the impossibility of locating any one observable point as that which is responsible, by its presence or absence, for causing the child to develop normally or abnormally.

Child observation feeds the fantasy that one can see certain kinds of relation between child and care-giver, can see what is happening now and by implication predict what will happen in the future (Miller *et al.* 1989; cf. Burman 2008; Groarke 2008). It is of a piece with a psychological narrative – of observation, prediction and control – and leads us away from an attention to fantasy as such and away from the peculiar convoluted ways in which fantasy is reworked and recounted to the analyst. The truth of the subject is taken to be there to be observed in this kind of practice; it is fixed by a certain kind of knowledge of developmental sequences – knowledge confirmed by psychological knowledge – rather than being a truth that is enunciated, in process, as one reflects on who one is and how the knowledge that one has of oneself functions.

Organising analysts

Lacan's attempt to found a school that would enable horizontal rhizomatic connections between its members, and would be set against the vertically-oriented bureaucracy of the IPA, anticipates later ostensibly non-Lacanian philosophical approaches around the writings of Gilles Deleuze and Félix Guattari (1972/1977). Deleuze, whose work is often seen as antithetical to psychoanalysis by many followers, was courted by Lacan (Smith 2006: 39); Guattari (1984) was already a member of Lacan's new school (cf. Guattari and Rolnik 2008). The formation of clusters of workgroups, 'cartels', which would assemble and dismantle themselves before reforming with different members – proposed by Lacan (1987c) to prevent the sedimentation of hierarchy in a psychoanalytic school, a proposal derived from his early brief forays into group processes (Lacan 1946b, 1947/2000) – is in itself a rather Deleuzian practice.

There were a number of innovations in the organisation of the École freudienne that were designed to ensure that this group would not fall prey to the crystallisation of a ruling layer guarding what it took to be the orthodoxy. There have, of course, been charges during later purges and splits in the new international that this is exactly what happened, and accusations that Lacan's own authoritarianism did not help matters. Notwithstanding this, the innovations in technique that Lacan was condemned for – 'variable length' sessions being the most often cited by his enemies in the IPA – and the theoretical transformations of psychoanalysis that were already taking place before 1964 were now complemented by some striking practical proposals concerning how analysts might train and coexist in the same group. It is possible to read these proposals as a critical response to processes of psychologisation that had played a part in warping the kind of psychoanalysis Lacan left behind.

One innovation was a clear response to the administrative measures taken by the IPA against Lacan, the decision that he should not be permitted to continue as a 'training analyst' in the organisation. Those who are deemed to be 'training analysts' in the IPA groups around the world, and in satellite organisations training psychoanalytic psychotherapists that are modelled on the IPA training structures, are of course senior members of the organisation. This is a privileged position, one of very much higher status in the group, and it gives a certain cast to the debates that take place within it, including a notion of what special kind of analysis a 'training analysis' should be. This role has been venerated in such a way that – with the average age of 'training analysts' in the US currently being well over retirement age – orthodoxy in the training system is sedimented around a gerontocracy (Malone 2006).

There are a number of theoretical problems here, and psychology of one kind or another works its way into each. The first is that 'training analysis' is separated off from other kinds of analytic experience and comes to be defined not only around the sagacious figure who administers it but also by a defined procedure and an expectation of where the analysis will lead the analysand. The classic 'training analysis' then comes to be characterised by a degree of education as well as insight, and the danger is that the course of the analysis is directed not so much to the Delphic injunction 'know thyself' as to 'knowing psychoanalytic knowledge'. This is all the more problematic for Lacanian psychoanalysis, which is not concerned with how knowledge of any kind should be attained – as if, for example, there was a 'knowledge' of the self that the analysand could arrive at – but how the subject changes their *relation* to knowledge. Knowledge of the kind offered and enforced in something conceived from the outset as 'training analysis' is liable to degenerate into a form of psychology: the idea that the self is of a kind that can be known and that it is necessary to know what selves are in order to change people.

To believe that one should commence a 'training analysis' marks out the analysand as one who should be 'trained', and it tends to preclude the possibility that psychoanalysis may enable the analysand to decide that they do not want to be an analyst after all. The figure of the 'training analyst' also slots all too neatly into the Russian doll set of identities that invite an 'analyst' to imagine that they are a certain kind of being, not that they merely function in a certain position in certain circumstances some of the time. The lure of psychology thus operates at the level of identity as well as in the specification of criteria for training and the transmission of a certain kind of knowledge (Safouan 1983/2000).

Lacan's solution to these problems was to abolish the figure of the 'training analyst', and so today Lacanian psychoanalysis is an analysis as such set in motion by a request to an analyst to speak. This enables a questioning of the relation to the knowledge that one has acquired of oneself as a function of a peculiar set of signifiers, a set of signifiers that gives rise to the idea that we have an identity of some kind. It may be an identity, a form of 'psychology' that we become attached to which is organised around symptoms that give pain and pleasure – that is jouissance – and sometimes too much pain. And, at the end of this process, whatever the 'end' of the process is, it is possible that one decides that one would want to take up the position of analyst (Lacan 1967–1968). Then, only after the event, retroactively, does this analysis turn into what it always was, a 'training analysis'. For Lacanians every analysis could turn out to be a training analysis, and it does not lead to a form of identity, merely the ability to take up a certain kind of position in relation to an analysand. The influence of psychology inside psychoanalysis, however, has led to a number of distortions of practice that Lacanian psychoanalysts have had to struggle against.

Identity

Lacan deepened his critique of 'identity' in psychoanalysis with a series of attacks on the 'identity' of the IPA as the one organisation claiming the right to speak for psychoanalysis. Needless to say, this enclosure and segregation would have left the Lacanians outside the field, and so it is 'identity' as such that becomes a target. Some who defend ego psychology have argued that *émigré* analysts did indeed adapt to US capitalism, and that there is nothing necessarily wrong with that, even suggesting that free-market capitalism is the only alternative to Soviet-style Marxism (Zeitlin 1997). This does at any rate open a series of theoretical questions about the identity of Lacanians in relation to psychoanalysis as well as how a dismantling of identity is to be understood by those who claim, and those who refuse to claim, identity as a persecuted minority, and for whom 'identity' operates as a form of defence.

The presence of Jews in the history of old psychoanalysis, that which Lacan claimed to be returning to, and the consequences of cutting himself off from an international association that had needed to define itself against a hostile world, and so against a world hostile to its existence as if it were a Jewish science, has been a recurring motif in Lacan's work. Lacan (1991/2007: 135) insists, for example, that analysts be interested in 'Hebraic history' because 'it is, perhaps, inconceivable that psychoanalysis could have been born anywhere else than in this tradition' (see Reinhard and Lupton 2003).

The notion of 'extimacy' can then be used to describe how an object, object of enjoyment, that is ostensibly 'intimate' to the subject is experienced by them as outside so that others might be seen as responsible for the 'theft of enjoyment', enjoyment that the subject never actually possessed. This notion has been deployed to describe racism, and Miller (1986) also makes the point that psychoanalysis as a practice has been defined by the 'extimacy' of the Jew as a figure intimate to the practice but at the same moment exterior to it. There are some significant steps here to conceptualising how it is that psychoanalysis has been formed as a Jewish practice that is also at the same time haunted by anti-Semitism (Frosh 2005).

There is therefore in this trajectory of a critique of 'identity' also a critique of individual psychology as a threat to psychoanalysis. Lacanian psychoanalysis provides theoretical tools to understand the insidious psychologisation of the subject now, but also of the way certain human groups are segregated under capitalism. And there is a crucial link with the history of anti-Semitism and the place of anti-Semitism under capitalism (Leon 1946). The motif of 'identity', and the paradoxical demand that ethnic rights be recognised at the same time as groups assimilate themselves to the dominant culture, operates at the level of symbolic allocation of roles and at the level of imaginary rivalries.

Natural science and psychology

From the earliest days of the École freudienne there was active participation of psychologists and priests (Roudinesco 1990). This participation has then also characterised the formation of Lacanian groups around the world, with the role of psychologists in the emergence of local forms of Lacanian psychoanalysis more prominent in some countries – Japan, for instance – and the role of the Catholic Church very important in others, Brazil being one such place (Dunker 2008; Parker 2008).

The bid for psychoanalysis as natural science has had a double impact, buttressing two contradictory forces that, in turn, reproduce antagonistic historical political-economic formations. At one and the same moment, the signifier 'science' appears to warrant medical psychiatric conceptions of diagnosis and treatment, and so reproduces a feudal relation between doctor and patient, and appears to operate within a more open democratic field of enquiry in which analyst and analysand speak as contractually-equal, if asymmetrically-positioned, bourgeois subjects. 'Science' in this second sense of the term becomes part of a domain of empirical hypothesis-testing and observational work in which there is shared understanding that there will be some kind of incremental accumulation of knowledge. This enterprise requires balanced judicious investigation, and there is indeed also at work within it a balance between a pragmatic view of the 'truth' that this knowledge yields – truth as that which works – and a more empiricist expectation that 'truth' as such will be unveiled by those who search rigorously enough, and here truth accompanies the knowledge that renders it visible, as illuminating if sometimes unpalatable (Glynos and Stavrakakis 2002). For Lacan (1976–1977: 78), psychoanalysis is 'not a science at all, because it's irrefutable. It's a practice, a practice that will endure, or not. It's a babbling practice.' This means that attempts to measure Lacanian psychoanalysis against evidential criteria demanded by psychology are mistaken (*pace* Billig 2006; cf. Stavrakakis 2007a).

Positivist science under capitalism, especially in the disciplines that comprise the psy complex, has oscillated between these pragmatic and empiricist poles of attraction, and through the twentieth century there was an ideological aspect to this oscillation. Pragmatist tendencies have been more powerful in the US and parts of the world where capitalism flourished on an ostensibly empty terrain, as if technological capabilities, social relations and even forms of subject could be developed from scratch and flower out into apparently limitless possibilities. The question here is what can be achieved, just that, and so adaptation of psychoanalysis to this kind of New Deal for the subject was, among other things, to what the future holds rather than on what is still present of the past. Empiricist tendencies, in contrast, have tended to give a more pessimistic cast to what knowledge reveals of possibilities for change. In England, for example, the weight of the past on the minds of the living is composed both from the inheritance of feudal traditions, an enclosure of mental space that draws attention to limits, of what is possible, and from the arrival of a more tragic continental European sensibility which chimes with motifs of constraint and inevitability. On the one side of the Atlantic it is as if space is the final frontier and on the other side it is as if time will take its toll on those who hope for too much (Parker 2007).

These are the strait-gates through which Freudian psychoanalysis already freighted with romanticism – in which, it is said that the most that can be hoped for is 'common unhappiness' which defines the human condition – is transformed into a French psychoanalytic blend of phenomenology and structuralism, existential dread and castration by the signifier. To summarise Lacan's return to Freud in these reduced terms is to simplify a contradictory nuanced reading and reinterpretation of psychoanalytic texts, and to already close down what Lacan opens up there. Even so, it is necessary to appreciate how, on the one hand, Freud in France does get mired in a positivist tradition of scientific research that was still torn between what remained of the old dispensation – aristocratic residues in the organisation of scholarship and the professions – and Enlightenment culture, albeit refracted through images of freedom as entailing a delirium close to madness in, for example, versions of a call for individuals to be dutiful or to transgress the law (Descombes 1980; Roudinesco 1990).

Lacanian psychoanalysis encountered forms of psychology – local variants of subjectivity decanted through disciplinary mechanisms that are necessary to the functioning of capitalism – and it is psychology more than psychiatry that filters out what is thought to be scientifically valid in psychoanalytic practice according to the twin precepts of empirical evidence and pragmatic utility. What should be noticed about scientific knowledge here is that under capitalism it begins to operate as a kind of machinery which presupposes a kind of truth that it mobilises for strategic purposes or reveals as the warrant for decisions to be made about well-being and health, including 'mental' health.

Human science and faith

On the other side of the debate over the opportunities and distortions that an alliance between psychoanalysis and medical science would bring were many leading figures who argued their position from the margins of the IPA, or from the outside. There were a number of analysts who left the international and abandoned psychoanalysis altogether in the post-war period precisely because the adaptation to positivism was not far-reaching or fast enough. One trajectory of psychoanalysis in the US was toward cognitive behavioural approaches, toward a rapprochement with psychology as a discipline that had tried to cut its links with Freud and Freudians some time before. Many key figures in the history of psychology have past psychoanalytic allegiances erased from their work in psychology textbooks. For example, Jean Piaget, whose cognitive-stage conception of child development is often counterposed to analytic perspectives, was a member of the IPA, conducted analyses, and gave papers at psychoanalytic congresses (and was probably present at the session where Lacan first outlined the 'mirror stage') (Schepeler 1993).

While Lacan is the most well-known casualty of the concerted campaign from before 1953 by some figures in the leadership of the IPA against the French dissidents, he was by no means the only one. Other analysts such as Françoise Dolto had also strayed too far from the line of the international or gone too far over the line the organisation had drawn to protect what it took to be analysis as such. There were analysts who left, but also some who were able to stay inside one of the franchise groups because they effectively accepted the prohibition on training that Lacan would not. It seems very likely, for example, that Erik Erikson in the US would have also been excluded if he had insisted on training analysts, and deviations from accepted IPA practice were tolerated providing that these deviations were not transmitted to others (Roazen 1996: 323).

The cognitive behavioural closet psychoanalysts have swung around outside and against old psychoanalysis as one half of a pincer movement to enclose it within another existing interpretative framework and so discredit Freud. Meanwhile, the humanist reinterpretations have functioned as the other arm of this psychologising enclosure. On the one side then is the insistence that psychoanalysis should concern itself with 'cognitive' strategies, by implication with what is faulty in the patient's reasoning; on the other is the insistence that what the patient says should be filled with meaning, by implication with the meanings they feel are already present but hidden even to themselves. In stark contrast to both, Lacan insisted that what the patient 'thinks' and even the unconscious itself is not inside the person at all but is a product of symbolic practices that, in bourgeois society, invite each subject to imagine that they are, or should be, an enclosed individual. Psychoanalysis is, then, a process of unravelling connections between signifiers; far from filling them with the meaning that was always present, as if it should be turned from something 'latent' in the signifiers into something manifest to the patient, the task is to reduce their meaning (Lacan 1964/1973: 250). Lacan (1991/2007) argued, therefore, that we should be aware that 'latent' content was something produced by the analyst, not excavated by their masterly interpretation of the patient's dreams or other formations of the unconscious such as jokes, slips and symptoms.

Cartesian separation – the reification of knowledge about human nature sustained by scientific discourse and deification of the subject invited to assume command of that knowledge – is one of the characteristic ideological forms that thrive under capitalism, ideological forms that capitalism feeds upon to sustain the self-conception of human beings under these peculiar political-economic conditions, and the belief that they enter into a contract freely to sell their labour to others. Lacan (1965) gives us the conceptual tools to understand how this separation operates. Science develops under capitalism such that there is an alienation of two principles that are dialectically intertwined in psychoanalysis: reason and faith (Nobus and Quinn 2005).

Enlightenment reasoning

Science under capitalism, for all its pretensions to provide a system of open democratic investigation which harnesses speculation to an apparatus of hypothesis-testing and ever-more refined modelling of its objects of study, confronts the individual subject as an accumulating corpus of knowledge. There is, at its heart, an alienating dimension of the way scientific knowledge operates which betrays its promise to lay out an expanding space of reasoned enquiry, a promise that each and every participant will understand more of the world and more of their own nature. This double game replicates and reinforces one of the most disappointing motifs of bourgeois democracy; it pretends to include every citizen in the decision-making machinery but then excludes discussion over underlying ground-rules of debate concerning private ownership of the means of production and distribution of resources (Žižek 2008). Disappointment over the gap between what is promised – transparency, accountability, universal rights – and the reality of the apparatus then becomes one of the deepest and most pernicious motifs of democratic life. And the message that we should come to awareness that we cannot change the world within these given parameters, and that these given parameters are the only ones we will ever experience, then comes to define the limits of what is vaunted as mature reason.

If the Western Enlightenment, flowering in the bourgeois revolution against feudal society, was supposed to have been characterised by the injunction that we have the courage to think for ourselves – this is Immanuel Kant's (1784) catch-cry to end the 'self-incurred tutelage' of human beings – then capitalism, and forms of science factored into the production of knowledge under capitalism, transforms that injunction into one in which we should traverse the triumphant experience of such courage to arrive at the courage to accept what cannot be changed (cf. Foucault 1984). Psychoanalytic social theory derived from the adaptationist tradition Lacan excoriated draws out the lesson directly and openly, turning it into a moral stance to be declared and advertised to all as the 'importance' of 'disappointment' (e.g. Craib 1994). But Lacanian psychoanalysis is still often also trapped in this limited mode of engagement with politics, and names this disappointment 'lack'. The precise coordinates of 'lack' in clinical work thus need to be differentiated from disappointment in the political realm. A starting point for making that differentiation comes from Lacan's own careful interpretation of how a particular kind of subject comes to lie at the heart of capitalism and Western science recruited to that alienating political-economic system. Now it is possible to develop an interpretation of Lacan's own account to show how his analysis of science also entails a critique of capitalism.

The focal point of Lacan's analysis is the reasoning individual that appears centre-stage in the writings of Descartes (1641/1996: 68) as the 'cogito', that which doubts everything save its own activity and existence as something that is thinking. Even if there were an evil demon that was misleading us about the nature of reality, that sabotaged scientific investigation, there would still remain *thinking* and this very doubt about the nature of reality operates as a defining property and safeguard for the fact that 'I think therefore I am' ('*cogito, ergo sum*', in some formulations 'I am thinking therefore I am'). However, there is a crucial gap in Descartes' formulation of the nature of this thinking substance, which it is then possible, as a second step, to magnify such that it becomes a gap in being and defines the human subject as marked by a 'lack'. To take that second step is to introduce a potent ideological element into the equation, and we will need to take care to circumscribe our account of Lacan's reading now so that we do not inflate this precise theoretical point into a moral lesson. Lacan points out that the 'I' of the 'I think' ('*cogito*') is not necessarily self-identical with the 'I' of the 'I am' ('*sum*'), and that the 'therefore' ('*ergo*') of the equation glues the two forms of 'I' together. It is a linguistic operation with metaphysical consequences, consequences for how the Cartesian subject will come to think of itself as 'itself' and warrant its existence as something separate from other subjects defined as discrete individuals.

An entire mental landscape operating on particular epistemological and ontological principles is thereby opened up for the subject, a mental landscape which enables the subject to map themselves ideologically into capitalism. This mental landscape is eventually filled out by the discipline of psychology, but there is already an incipient and necessary psychologisation of the subject at work in Descartes' reasoning about reason, reasoning that

Lacan unpicks. Descartes' account works under capitalism, it corresponds well to it, but it does so on condition that there is something else that guarantees that we can move out from our own separate individually-enclosed spheres of reasoning into a knowledge of the world. The guarantee comforts those individual subjects who are alienated within that knowledge as scientific knowledge they cannot fully comprehend. And that something else is God, for while there may be those who work like the evil genie in this world and mislead us about the nature of reality, there is, Descartes argues, a benevolent God who ensures that the universe is arranged in such a way that our investigation will bring us to more complete knowledge of it.

Scientific knowledge under capitalism thus rests at a deeper level on faith, and Lacan repeatedly draws attention to the way that a simple refusal of a spiritual dimension covers over the hidden presupposition that there is a God. Atheists may declare that God is dead, but the attempt to dispatch him too quickly results in that omniscient being – a 'subject supposed to know' as condition for us knowing anything at all – having a more profound function which is captured in Lacan's (1964/1973: 59) comment that under current conditions it is not so much that the deity has been finished off altogether but rather, as 'the true formula of atheism', that *'God is unconscious'*.

Two psychological subjects

This argument corresponds with a reformulation of the *'cogito'* as such in Lacanian psychoanalysis. There is an intriguing reversal of Lacan's argument in the course of his work concerning the relationship between the 'I think' and the 'I am'. As we have noted, Lacan conceptually differentiates the two ways the 'I' appears. At one point in his writing, the signifier 'I' that is thinking is treated as a fictitious thinking substance, the *'cogito'* as something very like the 'ego' in psychoanalysis, and we know that Lacanian psychoanalysis treats this ego with suspicion. This ego as 'the mental illness of man' pretends to function as the centre of the self, perceiving and appraising reality, working on the 'reality principle', and is then neatly assimilated to an 'ego psychology' and then to psychology as such; for Lacan (1975/1991: 16), in contrast, 'the ego is structured exactly like a symptom. At the heart of the matter, it is only a privileged symptom, the human symptom *par excellence*, the mental illness of man.' The ego is treated as the site of cognitive and creative imaginative functions, and the human being in which the ego is to be reinforced so that it can healthily adapt to reality is configured as a psychological being. This is a psychologisation of psychoanalysis that Lacan combats when in the IPA and then attempts to circumvent in his return to Freud in his own school (cf. De Vos 2005).

Against this ego – the misleading 'I think' of the subject – there is 'I am', being which is occluded by reality and which it is the task of an authentic psychoanalysis to make present. A linguistic operation which divides 'I think' from 'I am' in Cartesian reasoning is the basis for reworking the division between consciousness and the unconscious. Psychoanalysis then becomes one of the places in which the human being can speak as it is, 'I am', and this process of speaking Lacan refers to as the moment at which the 'subject of the enunciation' appears in and against the 'I think' celebrated in everyday speech and scientific discourse about the human subject as a psychological subject, that which Lacan (Lacan 1964/1973: 139) terms the 'subject of the statement'.

The dramatic shift Lacan makes later in his writing is to treat the 'I am' as that which appears, albeit momentarily, to consciousness. Now it is that which manifests itself as the 'subject of the statement', and he treats the 'I think' as that which is driven into the unconscious. To 'think', to reason, is here seen as a function which appears as a 'subject of the enunciation' when the subject is able to voice connections and locate itself in relation to others and its own history (Dolar 1998). We can read this shift in Lacan's work as a necessary reversal of perspective that draws our attention to the way the 'I' has been captured by the burgeoning discipline and popular configuration of 'psychology'; it is a shift of emphasis that draws attention to the increasing psychologisation of the subject. Psychology is a set of disciplinary specifications for what the human subject is like as if it were a mechanism which thinks and behaves and which can be predicted and controlled.

This psychology not only pertains to how the subject 'thinks' – leaving more profound aspects of human existence to the domain of faith or, perhaps, a form of psychoanalysis – but it now extends its reach into how the subject feels itself to be. Lacan's reversal of perspective underscores the division of the subject rather than placing bets on where reason really lies. Unlike the 'subject of the statement' – insofar as it is alienated and reified – the 'subject of the enunciation' cannot be substantialised and so speaking in this quite different way about desire opens a space for reasoning about existence that is, as a process, antithetical to 'psychology'.

Psychologisation of human experience extends into the 'I am', revels in the experiential depth of the individual and defines how it should be and how it might best realise its potential as a positive healthy well-being. Critical reasoning about our place in the world is side-lined and must be struggled for and spoken in attempts to reconstruct and map ourselves as something that thinks, 'I think'. It is as 'subject of the enunciation' that I am able to think, and this process of speaking while thinking enables, in psychoanalytic clinical space, a distance to be struck from the psychologised banal representations of what I am as 'subject of the statement', that which captures and limits my being.

This tactical manoeuvre has wider implications for how the 'subject' is grasped theoretically and clinically by Lacan. The reversal of the Lacanian opposition between subject of the statement and subject of the enunciation draws attention to a crucial feature of the divided subject, which is that neither subject is treated as definitive substance which exists as such waiting to be revealed. In Lacanian psychoanalysis the unconscious is not a place from which a true subject of any kind can be discovered and released, and in this respect there is a significant difference from the way psychologised versions of psychoanalysis have developed in the English-speaking world. Here, particularly in the Kleinian and object relations traditions, the terms 'introjection' and 'internalisation' function to enforce a divide between inside and outside that Lacanian psychoanalysis questions: 'the very terms that were used to damn the model of "internal-external" would become exactly the terms that sustained it' (Leader 2000: 52). Against the falsity of the ego, falseness reinforced by psychological conceptions of the ego whether conceived of as something that is that which thinks, or as something which is the substantial being of the subject, there is a truth of speaking. The subject factored into psychologised modes of representation of the human being under capitalism, in contrast, is as a product – specified as having a certain shape and engaging in certain kinds of mental operations – and there is a corresponding commodification of the objects of desire which it chases after.

Mentalisation

The historical transformation of feudalism into capitalism is unfinished business, and this is no more evident than in the biopolitical management of populations and individuals. This problematic, in which medical psychiatric practices compatible with late feudalism inform the psychologisation of individual subjects under capitalism, is one that psychoanalysis has been influenced by and sometimes colluded with. In modern biopolitics there is a twofold process at work by which the body is still the target of sectors of the psy complex concerned with the healthy functioning of social systems – now the 'behavioural' element of psychological treatment – while, at the same time, the mind is abstracted as a mechanism responsible for faulty perception and 'cognition' which can, in principle, be corrected.

Under these conditions individuals are marked out as separate from one another, but in a particular relationship to the state, 'surrounded by a boundary that simultaneously isolates and protects them' (Esposito 2008: 141). This, a 'double enclosure of the body', signals the limitations of bourgeois-democratic alternatives to sovereign power, and the role of psychology as a reductive enterprise that promises personal freedom only within the horizon of a political-economic system revolving around private property, and as private practice revolving around good mental hygiene that it reduces even further now to 'mentalisation' of bad feelings (e.g. Bateman 1995).

Lacanian psychoanalysis is also complicit with psychologisation insofar as it conforms to abstracted and reductive specifications of pathology and with a model of individual 'accountability' that encourages each individual to take responsibility for their own enclosed privatised fantasies about what might bring them pleasure, if not jouissance. Its practice is often carried out in such a way as to enforce the lesson that each individual subject's fantasy must be addressed 'one by one' in a relationship with one other that is not really a relationship at all. However, there are theoretical resources within this psychoanalysis that enable us to rebel against as well as revel in bourgeois-democratic ideology together with an individualised distributive ethics which characterises life under capitalism. So, it is to psychological ethics as a problem for psychoanalysis that we turn next.

Chapter 4
Distributed selves

This chapter examines the dominant conception of ethics that psychology appeals to, one which Lacanian psychoanalysis refuses. Psychology as a disciplinary practice configures itself as a particular kind of ideal, of the good as a field of utilitarian ethical calculation. Lacanian psychoanalysis, in contrast, lays the ground for a reformulation of how psychological categories are crystallised as structural positions in relation to language, and these structural positions are embedded now in distinctive subjective orientations to capital and the labour process. Further political implications of crucial differences between psychoanalysis and psychology are spelt out with respect to the different notions of sexuality that are employed by the two approaches in clinical practice. The claim made by Lacan and his followers to have provided a radical alternative to dominant conceptions of gender is examined; a distinction is marked between notions of 'gender' and 'sexual difference', and consequences for psychoanalysis are discussed.

Allocation

The transformation of feudalism into capitalism required in some parts of the world a social revolution which definitively ended aristocratic rule, and in other parts of the world it occasioned uneasy compromises in which local elites struck a deal with colonial entrepreneurs. Even in what were to become imperialist heartlands of the new global economy there was a complex concordat between the remaining elements of feudal power structures and the bourgeoisie. In France, for example, the break between the two systems seemed more complete than was the case in England, where the bourgeois revolution was more obviously unfinished (Anderson 1979, 1980). However, the transformation and recomposition of class power in both European countries, as well as in the New World and the new colonies of Europe and the United States, took place on another yet deeper and more historically-enduring pattern of oppression, patriarchy. If bourgeois democratic politics compatible with capitalism still reproduced patriarchal power as the domination of women by men and of younger men by older men (Millett 1977), it nonetheless rendered that power visible. Early reform movements in nineteenth- and twentieth-century first wave feminism put the question of women's emancipation on the agenda, as they did the question of slavery (Beechey 1979; Eisenstein 1979).

In place of differentiation between the sexes as taken for granted, either as God-given or biologically hard-wired, there opened up a space for interpretation of what this differentiation might mean and even for how the ostensibly different worlds of men and women might themselves be reinvented. One of the characteristic motifs in early psychoanalytic writing was that another differentiation be made between sex as biological binary opposition and gender as socially ascribed difference (Grigg *et al.* 1999; Verhaeghe 1999). Freud (1905: 220–221) drew a more subtle differentiation between biological difference (between males and females), social role (that defined the position of men and women) and personal identity defined by one's masculinity or femininity. The logic of this triple-layered differentiation of human sexual relationships was that sexuality as such could conceivably be reconfigured outside the binary operations that most forms of patriarchy were predicated upon. Freud hints at this possibility and then draws back from it; at one moment the infant is described as 'polymorphously perverse' and at another as 'constitutionally bisexual', and the trajectory that the growing child must follow in order to enter the adult world of compulsory heterosexuality is thereby questioned but then reaffirmed (Freud 1905: 148; cf. Worthington 2008).

The political lesson that Freud, who translated texts by James Stuart Mill on the rights of man, himself draws is that there are indeed underlying differences between men and women, and the task of an enlightened scientist is to ensure that there is a sensible differentiation and distribution of rights and responsibilities (Gay 1988). (Bertha Pappenheim (Breuer's patient referred to as 'Anna O.') translated Mary Wollstonecraft's *Vindication of the Rights of Women* into German in 1899 (Appignanesi and Forrester 1993: 78).) Here we pass from the domain of psychiatric differentiation – which searched for biological differences – and psychological differentiation, which looked for a more balanced account of how human subjectivity might be distributed across what still must be taken as given. In this, psychoanalysis often sustains in its clinical practice an ethics of sexual difference and a range of other human differences – of class, race, ability – that have been psychologised (in an attention to individual responses to unjust treatment). There were intimations of different forms of ethics elaborated in the course of the Western Enlightenment at the birth of capitalism, but psychoanalysis in one of its modalities – that is, as a form of psychology – opted for ethics organised around the allocation of *rights*. There was an assumption that there should be a distribution of pain and pleasure, of the costs and benefits of coexisting within a society concerned with commodity exchange. This assumption is one of the aspects of traditional ways of thinking about ethics which Lacan (1986/1992: 303) refers to as the 'service of goods' (see Rajchman 1991).

Capitalism rests on a particular conception of individual rights, and there is a balance presumed in bourgeois-democratic ideological systems between the rights of those who own the means of production to employ others for profit on the one hand, and the rights of workers to sell their labour power on the other. The exercise of the employer's and the employee's rights is viewed as taking place within an exchange that operates as a kind of contract that both parties consciously and freely engage in. In this ideological universe it is presumed that it is possible for judicious administrators to determine what will be good for people and bad for them, and to arrange roles and responsibilities so that the greatest possible good is distributed among them. Psychology as a discipline comprises elaborate models of human behaviour to warrant this version of ethics, and even some of the strands of work in the behaviourist tradition, for example, which seem to refuse to adopt a specific moral standpoint, do still actually rest on notions of what healthy and unhealthy patterns of behaviour are and how 'contingencies of reinforcement' might be engineered to distribute benefit to all (Skinner 1969; cf. Napoli 1981).

This conception of ethics rather conveniently overlooks, as does behaviourism generally, what the stakes are for the individuals or groups that arrange the distribution of goods. Some kind of neutral disinterested position outside the system is presupposed from which decisions are made, decisions which are not themselves induced by certain benefits for those who decide what is good for everyone else. However, conscious decision-making and the presumed goodwill of those distributing the rights of others are the least of the problem. The rights of each individual are limited conceptually and clinically by an elusive domain of the subject, the unconscious, and this domain remains forever out of reach, outside the domain of 'rights'.

Obsessional alienation

The rationality of capitalism as a political-economic system is underpinned by a scientistic view of social and personal enlightenment. The ideological armature of science under capitalism is then set against alternative systems which are derogated as pre-scientific, uncivilised and 'irrational', or may be romanticised as non-rational and intuitive, but usually in such a way as to prioritise the rationality assumed by each individual seeking further enlightenment from them. Psychoanalysis itself, despite Freud's (1933: 181–182) own warnings, often adheres to a distinctive worldview which it assumes to be universally true, and which is sometimes buoyed up by appeals to science, to scientific method, or in claims to be underwriting the subject of science. These forms of truth are sometimes given a publicly-accountable frame as warrant for a psychological reduction of truth to what can be defined as correct. In that case there is an adherence to 'evidence-based' standards and explicit rationalism, and sometimes this mode of reasoning is given a hermetic cast, in which case the internal logic is valued as specifically scientific and even more rigorous than that of mainstream science. This is why it is said that Lacanians 'must expose any attempt to accuse us of being amongst those who promote and identify with the ideal of effectiveness' (Laurent 2002: 100).

A peculiarity of subjectivity under capitalism is that the human subject – the nature of their being in the world and their reflexively elaborated relation to others – is of that subject as an isolated individual. From this separation of each subject from others, individualism thus defines the ground on which someone will conceive of themselves as electing different options, as if choosing commodities. The obsessional neurotic is actually the quintessential psychological subject. Another peculiarity, which coexists in a dialectical relationship with individualism, is that the individual subject is torn between a relation to capital and a relation to the labour process.

On the one side, capital as a system of commodity exchange in which labour power is itself treated as a commodity produces a further reification: of relations reconfigured as if they were things. On the other side, the labour process is the site for the exercise of creative powers of the human being, but it is creativity betrayed as those powers are turned against the subject through different aspects of control, deskilling and unemployment (Mandel and Novack 1970; Braverman 1974; Shotter 1987). It is possible to conceive of this second side of the equation as the site of alienation, but theoretically more productive to treat alienation as the *split*, the gap between the relation to capital on the one hand and the relation to the labour process on the other. Attending to this split we are able to develop an account of alienation that is at one moment materialist – grounded in the specific nature of capitalism – and Lacanian. Or, another way of putting it, a Lacanian account of alienation as the division of the subject also provides a materialist account of conditions of production, including production of the subject under capitalism.

This divided subject under capitalism – alienated both in their condition as commodity and as source of surplus value – feeds psychologisation, and the relatively enduring reality of life under capitalism provides the conditions in which certain clinical 'structures' take on a life of their own. Conditions of psychologisation sediment a process of pathologisation, and the distinct psychiatric categories that psychoanalysis adopted – of obsessional neurosis, hysteria, psychosis and perversion – seep into the life-worlds of subjects. Their individual experience of distress also speaks of a pathological compliance with and revolt against exploitative alienating society. Under capitalism alienation comes into its own as a Lacanian psychoanalytic category, alienation no longer as some quasi-existential 'lack' which may either, at best, give the space for critical distance from existing conditions or, at worst, confirm bitter disappointment as the end point of reflexive enquiry into the human condition. Instead, alienation plays a much more fundamental role in the position of the subject, and it does so as real, in two senses of 'real' elaborated by Lacan (1964/1973).

First, alienation is 'real' in its status as the necessary underlying condition for becoming a subject, for one must both sell one's labour power and consume to survive. Whether selling or buying to confirm one's being – as one's 'justification for existence' – and torn between the two, one is faced with something impossible, the real as impossible (Lacan 1964/1973: 167). The real is impossible to grasp, and appears only transitorily at moments of traumatic revelation; it is resistant to symbolisation, and it is understood only in imaginary and symbolic terms when it is covered over, given meaning. Here, in this first sense one might speak of the material 'base' of capitalist economy, but only if one gives up the idea that this base can be bit-by-bit excavated and re-presented to us as it is, as if a 'metalanguage' can be spoken (Lacan 2006: 688).

Second, alienation is 'real' as gap in the symbolic, as a necessary contradiction that sustains the way we account for where we are in this political-economic 'reality'. Within the very texture of capitalism as an ostensibly rational system of production and consumption and as terrain on which each individual is free to enter into different kinds of commercial and interpersonal contract with others, there are moments of unbearably excessive irrationality when relations between subjects break apart. This aspect of alienation which haunts everyday reality breaks the trust which glues market trading and the civil community together, and this alienation is 'real' as that impossible point at which the subject is torn, divided between commodity exchange and the labour process. Here the subject as such is vaunted in ideology as the psychological individual – perceiving, cognising and electing between alternative courses of action – but, in its pathological condition of obsessional neurosis, it is the subject as product of capitalism.

Uncertainty, procrastination, powerlessness, resentment and secretive victories over a world that renders it guilty at its heart for its failure and complicity with exploitation: this is the condition of the subject which may be crystallised in a symptom taken to analysis, and then this structure of the subject can be laid bare as obsessional 'clinical structure' and the subject can speak something of the truth of the alienation that forms it.

Hysterical truth

The quasi-contractual basis of life under capitalism sustains the illusion that there is potential if not actual transparency of social relationships, but this ideological trope of transparency itself functions to intensify alienation suffered under capitalism. This alienation, together with individualising descriptions and explanations of it, serves to obscure the conditions of life and work that separate each individual from their creative work. Lacanian psychoanalysis aims to enable the subject to grasp that there is no escape from alienation, and some form of alienation is viewed as a condition for being a subject, a subject of language. Claims to freedom have always been treated with suspicion in the psychoanalytic tradition, as forms of illusion or delusion. It is, instead, thought necessary that there be forms of defence against the temptation to abolish the social constraints that make us human, and, when it buys into and sells that argument to the general public, psychoanalysis itself thereby also functions as a form of defence. It is one of the defence mechanisms capitalism utilises to warn those who rail against alienation that they will most likely end up with something worse. There is thus a tense, sometimes uneasy, but mainly compliant relationship between psychoanalysis and capitalism, one which this book aims to break (cf. Kovel 1981, 1988).

Obsessional neurosis replicates and condenses a certain form of masculinity, and this link between one form of pathology and gender identity is reinforced by their shared overlapping dominance and prevalence under capitalism. This is apparent in the way that individualisation intensifies powerlessness, and in identification with power or guilt at failure to achieve it as the overall structuring mode of being, actually or virtually, in reality or fantasy. Here one kind of domination as a characteristic of work – the command mode enforced by factory discipline and monitoring of productivity – meshes with that of the model nuclear family, and so capitalism feeds and is favoured by patriarchy in the public and private sphere (Kakar 1974; Zaretsky 1976). However, Freud saw obsessional neurosis as a 'dialect' of hysteria, and the common unhappiness we can expect under capitalism erupts from time to time as hysterical misery and even as revolt against the conditions that cause it, including against the attempts to define such revolt as 'psychological' (Ussher 1991). It has been pointed out that 'if an hysteric balks too much against the therapeutic alliance her pathology risks being considered as coming from the borderline field' (Maleval 2000: 125).

One of the characteristics of alienation as the distinctive division of the subject under capitalism is that there is resistance alongside compliance; and one of the characteristics of hysteria is that guilt – blame turned inward so that a paralysing circuit of agonising self-reproach locks the subject into their mind as an obsessional strategy – can be replaced by accusation. Shame is then mobilised and thrown out at others who have caused this distress, a distress that might be fixed upon a traumatic point but which speaks of wider systems of abuse to which the hysteric has been subject. So, at the very moment that the subject confirms that they have been rendered into the product of exploitative conditions – the condition of becoming subject to capitalism – the subject finds a deeper point from which to voice the truth of who they have become as they rebel against those conditions.

This condition of subjection and revolt that is hysteria is one that Lacan saw as a more fundamental underlying human condition that capitalism masks with another obsessional second nature as a necessary false consciousness that will enable the subject to navigate this historically-contingent reality. That this condition of the subject is stereotypically feminine is symptomatic of its marginalisation and the way it appears in spaces that are orthogonal to the world of work. Psychoanalysis becomes possible when hysteria is torn free from the female body, the hysterical symptom is laid into a *map* of the body, and the existence of 'male hysteria' indicates that femininity itself is in this map rather than in the body itself (Mitchell 1984).

If obsessional neurosis reveals something of the material 'base' of capitalist economy – alienation as real – then hysteria speaks in and against the ideological superstructure. The hysteric is called into being as a form of subject but refuses to be addressed, to be understood, and this form of subject has been particularly rebellious against its status as product, as passive object of capitalism functioning as a form of patriarchy. This refusal of recruitment by the ideological apparatus of capitalism marks the hysteric as one who has nevertheless begun to grasp how, as Lacan (1964/1973: 198) puts it, she is a subject represented 'not for another subject, but for another signifier'; she is determined by signifying chains that define who she is for others. The hysteric thus shows us something about the nature of ideology, shows how ideology 'represents the imaginary relationship of individuals to their real conditions of existence' (Althusser 1971: 153).

There is, therefore, a distribution of neurotic responses to conditions of life under capitalism, to the split that opens up between commodities circulating as if they are signifiers representing the subject for other commodities and a labour process that strips the worker of their creative capacities and turns work into dead time. This distribution itself operates ideologically, as an imaginary relationship to real conditions, and allocates stereotypically-gendered forms of misery to those who comply with existing conditions, albeit reluctantly and resentfully, and those who resist, whether in open defiance or through self-sabotaging strategies in the course of which conflict is coded in the body.

Of course, it is not only men who obsessionally conform – even though the oedipal pact which promises them access to power in culture at some point in the future is at the price of obedience now – and not only women who hysterically resist, even if they are to some extent not entirely at home in systems of power. Lacan (1975/1998) in his later writings redefined this ideological allocation of bodies to gendered positions in his account of the non-relation between the two, man and woman, as a non-relation. Here 'man' is completely enmeshed in language – and, we can say, power – and lured into the fantasy that there is a point of exception in which one man, perhaps the father, perhaps the leader, and perhaps even one day this man himself, will stand outside this system of subordination. Here 'woman' is enveloped by language and power, but 'not all' of her is contained by it, and there is an aspect of her existence which finds escape.

This neatly turns around Freud's (1914) argument that the super-ego is weaker, if not entirely absent, in women, and produces a revaluation of the incomplete acculturation of women to capitalism, to capitalist forms of patriarchy; the logic of this argument is expressed in the statement that 'Women don't need a superego, since they have no guilt on which the superego can parasitize – since, that is, they are far less prone to compromise their desire' (Žižek 1994: 69). Here again, however, we need to keep in mind that, for Lacan, 'man' and 'woman' are categorical distinctions – and we should say, ideologically-loaded categories – which may be occupied by biological males or females. Resistance to capitalism is, to some extent, necessarily 'hysterical', and is liable to be interpreted as such by psychoanalysis, and in this psychoanalysis is therefore not necessarily incorrect. What women's resistance to capitalism does is to configure the symbolic – the symbolic, that is, as it is constituted under capitalism – as a site of trauma, and Lacanian psychoanalysis provides theoretical elaboration of the extimate relation between a traumatic point 'inside' the subject and the 'external' world. This resistance, we might say, speaks truth to power, which is also a notion articulated in Marxist and feminist traditions (Budgen *et al.* 2007; Lorde 2007).

Psychotic knowledge

Under capitalism economic relationships are ratified anew in the face of disparate ideological and moral challenges. This ratification elaborates the ideological horizon within which capitalism is questioned and confirmed, this in such a way that there is sedimentation of taken-for-granted ground-rules for production and relationships, ground-rules that are not immediately open to question. Obsessional neurosis operates within these ground-rules, replicates them, and hysteria breaks them, questions them. But the demand that each subject accede to a position of power within a hierarchically-organised gradation of rights and responsibilities includes within it another demand, that the symbolic apparatus that confirms the legitimacy of the system itself be confirmed. There is, in other words, a demand that knowledge itself be accorded agency and that the subject should mesh itself with that knowledge and assume a precarious position within it that threatens to abolish the subject as such. Another position outside this symbolic apparatus, one which would provide some critical distance from it, is thus shut off, ruled out (Fink 1997).

As we have already noted, obsessional neurosis is one strategy for coexisting with this demand, and a private enclosed mental space is secured from intrusion by outsiders. The price to pay for this strategy is that the subject is also locked inside a maze of their own making, and finds it difficult to abandon the consolation that a fantasised relation with objects of desire – that of a barred subject in relation to the object a – provides. Hysterics play the game both ways, trapping conflict in the body in order that a coded message can thereby be sent to the outside world – to the Other – about their suffering, and breaking the rules in ostentatious displays of non-compliance. In both cases there are degrees of repression at work, a fairly efficient procedure which shuts out of consciousness what is unthinkable to the subject. What is shut out may then be rediscovered in analysis in another place, which some psychoanalysts think of as a place they call the unconscious and which Lacanians treat as a series of constitutive gaps in spoken discourse. There is also, however, a more drastic refusal of forms of law and order (including those forms that capitalism demands), and the operation of this existential choice and its sometimes disastrous failure characterises the predicament of the psychotic.

There is a risk here, that the 'psychoticising' strategies of psychiatry are relayed into psychoanalysis when the category 'psychotic' is employed. Much of what passes for 'psychosis' today is in fact a 'psychotic discourse' inhabited by professionals who are disturbed by those who, with great effort and pain, have broken from taken-for-granted ways of being in heteropatriarchal capitalism and have attempted to reconstruct an alternative symbolic universe which can only be understood by the psychiatrically-inclined as a 'delusion'. That this is painful and that the construction of an alternative universe may turn out to be as unbearable as the one that neurotics inhabit should not, however, be seen as grounds for psychiatric treatment. Lacanian psychoanalysis in its psychiatric mode does often collude with a medical response to this radically marginal way of being human when it presents as an emergency to the subject and to others. This is why the nature of 'psychosis' needs to be theorised in such a way as to embed it in the political-economic system against which it stands and of which it speaks (Santner 1996).

For Lacanian psychoanalysis the trajectory of each subject is the product of a particular determination, and sometimes, it is said, 'overdetermination', by familial relationships or chains of signifiers (Freud 1900/1999; Althusser 1977; Žižek 1989). These ground-rules for interpreting what our place in the symbolic means for us and others are, of course, thrown into question in analysis but there is no promise that the analysand will escape such determinations. There is merely the option of reducing signifiers to nonsense in the analysis and forging a different relationship with them outside the clinic. Some forms of psychoanalysis insidiously ratify the social forces they explore, and the analytic process can often end in a blend of stoicism and cynicism in the face of an outer world that must remain the same as it was before. Lacanian psychoanalysis does at least set itself against the distillation of the psychiatric category of psychosis into a set of symptoms that can be addressed by a psychologist. Such a psychological 'reconstruction' of psychiatric categories evacuates the category of psychosis of its political reference points (e.g. Bentall 1990).

We should take seriously both elements of Lacan's account of psychosis in different periods of his work, of it as 'foreclosure' and as 'knotting'. Lacan (1981/1993) first defines it in terms of 'foreclosure' of a signifier, the 'Name-of-the-Father', and the fact that this is such a potent signifier, one that Lacan was to reformulate as a 'master signifier' in later writings, draws attention to prevailing forms of patriarchy. It is then said that psychosis for those subjects who are already characterised by psychotic 'clinical structure' can be 'triggered' by an encounter with this signifier, with, for example, the impending status of fatherhood or the attainment of some other position of power that carries with it the semiotic connotations of leadership as fatherhood, what has been termed 'an investiture crisis' in a system organised around the transfer of power and knowledge (Santner 1996: 32).

Lacan later shifts attention from 'clinical structure' defined by modes of defence – 'foreclosure', 'disavowal' or 'repression' – to forms of 'knotting' which enable the subject to weave together the registers of symbolic, imaginary and real around a specific symptomatic formation, condensed as a symptom as such in the clinic (Ragland and Milovanovic 2004). This 'symptom' is no longer reduced to foreclosure of a signifier functionally homologous to that name for the subject – whether of the 'Name-of-the-Father' or other master signifier – but is a sometimes heroic attempt to re-found some place in language, something that psychologists would assume to be an 'identity'. Under capitalism, where the symbolic system is a site of traumatic exploitation for the subject and alienation is real, it is language as such that operates as a knot. The 'language disturbances' that are supposed to characterise 'psychotic speech' are actually disturbances that a professional constructs in order to explain to themselves why they do not understand what they hear (Georgaca and Gordo-López 1995). Lacanian psychoanalysis breaks from psychiatry and provides a space in which the subject speaks and reconstructs anew a different place in conditions of life under capitalism (or in another world that is fabricated as if completely outside it).

Perverse objects

The presumed binary relation between normal neurotic subjects – obsessional neurotic men and hysterical women – is unravelled by those with a sexual orientation quite other, those who do not look to the conventionally prescribed 'other' sex as their object of desire. This binary relation could be unravelled by analysts, and best practice of Lacanian psychoanalysis is that this ideologically-potent assumption about the nature of human sexuality as always reaching across to what is already known as the 'other sex' is thrown into question. Analysis questions what 'heterosexual' object choice is for the analysand as intensely as it questions 'homosexuals' about what they want. Psychoanalysis that presumes heterosexuality as a standard for mental health is bad psychoanalysis, something more like psychology. Then we really would be in the realm of a specific kind of ethics concerned with the allocation and balance of pleasure between two quite different kinds of being – man and woman defined by their biology – but with a twist. The twist is that ethics, which concerns the grounding of human action, is turned into morality as a set of standards or as a kind of glue to bind a community together (Badiou 1998/2001).

In such moralising versions of psychoanalysis those who disrupt the boundary are placed in a pathological category all of their own, perversion. Some deviant strands of Lacanian psychoanalysis fall in line with this vision and offer moral-political diagnoses of the state of youth today while bewailing the effects of homosexuality and same-sex marriages (Dufour 2008), but this is against Lacan's own practice. Lacan saw gay and lesbian analysands and, unlike some national sections of the IPA for example, it is as 'normal' for such analysands to train as Lacanian analysts themselves as it is for those who believe themselves to be heterosexual. There has usually been no big deal made about this because our psychoanalysis has tended to question any form of declared 'identity', whether that concerns sexual or ethnic orientation. At the same time, as with the use of other clinical categories, 'perversion' can still be crystallised into an object, 'pervert', and so we need to understand how this object is constituted in the gaze of those who think they are the non-perverts.

Lacanian psychoanalysis gives a precise formulation for 'perverse' clinical structure that captures well what is required of the subject in capitalist society. While neurotic subjects, the closest to what Lacanians would recognise as 'normal', are defined by a fantasy structure that links the barred subject to object a, the 'perverse' subject reverses this formula so that they are positioned as object defined in relation to a barred subject. This simple reversal can be read as a repetition of Freud's (1910: 100) diagnosis of narcissistic homosexual love in which the subject takes the position of their first love object, the mother, and finds another to love as their mother once loved them. If the formula for fantasy of the perverse subject is read in this way we arrive at a definition of the ideal subject of capitalism, one in which the individual is able to configure themselves not only as one who chases after commodities, objects of desire, but also as an object to be consumed by others. One might then interpret this clinical structure as one of the logical, pathological, responses to the split in the subject formed by the division between commodity exchange and the labour process. Capitalism is a political-economic system in which there is exploitation that requires control, if not now always immediate ownership, of the means of production which is organised around profit obtained from surplus value produced by workers.

There is a further crucial link with narcissism as it is understood in classical Freudian theory, and this form of psychopathology testifies to the way that otherness is configured by capitalism as something imaginary. Rather than the 'other' taking the place of the object, the object being searched for in another person, the subject who takes the place of the object constructs an image of the other as subject, as they themselves could or should be – as the kind of subject desired by those once close to them – and this idealised image is assumed to be transparent to them, as someone who will understand them (and then who will bitterly disappoint them when there is no such perfect understanding).

Psychoanalysis disrupts this illusion of transparency, and does so through the key clinical device of transference in psychoanalytic work – the re-enactment of signifiers from the past of the analysand in the present in relation to the figure of the analyst – and as clinical practice psychoanalysis itself requires a conceptual apparatus of ownership and self-management. It also, of course, operates within discrete privatised financial arrangements in which the analysand must pay the analyst, and transference therefore entails the reproduction of relations of power, relations in which the subject has been constituted. In this practice, psychoanalysis is itself always operating as a perverse practice. Here the formula Lacan offers for analysis is identical to the formula for perversion; the analyst configures themselves as semblant of the object a in relation to the analysand as barred subject, as the one hystericised to question who they are by questioning the other they address in analysis (Hoens 2006).

Perversion is defined by Freud and Lacan by way of a specific defence, 'disavowal', in which a fetish object is conjured into being which operates as a stand-in for the mother's phallus. The supposedly frightful absence of this phallus is refused, 'disavowed', and the fetish is, for the pervert, something which is present to them as an object which becomes a condition for sexual gratification. But then, the 'pervert' itself has become a fetish in patriarchal society that insists that the mother should not have a phallus. Once we shift from Freud's often concrete reference to the 'penis' as phallus and take seriously Lacan's indication that the phallus is an 'insignia', a marker of power historically attributed to men, we find every subject implicated in perversion, fetishism, and then necessarily falsely-conscious of a world organised around commodity fetishism (Easthope 1986; Butler 1993).

The normal obsessional fantasises that they are a pervert, for example, and so the figure of the pervert comes to function as a fetish for this most quintessential subject of classical capitalism. The analysand thus constructs a personal ideological device for experiencing and explaining what exploitation is, and this then may operate in analysis as a narrative device by which we work through the fetishisation of objects of fantasy. This is where the 'pervert' comes to circulate as a moral-ideological motif sustained by a popularised version of psychoanalysis (with the existence of psychoanalysis as a warrant for pathologising what are assumed to be aberrant forms of sexuality).

Mindfulness

Psychoanalysis calls upon a particular kind of subjectivity, one that requires, it is sometimes said, 'psychological-mindedness' (Coltart 1988). There is here a potent representation of what the inner world of the patient should be like, that they have some awareness that there is an unconscious. There is also a stipulation hidden in this assumption that the analysand should speak of their internal mental states in the same kind of way that analysts have learnt to speak about themselves in their own analysis. This awareness is an effect of a certain form of subjectivity, of an individual abstracted from social relations who searches inside themselves for the meaning of life, and psychoanalysis, or something like it, is a necessarily ideological component of capitalist society.

Psychoanalysis, in different ways in different theoretical traditions, revolves around the problematic of the integrity of the subject. This problematic is not neatly solved in any tradition of psychoanalysis, but reappears through discussions of the nature of the ego as a 'bodily ego', of the nature of 'skin' as a surface of demarcation, of the 'I' who comes to be where 'it' was, of the 'subjectivising' of the subject, and of the value accorded to 'responsibility' even if conceptualised as being capable of giving response to, of accounting to others (e.g. Bick 1968). The territory of the individual thus complements the territory of the state as a place from which commerce with others might take place; the most popular name for this micro-national territory is 'psychology'.

Most forms of psychoanalysis aim to reinforce some form of identity, though there is some queasiness now about Freud's (1933: 80) recommendation that 'the work of culture' and psychoanalysis is that the domain of the ego be enlarged. Some traditions are suspicious of the ego as the central organising instance, but then there is often a risk that the 'subject' as such, even if conceptualised as a necessarily 'divided subject', is treated such that some form of identity is smuggled in the back door (or through a kind of trapdoor leading to the unconscious). If relationships and sedimented individual identities as their component parts are not explicitly essentialised, acceptance of the law, which always also pertains to identity, is effectively reinforced. There has also been a powerful impact of these ideas even on those using Lacanian theory to reduce class analysis to class identity, to seeing class solidarity as merely a question of 'identity politics' (Laclau 2000: 203).

Imaginary alienation

Alienation is given a specific double-quality under capitalism; it acquires a distinctive meaning in Lacanian psychoanalysis, to describe the process and effect by which a subject becomes subject to signifiers, alienated in the signifier before a separation from it enables the newly constituted individual to use language as if it were a tool for communicating to others. On the other hand, alienation operates as a theoretically-grounded account of the separation of the worker from their labour under the peculiar conditions of exploitation in capitalism. But this alienation also has a further potent ideological quality by which our understanding of it is distorted, distorted by virtue of the very mystifying processes it is designed to explain. Alienation is often treated in everyday discourse and academic discussion as an 'experience', describable and even measurable so that steps can be taken to ameliorate it and increase well-being (Therborn 1976; cf. Mandel and Novack 1970). The problem, as much an obstacle to its easy deployment by critics of capitalism as useful for apologists, is that alienation cannot be captured and observed as such. It is, rather, only ever captured and observed in its psychologised form, and it is here that it becomes part of the apparatus of the register of human life that Lacan calls the imaginary.

This category of the imaginary thus becomes crucial to our theoretical understanding of alienation in the conditions under which psychoanalysis has been formed, and it is an invaluable conceptual resource for Lacanian clinical practice. First, it enables us to make a distinction between individuality and singularity. Decisions taken by the exploited to sell their labour power, as well as decisions of the exploiters to invest, as if they played on a level playing field, are treated as individual decisions in ideologically-structured commonsense reasoning, and this individuality is often invoked by supporters of the present dispensation as a marvellous defining principle of capitalist society. There is then a corresponding and necessary individualisation of the domain of subjective experience so that even attempts to make capitalism run smoothly are viewed as 'state interference'.

There is a paradox, which is that this supposed 'individuality' of human experience – the complex unpredictable idiosyncratic way that interaction with others is reworked in fantasy for each subject – is betrayed by the disciplinary apparatus that pretends to give voice to it. Psychology is intent on valuing the 'individual' as its object of study, but every procedure it uses to define 'normal' and 'abnormal' development homogenises what it assumes to be the underlying first nature of the self, renders it into the same stuff while separating each individual from others. Psychology thus engages in its own second-level process of alienation and separation, describes that process as if there was a metalanguage, and locks the subject into a fixed second nature which has its own particular imaginary features.

Here, the imaginary is indeed part of reality – reality that Lacanians differentiate from the real – and conforms with it well enough to give a necessary illusion of understanding other subjects, 'the symmetrical world of the *egos* and of the homogeneous others' separated from each other by what Lacan (1978/1991: 244) calls 'the wall of language'. The imaginary is that dimension of interaction organised around understanding, a presumed transparency of the other to oneself that also incites competition with the other; it appears both when another appears to be too much like oneself and when they depart from that presumed likeness. It is, then, a 'dual relation' which looks for understanding and agreement that will also serve to confirm one's own self-image – Lacan (ibid.) is careful to say that it is part of reality rather than illusion – and it does also confirm a misleading imaginary representation of some kind that conforms well enough to reality; 'The imaginary gains its false reality, which nonetheless is a verified reality, starting off from the order defined by the wall of language.' This is what Lacan will later refer to as the symbolic, as is clear from the continuation of this point: 'The ego such as we understand it, the other, the fellow being, all these imaginary things . . . are indeed objects, because they are named as such within an organised system, that of the wall of language.' We are 'falsely-conscious' that who we are could be reducible to our ego as site of conscious awareness of ourselves and others. This illusory aspect is also underpinned (and warranted in psychoanalytic reasoning that operates as a form of ideology) by the narcissistic aspect of the ego, of images that we attach ourselves to in order to shore up our sense that we are 'individual' – as if we were actually discrete undivided beings – and it therefore leads to a relation to knowledge that is somewhat paranoiac.

When Lacanian psychoanalysts in the clinic distinguish between imaginary, symbolic and real, the imaginary is here marked out as the necessary condition for communication to take place but it is not treated as the basis of a 'treatment alliance' or, still less, as a shared understanding of the nature of the symptom that the analysand's talk crystallises in the transference (e.g. Sandler *et al.* 1970). The symptom is reconfigured in a certain kind of way for a certain kind of audience as, we might say, a signifier that represents the subject for another signifier. That is, speech is geared for the analyst as other for whom the symptom operates and which carries the analysand into another place as they speak and are spoken by the signifiers that appear in the analysis; this is how the symptom assumes form in transference. Circumspection concerning the imaginary register entails that the Lacanian analyst effectively constructs a space which 'depsychologises' the experience of the analysand.

Lacanians are suspicious of images in general, and they should have good reason to be suspicious of images of pathology that were the stuff of nineteenth-century psychiatry, and, for that matter, wary of 'recognition'. At the same time as the analyst does not pretend to offer 'recognition' to the analysand – the pretence to understand and empathise with the anguish that has brought them to analysis – there is no demand, as the flip-side of this master–slave dialectic, that the analysand recognises the analyst, no demand that the analysand conforms to or confirms psychoanalytic expert knowledge; 'It is in the name of psychoanalysis itself that the ideology of expertise must be resisted, as it is a totalitarian ideology' (Roudinesco 2006:

370). Unlike psychiatry and psychology, knowledge in Lacanian psychoanalysis is not relayed from one subject to another, still less from knowledgeable analyst to naïve analysand; rather, the analysis provides a space in which the analysand's relation to knowledge can be changed. The analyst is at a distance from the imaginary and so does not lure the analysand into identification with them as good outcome of the treatment, as an equalising of the share of knowledge that would be part of the ethics of allocation that governs psychology.

This also means that Lacanians do not treat aggression as a psychological category, for the 'aggressivity' that erupts in the imaginary is seen as the function of a particular dialectic of identification and rivalry rather than as biological or cognitive process, of instinct or error (Lacan 1975/1991: 177). And the infant in front of the mirror at 18 months old, a 'stage' to which Lacanians trace the imaginary, is not treated as a developmental psychological process. This 'mirror stage', in which the infant attains a jubilant sense of unity as it models itself on the other it sees in an actual mirror or the mirror of another's responses to it, using that model of self to understand others and what others are, is not a 'phase' through which they pass before maturity but a 'stadium' in which they will be caught many times in adult life, including in bad analysis (Lacan 2006: 233). There is another paradox hidden in this Lacanian category, which is that while it is predicated on the idea that the individual is separate and self-contained, the imaginary is dependent on the symbolic.

Symbolic

Mirrors, and the dual relations elicited as we face the image of our own self in the mirror, are products of certain kinds of technological process, and the 'mirror' as a metaphorical trope is itself only recognisable as such in relation to a third position from which we are able to triangulate our self and the image. That 'thirdness' which is a prerequisite for the subject to know what a 'dual relation' looks like is a function of the semiotic process that the symbolic makes possible (Muller 1996). Even as we home in on the mirror stage as if it were a significant developmental moment, it becomes clear that the presence of others is necessary as part of the symbolic apparatus through which the infant is guided to recognise itself and position itself as if it were an ego, as it 'gains its false reality' (Lacan 1978/1991: 244). There is no imaginary if there is no symbolic, as Lacan came to see as he elaborated these two orders in relation to one another from 1953 (the year the rupture with the IPA began), and the intermeshing of these orders with the real was to become all the more important in the final stage of his work. In the clinic the symbolic is the point of reference from which the lure into the line of imaginary is resisted, and for Lacanian analysis the symbolic is a guiding theoretical concept, which we can now also use to connect psychoanalysis with analysis of the social formations in which we work.

In the clinic the analyst needs to grasp how the imaginary and the symbolic operate, but there is also an imaginary temptation to treat the symbolic as yet another place which it is possible to 'know', as if there was another point beyond it from which it was possible to know it, an imaginary temptation to be resisted. This is why it is so important not to try to 'understand' in psychoanalysis, but rather to grasp our place in the world through a form of 'mapping' (Žižek 1995). Our task is to be in the symbolic, to make use of it, to position oneself in the symbolic universe of the analysand, without imagining that the analyst is outside that universe in a 'metalanguage'. Furthermore this is why, with respect to the analyst taking care to resist the lure of the line of the imaginary and the temptation to speak from within a metalanguage (to interpret transference, for example), Lacan points out that resistance is on the side of the analyst. Freud (1900/1999: 336) commented that *'whatever disturbs the continuation of the work of analysis is resistance'*, but this 'resistance' needs to take account of the unconscious, which is not located 'inside' the subject. To speak of 'resistance of the subject' implies a pre-existing self-sufficient ego responsible for psychic phenomena (Lacan 1964/1973: 68); instead Lacan (1958: 497) avoids 'psychologizing superstition' to localise resistance on the side of the analyst.

In some formulations, the analyst positions themselves within the symbolic as the big Other, as that aspect of the symbolic which is evoked in any act of communication – the Other is the particular face of the symbolic for a particular speaking subject – and this is one reason why quite early on Lacan (1991/2007: 244) comments that 'speech is founded on the existence of the Other' (cf. Verhaeghe 1999; Hook 2008). In later writings on the place of the analyst, Lacan (1991/2007) argues that the analyst should take the position of the semblant of the object a.

The psychoanalyst's refusal of recognition – not to fall into the line of the imaginary – enables a sublation of the psychiatric gaze rather than a repetition of it. That is, this refusal indeed 'objectifies' the analysand in some way, and it is a refusal of recognition of their pain and of sharing the experience of it. In this way psychoanalysis differs from humanistic approaches that have a reading of Hegel in which it is necessary to transcend the master–slave dialectic by arriving at a state of mutual recognition (Tudor and Worrall 2006). Lacanian psychoanalysis, in contrast, encourages a quite different kind of objectification, 'objectification' by the analysand of the analyst. The analyst takes the place of the object a, and so there is a peculiar reduction of each, of the other for each, to the status of object. The difference from humanistic approaches is that this 'object' is not simply the object of 'objectification' as an alienating reification of a human experience, but it is an objectification as necessary to the production of knowledge and a different relation to knowledge.

The symbolic is riddled with paradoxes that are utilised and stretched to breaking point in psychoanalysis, and the most important of these paradoxes is that this Lacanian symbolic is a law-governed system of semiotic operations. In this way it functions as the site of the laws of human 'second nature', a site which Lacan often capitalises as Law as such. But at the same time as this second nature gives substance to its own reference points, analysis *desubstantialises* what it refers to and seems to require as a condition of its own operations. In this respect, and the connection is not entirely accidental, there is a dynamic logic in the analytic composition and decomposition of the symbolic which parallels the creative and desubstantialising power of capitalist production (in which it is as if everything that is solid melts into air). Lacan argues at one point in his work that speech is founded on the existence of the Other, but he then rapidly moves from the dictum that there is no Other of the Other – a lesson of analysis – to the claim that there is no Other full stop, no Other (Chiesa 2007).

In Lacanian psychoanalysis, then, it is possible to learn something about the operations of the economy at the very same time as one learns about the production of the self and its objects. In capitalism the fantasy that gold has absolute value which gives meaning to money, for example, is replicated in each subject's fantasy that the phallus confers some power of which every other signifier is a mere semblant. Once again the analysand comes to change their relation to knowledge. Knowledge that circulates with reference to a hidden master signifier dissolves in true speech, full speech, dissolves into nothing (Shingu 1995/2004).

Repeating sex

There is a revolutionary transformation in psychoanalytic theory when Lacan returns to Freud's account of the death drive, and this transformation hinges on the way the subject's 'being unto death' – the fact that each individual will die and at some level knows this – is conceptualised in relation to repetition. Death already figures early on in Lacanian psychoanalysis as a phenomenological category – of finitude and nothingness – rather than as a biological process. When the motif of a struggle to the death in the master–slave dialectic is evoked by Lacan it is to shift emphasis to the properly human domain of 'aggressivity' in relation to the other, away from wired-in animal aggression, to drive from brute instinct. This transformation complicates the conceptual apparatus Freud (1920) elaborated to explain in more detail why it was that his patients seemed driven 'beyond the pleasure principle' toward something more excessive and deadly. Lacan lifts this notion out of biological matter and reconstructs it in the domain of the signifier. The more intense enjoyment that brought the subject to the edge of destruction and from which they then shrank – a repetition of a relation to something real beyond pleasure that then left traces of anguish and failure, shame and guilt – Lacan called jouissance.

Repetition as 'the insistence of speech' can now be employed to grasp two clinical phenomena (Lacan 1981/1993: 242). First, how the analysand organises their life around something self-destructive, but from which they are unwilling to break, that which is crystallised in the clinic as a symptom. Second, how the analysand organises their life in the clinic around the analyst as an object through which they repeat relations to significant others, that which manifests itself as transference. This reformulation of repetition around signification then enables Lacan to reconnect with the phenomenological tradition, in particular with existentialist concerns with death (as we saw in Chapter 2 in discussion of the quaternary character of the Oedipus complex). Now every drive is a death drive and the impulse to gratification always contains within it a secret – a repressed, disavowed or foreclosed secret – which is that fantasy is haunted by the intimation that, as Freud (1920: 38) put it, *'the aim of all life is death'*.

The apparent linearity of capitalist development, and of the natural development of capitalism out of earlier modes of production, is replicated conceptually in causal descriptions of natural and social processes and in the temporal ordering of the working day and of an individual's life-span. There is often a causal developmental sequence identified, a temporality buttressed by psychoanalytic appeals to evidence from developmental psychology. This temporal relationship can be conceptually reworked in ostensibly Lacanian analyses of the production of cause through deferred action by which certain events only become traumatic after the event. The danger is that this merely serves to enclose the history of the individual subject within a narrative that is more efficiently stitched in place by threads that loop back and make the present into something that will always have been the case. Even the most reflexive histories of capitalism use the same kind of device, to find in its origins what it will become so that economic history is caught in a closed circuit (Mandel 1971). So now can we break that closed circuit?

The clinical phenomena that Lacanian psychoanalysis conceptualises as forms of repetition are signifying operations, and so they connect the subject as analysand with their life outside the clinic, whether life as citizen or as bare life on the edge of the polity, or at some precarious point between the two. We need to attend to the *disjunction* between private life – that of the family, that which tends to be replicated in the clinic – and public life, domains of work and love outside the home. This disjunction gives a particular character – a psychoanalytic character – to the distinction between sex and gender.

On the one hand capitalism opens up a vortex of innovation, of rapid development and perpetual movement, which stands in opposition to stable family structures and to the attempt to maintain temporal integrity of the self. On the other hand, there is a replication of power relations, including of the relations of production, and this is counterposed to the entrepreneurial dynamic ideologically embedded in each individual. This double articulation is also a double contradiction that divides the subject between what they know of their sex and their gender. Here the separation between private and public life becomes crucial, and that separation opens up two ways of conceptualising the distinction between sex and gender. One way is to treat the family as the site of sex, unchanging and universal ground for sexed identity, and see the public realm as that in which gender operates as another layer which offers opportunities for the individual to change themselves and manage threats to the security of the family. The other way is to see the family as the place where gender roles are allocated, where gender identity and sexual orientation are enforced, and to see the public realm as the place where gender is sedimented ideologically as if it were sex, site of compulsory heterosexuality.

This separation between the two domains, a separation which is replicated in the separation between the clinic and the outside world, can either be managed in such a way as to heal the division between the two, perhaps articulated so that the two domains can be balanced – and this is what psychology does – or the ideological effects of the separation can be grasped and dismantled, which is what Lacanian psychoanalysis does. In this way analysis facilitates the desubstantialising of categories dear to the heart of psychology, those of 'sex' and of 'gender' (Klein 2003). This argument repeats Lacan's de-psychologising of the subject of the enunciation, now reconfigured as the speaking of truth.

Psychoanalytic interpretation

Lacanians refuse to adapt their analysands to social norms, and they also actively disrupt the ideological elements of capitalist society that are the building blocks for the discipline of psychology. They disrupt the still-potent psychiatric objectification of the patient and treatment of that object as a constellation of signs of disorder, and this is why interpretation is concerned with enabling the analysand to speak rather than to shut them up. They disrupt the idea that a good patient is one who passively accepts the treatment that follows accurate diagnosis, and this is why interpretation does not treat the unconscious as a place from which hidden meanings are dragged out into the open. They disrupt the idea that this knowledge is anchored in true eternal facts about human nature and social development, and this is why interpretation avoids explaining distress directly with reference to constructs like trauma. And they disrupt knowledge as the systematic taken-for-granted accumulation of cognitive skills into which each individual should be inducted, and this is why interpretation is not concerned with spelling out what a symptom or dream really means unbeknownst to the analysand. There are consequences here for the way we must now grasp the direction of the treatment, for psychoanalysis that is able to break definitively from psychiatry and psychology.

First, we need to take care not to psychiatrise the unconscious, and this leads us to re-theorise what psychotic and perverse clinical structures are. We have seen how psychiatric practice psychoticises and perversionalises through its own discourse categories of subject, and how capitalism encourages the sedimentation of these aspects of subjectivity so that they become real. There are ambiguities, fruitful ambiguities, in Lacan's (1981/ 1993: 143) comments on psychosis and perversion, when he notes, for example, that in psychosis 'the unconscious is present but not functioning', and that in perversion there is simply no demand for analysis.

These ambiguities, and further transformations in capitalist society after Lacan, lead us now to a clinical orientation in which every subject is divided between a psychotic and perverse mode of being. The psychotic aspect should not, however, be understood as a psychotic 'core' which lies deep in the unconscious, and perversion is not a conscious manipulative narcissistic game; those would be arguments that would facilitate a connection between Lacan and the post-Kleinian tradition in psychoanalysis (White 2006). If anything, the relationship between the two is reversed, with psychosis as the face of consciousness and perversion as the organisation of unconscious desire (as indeed Lacan points out in his formula for fantasy). These are the first faces of the subject that are presented in analysis, and it is from this starting point that analysis does or does not proceed. This means that every analysand is treated first as if they were 'a psychotic', and every subject is treated as if their unconscious, when it starts to function as a condition of being in clinical space, will bring to life a 'pervert'. This orientation maintains the cautious approach to the question of the presence of psychosis, and the potential that psychoanalysis may 'trigger' a psychotic episode, that characterises contemporary Lacanian practice. However, it also thereby sidesteps the psychiatric categories which tell us that a psychotic is always a psychotic and that a pervert is always a pervert.

Second, as we now turn to forms of neurosis, we need to take care not to psychologise the unconscious. Once we are inside clinical space as something that has opened out into something analytic, which is possible when there has been a demand for analysis and the analysand starts to follow the rule of free association, we meet an obstacle that we call 'obsessional neurosis'. Obsessional neurosis, which is still stereotypically the preserve of men who do not want to speak openly about themselves in analysis, is thus treated as a position of the subject. It is, of course, a position that repeats and maintains a position that the analysand has rehearsed at length in the outside world, but it is no less a *position* now in relation to the analyst. Interpretation here is designed to 'hystericise' the analysand, to provoke them to speak, but this kind of interpretation still does not suppose that the analyst knows what the unconscious contains or what the analysand means.

In contrast, the hysteric speaks enough, and the tendency to accuse others for being responsible for exploitation and abuse characteristic of this category of person – a category that is borrowed from psychiatric discourse and which is loaded with attributions concerning gender – makes them already into 'psychoanalytic subjects'. The danger is that a 'psychoanalytic subject' is itself seen as a category, an identity, that renders them into a psychological being, and so the direction of the treatment calls for the kind of interpretations that will question this identity and invite the subject to locate themselves as agents in the exploitation they describe.

The unconscious is 'the discourse of the Other', not some hidden material to be divined or excavated from under the surface. Lacan (1991/2007) emphasises this in his argument that 'latent' content is not what is dug out from the analysand but is produced by the analyst; an 'interpretation' in psychological mode, the giving of meaning to the client, is a construction. Interpretation as Lacan described it opens the unconscious as an authentically psychoanalytic phenomenon, a phenomenon that is distinctive to the clinic; interpretation as 'cut', as 'interpretation in reverse' also opens this unconscious (Miller 1999a). It also cuts against a psychological redescription of the unconscious that has become a pervasive ideological motif under capitalism. In order to open the unconscious when we interpret, we need to cut against the psychologising of the unconscious.

Competition

Psychology is part of the imaginary reality of capitalism, which Lacanian psychoanalysis unravels. But we need to grasp how this place of psychology as a specification of subjectivity congruent with capitalism is not analogous to the place of psychiatry in late feudalism. To treat the two forms of knowledge as equivalent, as serving the same kind of function in quite different political-economic systems, is to misunderstand the particular way that knowledge of the subject is produced under capitalism. There was no widespread 'psychiatrisation' under feudalism because that system did not call upon ideology in the same way as a legitimising force. There is indeed psychiatrisation of society now, but this is as a feature, one face of the increasingly prevalent psychologisation that is the necessary false consciousness of life under capitalism. Lacanian psychoanalysis thus gives us the tools not only to grasp how psychiatry and psychology operate in relation to knowledge, but also to grasp the difference between those two distinct disciplinary practices.

There is a requirement that there be a degree of regulation by the state of economic relationships, regulation that now operates in conditions of neoliberalism alongside deregulation and the privatisation of social welfare services. Capitalism maintains and warrants itself ideologically around the motif of the 'free market', yet the state has always been a necessary regulatory apparatus to ensure that there is 'competition' as well as ensuring that resistance to capitalism is quashed. Most versions of psychoanalysis enable the individual to function in adverse societal conditions, even if the psychoanalyst does not actually aim to bring about such adaptation. Adaptation to life conditions sometimes proceeds through the path of subversion of identification and ideals, but this then too-often leads to the giving up of political ideals, the idea that another world is possible, to living with and perhaps enjoying the symptom and an acceptance of 'lack'. Like the economic system that houses it, psychoanalysis recognises that the most adaptable processes are those that are able to work with rather than against innovation, on condition that innovation is contained by this system.

The clinic is part of capitalism, and the analyst is paid by the analysand for a service that enmeshes both of these two in a contract that appears to be freely entered into. This is one reason why an attempt to enforce standards of treatment based on psychological models of normal and abnormal behaviour or correct or incorrect thinking is antithetical to psychoanalysis. These psychological models fit seamlessly into the ethics presupposed by capitalist social relations, and they aim to adapt each individual to relations with others that are based on contractual obligations. There is therefore a necessary false consciousness produced in the clinical interaction that needs to be broken, broken by the analysand as they follow the rule of free association and discover that they are not 'free', and broken by the analyst when they interpret in such a way as to disrupt the notion that cure is a function of good education.

Chapter 5
Psychotherapeutic capital

We now turn to the relationship between psychoanalysis and psychotherapy. Lacanian psychoanalysis has powerful therapeutic effects, but this rather indirect link raises a crucial question for practitioners about the claims they make for psychoanalysis as a form of therapy as such. Psychotherapy is, among other things, a practice of self-understanding and self-development that is congruent with contemporary neoliberal capitalism, an ideological representation of subjectivity that reinterprets and distorts psychoanalytic conceptions of the subject. I locate the rise of psychotherapeutic practice inside and outside the clinic in contemporary society in the rebellion against capitalism by Marxism and the dire effects of the capture and caricature of Marxist politics by the Stalinist bureaucracy. The argument here is that ostensibly 'postmodern' fluid forms of subjectivity that psychotherapy values are a manifestation of particular political-economic conditions and of an ideological reaction against what an alternative to capitalism could be.

Representation

We are faced with a most curious problem now. The therapeutic effects that psychoanalysis aimed to produce have now taken form as something to be *directly* achieved; different psychotherapies either elaborate a version of psychoanalysis, are patterned on a mechanistic or humanistic representation of it, or they operate as route-maps to therapeutic effects that aim to bypass psychoanalysis, even pretending to bypass representation itself as they imagine they connect directly with what we feel.

Psychoanalysis began as a practice of representation, conceptualising and intervening at the level of representations of pleasure and pain, of what is thought to make the subject and those dear to them happy and what brings misery to each and all (Freud 1950). For Freud (1915a), psychoanalysis does not delve directly into the unconscious, and Lacan (1964/1973: 220) redefined this practice of representation in such a way as to differentiate it from psychology, insisting that the 'representatives' that psychoanalysis is concerned with are signifiers. For Lacan (1981/1993: 167), 'every phenomenon that comes from the analytic field, from the analytic discovery, from what we are dealing with in symptoms and neurosis, is structured like a language'. Likewise, it is the signifier as representative of affect rather than affect itself that is at issue as 'emotional' responses come to be structured and restructured in the course of analysis. This dimension of representation, and the figure of the analyst as the one who catalyses and purifies images of others that the analysand brings to them in transference, is then disturbing to many forms of psychotherapy that hope for unmediated contact between therapist and client as a model for how the client should relate to themselves.

Some variants of psychotherapy – those concerned with character typologies and life-plans – mimic psychiatric reasoning, and some cognitive and behavioural approaches to what has gone wrong, that try to patch things up, shade into psychology (House and Loewenthal 2008; Loewenthal and House 2010). Some variants which engage with numinous energies that flow from inside the self or from crystals and angels anticipate a model congruent with theological explanation (e.g. Rowan and Dryden 1988). Psychotherapy is a field of competing systems of knowledge about the self, and although there is disagreement between practitioners about what this 'self' is exactly they do all adhere to a set of images of a journey from misappraisal to self-understanding. Psychotherapy is now hegemonic as a form of commonsense about the nature of the self and it operates as a form of ideology – as banalised psychiatry, 'pop-psychology' – even of an everyday psychoanalysis.

The claim that we should search under the surface of spoken interaction and excavate a deeper reality behind language then serves to mislead us as to where the unconscious is and how it works. It is in stark contrast to this idea that Lacan (1964/1973: 131) argues that the unconscious as 'the discourse of the Other' lies in the gaps, stumbling points in speech; for the subject to speak from the unconscious is for them to find a way out of the romantic fantasy that there is something hidden that can be unearthed; instead, 'the unconscious . . . is *outside*'. This is why Lacan (1981/1993: 166) is very careful to point out that when he says that 'everything that belongs to analytic communication has the structure of language, this precisely does not mean that the unconscious is expressed in discourse'. Here again we have a sharp divide being marked between a materialist approach which attends to language, to the work of the signifier, and an idealist approach, which pretends to discover hidden meanings under the surface (for example, an 'unconscious' underneath language which is then 'expressed' in it).

Practitioners of a Lacanian approach will carefully attend to those moments in which the analysis slides into psychotherapy, and there will be times when the therapeutic aspects of the work will predominate. The unravelling of the self and of the comforting well-worn narratives of personal history that hold a sense of identity in place is often threatening. The task of reflexive deconstruction that an analysand embarks upon in psychoanalysis is very difficult, and they may hesitate at times for good reason, or for bad reasons that it may even so be necessary to honour. However, there are serious clinical implications for Lacanian psychoanalysis reducing itself to psychotherapy, and sensitivity to these issues means that it is even more important that the psychoanalyst is able, when appropriate, to direct the treatment to open the way from psychotherapy to psychoanalysis, to open the way to the unconscious rather than close it down; while psychotherapy preserves 'the consistency of the Other', psychoanalysis disturbs that consistency (Miller 2002a: 13).

Against this background, we can specify points of refusal that mark the difference between Lacanian psychoanalysis and psychotherapy. As we will see, psychoanalysis refuses many of the assumptions that psychotherapists make about the relationship between therapist and client, the therapeutic process and where it leads. It is possible to itemise each of these differences between psychoanalysis and psychotherapy, but the real problem lies in the way that each notion that psychotherapy values is linked to the other notions. Through an examination of these links we can start to appreciate how psychotherapy operates as an ideological system and we will then be in a better position to unravel connections between contemporary neoliberal capitalism and psychotherapeutic practice inside and outside the clinic, built upon and circulating as a particular kind of knowledge about the self.

Empathy and education

Psychoanalysis is concerned with truth, with truth of the subject as they speak, and it also has something to say about historical narrative truth, about the conditions in which it is possible for subjects to speak (Spence 1982; cf. Laplanche 2003). The injunction 'know thyself' carved into the entrance to the Oracle at Delphi and repeated through the history of psychoanalysis could make it seem as if this truth issues from careful introspection (Bettelheim 1986). Attempts by psychoanalysts to interpret the culture as if from outside it, as if psychoanalysis was a metalanguage, would also make it seem as if truth were equivalent to good empirical social science. In both cases there is a reduction of truth, treatment of the truth of the subject and of social conditions as an accumulation of tried and tested knowledge. One version of the Western Enlightenment would have it that the courage to think for oneself underpins psychoanalysis and that unequivocal truth is the illuminative quality of the knowledge that is produced from that kind of investigation of the self and the world (Adorno and Horkheimer 1944/1979).

Lacanian psychoanalysis indeed inherits that Enlightenment project, but it refracts the metaphor of light to insist on the place of darker matter that

Freud introduced into knowledge. There are two aspects of this refraction; one is the observation that we cannot speak the whole truth, it is but 'half-spoken', and the other concerns the gap between half-truth produced in the clinic and what we think we know about the world outside it (Lacan 1987a). This refraction poses a problem for those who believe that truth is a kind of knowledge produced through the acknowledgement, recognition and validation of what another thinks the subject knows about themselves. It is a problem for an interpersonal process organised around empathy as the comprehension of what it is the other comprehends. It also poses a problem for institutional practices predicated on knowledge as the accumulation of truth that can then be conveyed from one who knows to another who does not, conveyed as a form of education.

Here we begin to see how a psychotherapeutic framing of psychoanalysis turns it into a parody of the Enlightenment in which there is illumination of intersubjectivity and teaching and a peculiar equivalence produced between one and the other (Burman 2001; Ecclestone and Hayes 2008). What one knows about others harvested from intersubjective communication is treated as applicable to all the others who should reap this form of truth. The accumulation of psychotherapeutic capital then produces its own particular ideological twist on an already intensely ideological psychologisation of participants, whether of those directly involved in trying to understand themselves who then communicate what they have learnt to others or of vicarious consumers in thrall to media representations of this conception of the self (Furedi 2003; McLaughlin 2008). This ideological double-helix which works its way into the subjectivity of those involved, we can term – reluctantly, for it is yet another ungainly neologism – 'therapeutisation'. Therapeutisation, of clients and practitioners in different modalities of this increasingly popular approach to self-healing, and of psychoanalysis itself when it is treated as a kind of psychotherapy, becomes all the more potent through the link it forges between empathy and education.

This is why, despite there being therapeutic effects of its practice, Lacanian psychoanalysis must differentiate itself from psychotherapy in two key respects. First, in showing that the attainment of empathy serves to sabotage what is most radical about psychoanalysis, for the sense that one has empathised with another serves to make them the same as oneself. This is the fundamental error of hermeneutics that aims to 'understand' the other. Against this reduction to the level of 'imaginary' identification, the task of the Lacanian psychoanalyst is 'to obtain absolute difference' (Lacan 1964/1973: 278). Second, in pointing out that the idea that we should educate someone about what is right or wrong or as to how they should understand themselves serves to turn psychotherapy into the privilege of an expert caste. Every moment the analyst thinks they know best is a moment of ethical failure that betrays the task of opening a space for the analysand to make of their own analysis their own ethical practice.

Veracity and normalisation

There is another feature of Lacanian psychoanalysis that roots it in the Western Enlightenment tradition of sceptical enquiry into truth which is that the result of this enquiry – the courage to use one's reason – is that one thereby breaks from what Kant (1784) referred to as 'self-incurred tutelage'. One of the curious things about the history of Kant's answer to the question 'What is Enlightenment?' is the way that developmental metaphors come to be clustered around this journey to reason from wilful refusal to think, from what Lacan (1958: 524) called the 'passion for ignorance' that also often successfully sabotages psychoanalysis. That developmental framing of what is then taken to be an individual journey posits childhood as lack which is filled by self-possessed adult reason, and accords with a rendering of psychoanalysis as a form of psychotherapy (Foucault 1984; Burman 2008).

One reading of Freud would have it that the outcome of psychoanalysis could be marked by the signifier 'adult', and this reading is buttressed by a story of ages and stages, of failures, faults and fixations, and an image of the task of analysis as providing contained 'corrective emotional experience suitable to repair the traumatic influence of previous experiences' (Alexander and French 1946: 66). The analyst should then know how to configure themselves as a maternal presence in which this nurturing of the self can take place, as a paternal figure who will remind the analysand of the existence of others, and perhaps even as an other on whom they should model themselves. This kind of analyst knows what the path should be and what deviations from it look like. One thereby arrives at a product of analysis that can be captured by specifications of what society imagines to be healthy, and this version of analysis can answer to demands that it provide evidence of its efficacy, empirical products that correspond to a commonsensical view of reality to which individuals should be adapted (e.g. Westen *et al.* 2004).

This reading of Freud is given psychotherapeutic inflection in the notion that the adult that emerges from the clinic should still be attuned to their inner child and that there should be a balance between reason and feeling. One finds this notion at work in attempts to turn analysis toward projects for 'emotional literacy' as a political intervention, and to value the interconnection between the feelings of the analysand and emotional responses by the analyst in 'relational psychoanalysis' (e.g. Mitchell 1997). There are issues here to do with the supposed connection between clinical and political forms of feeling and with the role of 'countertransference' as a way of accessing reality (e.g. Renik 1999; Renik and Spillius 2004), issues problematic for Lacanians (e.g. Miller 2003).

In this respect Lacanian psychoanalysis challenges the idea that the outcome of clinical work should be an 'enlightened self'. The product of analysis, a subject who has traversed their passion for ignorance and so broken momentarily at least from their own self-incurred tutelage as they speak the truth, is also marked by loss, by the loss of the hope that there is a reality to which one should cling and in which one could thereby be normal (Verhaeghe 2004). One way of distinguishing psychoanalysis from psychotherapy is to attend to how each tradition comprehends signifiers that are produced in the clinic. For our psychoanalysis the signifiers are reduced to nonsense, and the analysand confronts and questions the way those signifiers have come to bear them and define who they are. For psychotherapy, in contrast, these signifiers are meaningful, and either injected with content by the therapist who already knows what they should mean or given meaning by the client which is validated by the therapist.

This is why Lacanian psychoanalysis subverts and radicalises the subject of the Enlightenment in such a way that makes it incompatible with psychotherapy; and there are two aspects to note. First, the notion that we should dispel illusion and bring about a more veridical relation to the social world serves to obscure the ways in which every image of 'reality' is always already suffused with fantasy. To speak truth in Lacanian psychoanalysis has nothing to do with accurate perception, and moments of truth for the analysand will precisely be those moments when they find a way of speaking in and against what is usually taken to be empirically true. Second, to attempt to normalise certain kinds of behaviour or experience may in the short term bring relief, but will serve to adapt the subject all the more efficiently to a debilitating idea of what is normal. Lacanian psychoanalysis does not need to work with disciplinary categories that divide the normal from the abnormal, still less does it treat the 'common unhappiness' that can be made out of hysterical misery at the end of analysis into something 'normal'.

Rationality and harmonisation

Let us turn to the stalling of enlightenment that takes place in 'postmodern' theory, to renderings of psychoanalysis as if it should become postmodern and of Lacan as if he were already a postmodern psychoanalyst (e.g. Loewenthal and Snell 2003; Pound 2007). This, it seems to some, is the route by which psychoanalysis connects with politics in relational mode (Fairfield *et al.* 2002). Unlike classical Freudian psychoanalysis, which makes its political interventions through the 'application' of theoretical notions to group processes or the personality formations of leaders and followers, postmodern psychoanalysis hopes for a more seamless connection between different domains where affect is intertwined with social relations (e.g. Trist and Murray 1990; cf. Miller and Rose 1988).

The 'postmodern' is pitted against the Western Enlightenment in two overlapping arguments that, even though they contradict one another, give undue status to postmodernism as if it were an alternative to that enlightenment.

The first argument rests on a spatial metaphor – this 'enlightenment' is problematic precisely because it is Western – and from a reflection on this geographical limit we can thereby unravel the way its Other is constructed, constituted as something to be admired or feared. Otherness of the Other is thus shown to be at work in orientalist racism and images of femininity, for example, and construction of the Other is from the standpoint of the Western enlightened subject as white and masculine (Ware 1982). Freud's (1926: 212) metaphor for women's sexuality as a 'dark continent' – a phrase tellingly marked out in English in Freud's original German text – neatly runs together these two motifs and reveals classical psychoanalysis to be mired in supposedly enlightened modernity.

The second argument is temporal in nature, and even though theoreticians of the postmodern actually insist that as a creative moment this often precedes the modern as such (Lyotard 1979/1984), the 'postmodern' condition is usually seen as something that succeeds obsolete modern enlightenment conceptions of the world and the subject. Freud is treated as out of date, and Lacan is enrolled in an ostensibly progressive shift from modern psychoanalysis to 'postmodern' psychoanalysis because he embraces the Other. That the unconscious is the discourse of the Other or that *'desire is the desire of the Other'* is seen as further evidence that Lacan (1964/1973: 38) provides a more open, generous and tolerant version of psychoanalysis in keeping with the spirit of the times, and 'post' is a signifier that surreptitiously links psychoanalysis with 'post-Marxism' (e.g. Laclau 1996) and so also explicitly or implicitly with 'post-capitalism', 'post-colonialism', even 'post-feminism' (cf. Bensaïd 2002).

Lacanian psychoanalysis does indeed drive the realm of Otherness deep into the heart of the subject and insist that the subject is also other to itself, an argument that is at work in the notion of the extimacy of the object a. However, our psychoanalysis does not thereby promise to make the Other reasonable to the subject – to turn it into a 'good Other' – or to harmonise relations between self and Other (Badiou 1998/2001). For Lacan, there is a question about what the Other wants that haunts the subject, and this question cannot be solved simply by appreciating intersubjectivity or interconnectedness. This is why Lacanian psychoanalysis sets itself against more open and flexible rationality and against bringing about a harmonious relation between the self and what is other to it. That more liberal rendition of psychoanalysis is undertaken by some psychotherapists and exemplified by the motif of 'multiculturalism' in US counselling psychology as a project of healing divisions in the self and promising an end to division between men and women and between the West and its Others (e.g. Atkinson *et al.* 2007).

Lacanian critique of psychotherapy as a project of locating the self in a domain of otherness which can then be reintegrated into a deeper more wholesome sense of subjectivity takes two forms which each demand a response. First, we argue that to promote rationality as the touchstone of conscious understanding serves to divide rationality from irrationality, and serves to reify both. Instead, Lacanian psychoanalysis opens a space for 'rational' reflection following those moments in which 'irrationality' comes into play through forms of 'act' that change the symbolic coordinates of a life and which then call for interpretation (Neill 2005a). Second, we point out that the attempt to bring about some form of harmonisation between aspects of the self will serve to cover over the contradictions that make someone into a human subject in the first place. Instead of trying to make the unconscious consistent with consciousness or, worse, trying to wipe it out altogether, Lacanian psychoanalysis attends to the ways in which each subject deals with their own dimension of impossibility, where they fail to coincide with what they want to be.

Prediction and pathology

Postmodernism as one of the ideological conceptual capsules of the subject congruent with contemporary neoliberal capitalism also promises – sometimes as a version of psychoanalysis and sometimes as an alternative to it – a greater sense of agency. Fluid, deconstructed and fragmented though the postmodern self is supposed to be, it is actually often vaunted as the site of greater openness to experience and source of illumination that exceeds anything conceived of in the Western Enlightenment (Loewenthal and Snell 2003). Again, we can see a spatial and a temporal argument at work. Notwithstanding the claim to transcend orientalism, the postmodern therapeutic self draws upon every form of wisdom and exoticises other places as it absorbs into itself images of enlightenment from around the world. This spatial metaphor for an expanded sense of agency is complemented by the temporal claim that narratives of the self can be reworked such that traumatic events can be dissolved into a new enlarged appreciation of the past (e.g. Singh 1999).

It is here that the ambition of the postmodern subject as agent outstrips what psychoanalysis ever offered, and now what Lacanian psychoanalysis provides. And here we have at one moment an uneasy alliance between postmodern versions of psychotherapy and Lacanian psychoanalysis insofar as they both oppose versions of psychotherapy that are simply applications of psychology, and at the next moment an insistence by Lacanians against full-blown postmodernists that the motifs of 'prediction' and 'pathology' need to be taken seriously (Copjec 1993). We can take each of these motifs in turn to show how this alliance and then division between Lacan and postmodernists operates.

First, Lacanians and postmodernists will agree, against some forms of psychotherapy, that to render treatment into a process that can be made susceptible to prediction as part of 'evidence-based' practice serves to close off what is most illuminating about the work of analysis (House 2002).

Lacanian psychoanalysis retrieves from Freud the notion of 'deferred action', remember, in which it is only after an event that we make it into something traumatic or something that may then be narrated in and out of the analysis. However, this traumatic point cannot be simply dissolved into a different narrative of the self, and the temporal logic of Lacanian psychoanalysis is concerned with how the symbolic work we carry out revolves around a real that cannot be completely symbolised. The role of punctuation points in a narrative that serve to reorganise the past of the subject in relation to its objects is so important precisely because narrative itself is a form of defence against this real (Laplanche 2003; Frosh 2007). So, while some forms of psychotherapy are problematic because they reduce change to a predictive controlled activity in line with psychology, other more recent forms of psychotherapy are problematic because they try to wish away the core around which every attempt to predict revolves (e.g. Young-Eisendrath and Muramoto 2002).

Second, Lacanians and postmodernists will agree, against some forms of psychotherapy, that to treat certain kinds of behaviour or experience as pathological merely serves to transform them from being things that the analyst may not understand into elements of a moral and moralising narrative (Fee 1999; Verhaeghe 2004). Lacanian psychoanalysis does not utilise descriptions of clinical structure in order to identify what should be changed, but to comprehend the direction of the treatment; and we have already seen that for Lacan (1959: 497) 'resistance', for example, is viewed as 'on the side of the analyst' not the analysand. However, these forms of pathology are not simply failures to appreciate the rich diversity of human experience, diversity incorporable into a fuller sense of what it is to be human. Again we see the importance of Lacan's critique of adaptationist psychoanalysis, for the critique concerns not only the adaptation of the subject as such but also the pathological nature of the society to which that conservative psychoanalysis aims to adapt the subject as ego. The trap that postmodern psychotherapists fall into is one in which pathology is replaced with a more inclusive normality, normalisation in a postmodern society which values narrative but which is still also pathological as such.

Immediacy

At a societal level the twentieth century saw the triumph and spread of capitalism throughout the world, first with the implantation of this political-economic system in different countries in the wake of colonialism – the moment of imperialist expansion – and then with neoliberal globalisation which insinuated entrepreneurial ideals around the world after the fall of the Berlin Wall. What should be noted about this second moment, one which deepens and intensifies what was once described as 'late capitalism' (Mandel 1974), is that psychologisation is now accompanied by and refracted through a concern with fluid forms of 'identity' nicely captured by the concept 'glocalisation' (Robertson 1995).

The paradox here is that critique in the socialist movement that accompanied the development of capitalism, critique that railed against its excesses in the early twentieth century, is now harnessed to that economic system; it is now as if the very political logic of the system is underpinned by experiential commitment to participation and equality of opportunity. The most powerful critique and alternative to capitalism, Marxism, has been at the one moment discredited – as if actually-existing socialism in the Soviet Union and China realised the worst of the oppression foretold by opponents of capitalism as its negative features – and at the next has seen its 'positive' aspects recruited to a newly humanised and re-energised capitalist world order (Foster 2005).

We can see this paradox at work in the motifs of 'change' and 'democracy' that have been retrieved from bad 'negative' Marxism and put to work as a positive contribution to the capitalism it was designed to comprehend and overthrow. A paradox homologous to this simple opposition between bad old and good new Marxism structures the absorption and neutralisation of psychoanalysis as a practice of self-transformation in which 'psychotherapy' starts to define what the goals of psychoanalysis should be. This journey through revolution as transformation to revolution as mere rotation takes us through the experience of Stalinism, an experience of promise and disappointment that betrays alternatives to capitalism and then even inspires, at the level of the individual, what we might characterise as a 'negative therapeutic reaction' to revolution as such; a reaction that involves 'exacerbation of the symptom and of the illness' (Freud 1933: 109–110).

First, with respect to an ethos of change, Marx (1845/1888) insisted that understanding the world necessarily entails changing it. The consequent refusal of any essentialism is underpinned by a dialectical mode of interrogation of reality which attends to and simultaneously facilitates transformation of social relations. This ontological commitment – to dialectical movement rather than to discrete essences – is displaced as the Stalinist bureaucracy crystallises, and relations become fixed in place, often with an appeal to identity categories such as 'the proletariat' and its leadership; and it is the appeal and the identity that is the problem rather than the category as such (Colletti 1970). Second, with respect to the expansion of democracy, Marxist interpretation is also an intervention designed to bring the working class and its allies up against the limits of capitalist exploitation and then through a necessary break from those limits in proletarian revolution. This democracy is defined as self-determination by associated producers of the organisation and distribution of natural and creative resources. This endeavour is betrayed by Stalinism; democratic centralism inside the workers' movement is replaced by centralisation of decision-making and prohibition of opposition in the rest of society (Trotsky 1936/1973).

Now motifs of 'change' and 'democracy', and many other such signifiers, have been appropriated by a renewed post-socialist capitalist economy and are pitted against a caricature of Marxism. The ideological claim now is that flexibility and precariousness actually give substance to a world powered by change and democracy as much as could ever be conceivable or desirable. If it was the case that early capitalism launched each subject into a vortex of change such that 'all that is solid melts into air' (Marx and Engels 1848/1965: 36), then latest capitalism takes us to the edge such that a revolution would take us beyond the limit of what could be tolerated. If contemporary capitalism is organised around pleasure, around the injunction to enjoy, then something more than that pleasure threatens jouissance that would be unbearable.

Radical libertarian attempts to break out from the binary of capitalism and Marxism – in surrealism, situationism, postmodernism or Deleuzian territorialisation of these projects – have failed to outflank capitalism, for now it relies upon and can satisfy the desire those projects promised (e.g. Hardt and Negri 2000, 2004). Each of these political alternatives aimed to break with the problematic of representation, representation as picture of the world that does violence to what it depicts – as if every word is the murder of the thing – and representation as deputising of authority to those who mediate the process of change and the institution of democracy (Lefort 1989; Stavrakakis 2007b).

Psychotherapy also works with representations, but its practitioners often pretend to arrive at a direct immediate comprehension which includes comprehension of that which lies underneath language. And so psychoanalysis is turned into its reverse, into a form of knowledge about the self that has displaced old psychiatry and even, to an extent, psychology in popular culture, knowledge that operates as a power to be wielded over others as a form of 'psychotherapeutic capital' (cf. Bourdieu and Passeron 1977). Psychoanalytic interpretation has been turned into its reverse through the insidious accumulation of psychotherapeutic capital that feeds what therapists imagine the unconscious to be, which is why Lacanians now do need to 'cut' into rather than endorse this kind of interpretation (Miller 1999a). We now need to map how this form of capital gains its currency. I will approach this task through an examination of four aspects of the way that psychotherapy displaces psychoanalysis, subtly shifting the focus of analytic work to render it into something suitable to the smooth running of contemporary capitalism.

Autonomy and reflexivity

The first aspect is knowledge. A cosmological conception of knowledge underpinned the elaboration of diagnostic systems in psychiatry, and this left each individual psychiatrist at the mercy of the very system of knowledge they needed in order to comprehend and treat their objects of study. A revolution in the status of knowledge occurred with the appearance of psychology as an ostensibly scientific discipline, and the prediction and control it aimed for meant that the psychologist could imagine they were in the driving seat.

Psychotherapeutic knowledge is of a quite different kind, however, by virtue of the position it occupies in relation to the therapist and their client. Therapeutic knowledge, as is the case for psychiatry, is a complete totalising system and, as with psychology, provides a grid through which the world should be understood and through which individuals should understand themselves. The lesson psychotherapy absorbs from psychoanalysis is that knowledge is not a categorical system into which different diagnostic types can be slotted, not a transparent system which will illuminate each individual as they learn who they are within it. This knowledge is unconscious, whether 'unconscious' means that it is the repression of a representation that lives another life inside the individual or whether it signifies absences in the representation we have available to consciousness. In both cases the knowledge that underpins psychoanalytic clinical work is something that is inaccessible, incomplete.

This slippery status accorded to knowledge that is so crucial to psychoanalytic conceptions of what we can and cannot know and how it is possible to know how not to know it all, is taken up and redefined in psychotherapy as if even this kind of knowledge is something hidden that should be brought to light. What is irreducibly and necessarily 'negative' at the heart of psychoanalysis is turned into something positive, and one of the characteristics of psychotherapy is precisely that it looks to accentuate the positive, to give substance to what is treated in psychoanalysis as the nothingness of human existence (Shingu 1995/2004).

We can trace this labour of psychotherapy, to retrieve something positive out of negativity, in the homologous trajectory of attempts at revolution against capitalism. It is precisely this trajectory that culminated in current conditions of possibility for the success of psychotherapy and its manifestation as psychotherapeutic capital. Let us take two elements of this trajectory, autonomy and reflexivity; it is a trajectory we trace through the fate of Marxism crystallised as its reverse under Stalinism.

First, for Marxism self-determination of associated producers reworks notions of autonomy such that human rights are defined in relation to freedom understood relationally in an ethical relation to creative labour. One can also see this relational conception of autonomy at work in psychoanalysis, an approach to the subject that refuses to buy into the image that individuals have of themselves in capitalist society as self-contained Robinson Crusoes. This ethical self-transformative capacity was betrayed by cynical strategic defence of the bureaucracy in which even opposition to capitalism as if it were merely a rival system to be displaced was instrumentalised. Stalinist instrumentality turned political struggle in each country into a diplomatic tool of the pragmatic needs of the bureaucracy (Mandel 1978). This mutation then also framed psychoanalysis, and pressed psychoanalysis into the image of it as an instrument which could use its knowledge to guarantee the good behaviour of those it cures.

Second, Marxism is an open self-transformative process of enquiry and change. The reflexivity necessary to Marxist analysis as a form of intervention is evident in its progressive recursive engagement with other social forces such as feminism, anti-racism and, more recently, ecological movements (e.g. Kovel 2007). Again, psychoanalysis has also been open to a political debate with such forces, and has been attractive to a variety of different Marxist traditions tackling questions of subjectivity. Stalinism, in contrast, operates on the assumption that some version of science will save the day, in its most grotesque forms as an identitarian 'proletarian science'; here 'scientific' dialectical materialism is turned to accumulating unquestioned truth about society and nature (Lecourt 1977). On the one hand this reductive form of materialism led to hostility to psychoanalysis in Stalinist states, but another effect of this reversal of fortunes for Marxism was that it became twinned with psychoanalysis as a warning as to where a science of human action would end up (M. Miller 1998).

Instrumentalised scientific knowledge thus becomes identified as an enemy, and an ostensibly more open and relativist capitalism emerges as an alternative in which relativism paralyses those who take a stance against it, this on the grounds that radicals are being dogmatic if they are steadfast in their political position. From a Lacanian standpoint, this is a parody of ethics that mires the analyst in 'relativistic moral stances' that make it difficult to assert an ethical position as such in politics and in the clinic (Oliver 2005: 671). It is this form of capitalism that facilitates psychotherapeutic capital as knowledge less certain and so flexible enough to assure new conceptions of the self comfortable with current modes of precarious entrepreneurship.

Freedom and meaning

Let us turn to a second aspect of the psychotherapeutic reformulation of psychoanalysis. This is an aspect that revolves around the role of key conceptual markers that hold a system of knowledge in place, 'master signifiers' (Lacan 1991/2007). As knowledge and our relation to knowledge changes over the course of history – knowledge is contested in different kinds of political struggle – so do such master signifiers. In order to approach the subtly different place of master signifiers in relation to knowledge in psychiatry, psychology, psychoanalysis and psychotherapy we also need to attend to how these anchoring points for knowledge may operate as dominant ideological motifs. Conceptual refinement of the role of signifiers in Lacanian political theory is useful here, and cues us into the different functions of, for example, 'floating signifiers' that may be articulated by competing groups or 'empty signifiers' that function to organise a field of debate but operate without an as yet determinate meaning (Howarth and Stavrakakis 2000; Glynos 2001).

Psychiatrists were once able to luxuriate in the status of such conceptual markers as if they too really were 'master signifiers', as if those individuals who incarnated them were the masters. The name 'psychiatrist' marked a position with some authority, and the name of the particular psychiatrist who made the diagnosis may have even, this for a lucky few of the masters, come to be the name of the medical category they brought to life. While such naming practices did continue in psychology, the historical accumulation of a more complete knowledge entailed a shift in the place of the name as such, of the key words that would hold this knowledge in place. As a new science of the individual, even as an empirical positivist science, psychology likes to refer and defer to names already accumulated, and citation practices in the discipline operate as a form of reference to what is already known about the phenomenon under investigation so that more knowledge can be added. It is this accumulation of citations, of reference to already-existing master signifiers, that makes 'prediction and control' conceivable (Danziger 1997).

Psychotherapy latches onto the signifiers produced as products, and is not willing to let them be lost again. The dialectical process that marks the progress of psychoanalysis from a Socratic questioning of the place of the subject in relation to their complaint to reducing the signifiers that bear it to nonsense is replaced with an attempt to give substance to the signifiers that emerge (Burgoyne 2007). This is despite the many genuflections to 'process' in psychotherapeutic writing and condemnation of the supposed reification of concepts in psychoanalysis, a reification and supposed 'consistency of the Other' that is indeed a problem, and which the return to Freud and returns to Lacan worry over and aim to work through (Miller 2002a: 13). One way of approaching this therapeutic attention to signifiers is to say that a distinction between the subject of the statement and the subject of the enunciation is still at work, but that it is not Lacan's distinction; it is rather a distinction which (like psychology) treats the subject of the enunciation as something whole, something that could and should find its own name.

Psychotherapeutic capital is thus accumulated as a symbolic resource which combines power and knowledge for the therapist who has access to a potentially if not actually complete system of concepts, and 'empowerment' is predicated on the production of self-knowledge offered to the client. In order for psychotherapy to circulate as symbolic capital in this way the signifiers that appear as products of the therapeutic process must be taken on good coin, as full of value at the moment they are discovered and as they are repeated in testimonies to therapeutic success. And as it is with the smug narrative of success in psychotherapy, so it is with the grander narrative of success now told by capitalism on the world stage. Let us turn briefly to two political-economic elements of the defeat of Marxism with the rise of Stalinism, and the self-satisfied lesson that neoliberal capitalism and its helpmeet psychotherapy draw from this failure.

First, Marxism is a theoretical and practical articulation of working-class consciousness as it grasps the nature of alienation under capitalism and constructs its own zones of freedom. It aims to overcome alienated conditions of production through a revolutionary process in which there are qualitatively greater degrees of free association, in which the free association of each is condition for the free association of all (McCarney 1990). Like the analysand, the working class grasps that its own identity is fabricated out of signifiers that mislead it not only with respect to what it is but with respect to the underlying assumption that it is something distinct and unchanging. Stalinism, in contrast, only offers the barest comfort in humiliating deference to elders and betters; the mystifying non-dialectical opposition to capitalism as a competitor is then repeated through the cynical and ironic complaint of those who positioned themselves as innocent victims of the bureaucracy. A simple reduced concept of 'freedom' is locked in place as if an abstracted individual agency that would enjoy that freedom could be possessed or not, and this also locks even those who lose out into an existence in reified social categories (Townshend 1998).

We have noted that one of the characteristic ideological forms that thrive under capitalism is that human beings freely enter into a contract to sell their labour to others. Freedom is factored into social relations in such a way that this self-conception is not an 'illusion'; insofar as it requires 'false consciousness', that kind of consciousness is grounded in an accurate appraisal of the world as it is under capitalism (Sohn-Rethel 1978). In this sense, individuals are indeed 'free' to sell their labour and the contract they make as they do so is to all intents and purposes 'fair'. The point is that from the vantage point of another world, a vantage point forged through historical practice which strikes a distance from capitalism, we can see that things could be otherwise and we can discern the deeper destructive effects of this form of limited freedom. Marx dismantles this theoretically, and of course psychoanalysis dismantles the idea that the contract between analyst and analysand is a 'freely' entered into contract between two individuals, an illusion that the ego psychologists pander to in the motif of a 'working alliance' (Sandler et al. 1970). Psychoanalysis compatible with a reduced image of freedom is then itself reduced in ideological framings of it to a lesson in humility and acceptance of what cannot be changed (Craib 1994).

Second, Marxism not only restores meaning to creative labour but also provides a world-historical meaning to the development of capitalism, and then to the activity by which it may be transcended (Lukács 1923/1971;

Žižek 2000a). Stalinism responds with simple appeals to authority and the closing of debates concerning the interpretation of history around one correct account (Mandel 1986). This totalisation also serves, of course, to ratify the power of the bureaucracy as the interpretative apparatus through which historical determination can be judged and measured. This is also the world of a caricature of psychoanalysis against which a supposedly more open and meaningful form of psychotherapy is able to posit itself as the solution to past mistakes, even perhaps self-styled as 'solution-focused' (e.g. De Shazer 1985).

Psychotherapy is fixed upon representations of 'freedom', 'meaning' and cognate notions which it treats as the hard-won products of its own activity when it has actually put its own knowledge to work and incited its clients to believe they have discovered those representations themselves. Psychotherapeutic capital is thus accumulated by those who misread and distort psychoanalysis in order that those who circulate it come to believe that they really do govern themselves (Rose 1996).

Resistance and history

One key difference of approach between psychoanalysis and psychotherapy, a third aspect of the difference between the two, concerns how one addresses the division of the subject. This dividedness is often factored into psychiatry as if it could be reduced to vulnerability, a notion that runs through to present-day explanations of the way environmental influences in mental illness operate upon 'predisposing' factors (e.g. Fonagy 2004). Today's 'bio-psycho-social' models of illness attempt to partial out the points at which the patient becomes susceptible to a breakdown, and to identify forms of treatment that will shield them from forces from without or that will seal over cracks within. One of the strategies psychiatry adopts to shield the psychiatrist and heal their own division is to enforce a sharp division between doctor and patient, to project onto the patient the vulnerability of the doctor. This dualist operation is easier to carry out if only the 'bio' and the 'social' are included in the equation.

When psychology emerges with its own disciplinary focus on the intervening term, 'psycho', there is a corresponding shift in the status of knowledge and the signifiers that anchor it such that failure, insufficiency or lack are arrived at in subtly but significantly different conclusions that the scientist comes to about their object of study (Bateman 1995; Shuttleworth 2002). Psychology, like psychiatry, keeps its object of study at a distance but it now has at its disposal a system of knowledge into which the assumption is built that every human being – taking into account that this 'every human being' is treated as a non-psychologist – is faulty, incomplete, prone to error. Psychologists worry away at what makes their objects of study tick, but with the result that all they produce is a reductive model of an imperfect being. One of the historical conceptual differences between psychiatry and psychology is that psychiatry tended to focus on what was excessive in those they diagnosed – organic process, affect, behaviour that spilled beyond what was normal – while psychology tended to assume that those they studied were deficient, a history that has led to some recent attempts to rebalance the discipline with a more 'positive psychology', which still, even so, tries to identify strengths in otherwise lacking subjects (Seligman 1998).

This brings us to the psychotherapeutic twist to the revolution in subjectivity that psychoanalysis introduces into psychiatric and psychological practice, a version of Lacan's subversion of the subject, and admittedly a contentious re-reading of Lacan's (1991/2007: 207) scornful references to 'revolution'. Psychotherapy, like psychoanalysis, addresses the subject in its division, makes it an object of concern, and psychotherapy also encourages the therapist to reflect on their own division. However, psychotherapy all too often treats the client as resistant, resistant to the knowledge that awaits them, knowledge that the therapist knows to exist as that which underpins their practice. Psychotherapy all too often retreats to a simplistic linear narrative of how distress appeared and how it might be resolved. This is because it is only through a linear narrative that the client can be brought to believe that they will arrive at a transparent view of their life as they look back to what they were and forward to what they can now achieve. Here psychotherapy, which profits in many other respects from a reaction to Marxism – at least to the form Marxism took in practice under the rule of the bureaucracy – actually replicates in miniature Stalinist versions of Marxism. Let us trace this through the trajectory of resistance and history in political-economic transformations over the last century.

First, Marxism enables and requires collective resistance to capitalism, and resistance to the strategies of divide and rule by which opposition is rendered into individual, ethnic or nationalist complaint. Psychoanalysis too calls upon the analysand to 'resist', challenge, question, and when this resistance manifests itself as resistance to change the analyst looks to how they are themselves implicated in the analytic process rather than blaming the analysand. Stalinism, in contrast, channels this resistance into obedience to a command-structure, a form of authority in which populism and state-sponsored re-articulation of power are assumed to be the only means of change (Mandel 1978). Psychotherapists do not, of course, deliberately endorse such a manipulative view of resistance, but we should note that neither do Stalinist cadres, for they do genuinely believe that they are good Marxists harnessing the activity of the working class to projects directed to progressive historical goals. The problem is that when a psychotherapist senses that their work is underpinned by knowledge of the self that their good clients are also capable of discovering for themselves, knowledge that will manifest itself in what the enlightened client discovers in therapy, resistance is, once again, embedded in a command structure.

Second, the historical narrative Marxism provides is one that learns from the past so as not to repeat it and provides a means by which past struggles against exploitation are redeemed. Marxist history is therefore also historical intervention in which combined and uneven development is characterised by unexpected connections and leaps which bring history alive again in the revolutionary process (Mandel 1979). Something somewhat akin to these redemptive moments is put to work in Lacan's (1967–1968) account of the psychoanalytic 'act' by which the subject reconfigures a response to trauma as what once will have been the case and rewrites the way such trauma figures for them now. This conception of history is betrayed by Stalinism which rewrites the past in order to favour the standpoint of the leadership. This fixity of sequence replicates the fixed position of the bureaucracy, and serves to justify alliances with the 'progressive bourgeoisie' of capitalist economies friendly to the leadership. It serves to fix the narrative into fixed sequences of stages of development so that they culminate in present-day arrangements. And, for all the radical pretensions of many psychotherapists who genuinely feel that they are marginal in contemporary society, their vision of the self nevertheless still corresponds to present-day arrangements.

Collectivity and cosmopolitanism

Psychotherapeutic subjects govern themselves as individuals but at the same time there is in many forms of psychotherapy the hope that a link with others might be forged, a link which sometimes comes to life through sharing one's experience of distress, exploring relatedness as a motif of the therapeutic process, or advertising the success of the therapy, even to the point of deciding to become a therapist oneself (e.g. Rowan and Dryden 1988). Themes of interdependence of self and other are shared with psychoanalysis, of course, but this is turned in a slightly different, significantly different, direction by psychotherapy. The distinctive mutation of psychoanalysis into psychotherapy revolves around the mysterious object that fascinates each subject, the object cause of desire that Lacan calls 'object a'.

This object drives the psychiatrist's search for the underlying cause of mental disorder, an underlying cause that they believe operates somewhere in the sick mind. This object cause of psychiatric attempts to categorise and group together similar instances of disorder, ideally in identifiable diseases and often in syndromes as clusters of symptoms, is perpetually produced and then lost. At one moment the cause is glimpsed and then it disappears from view. In classical psychiatry toward the end of the nineteenth century there were attempts to make the cause visible through an attention to what can be seen as disorder, and this is one reason patients were put on display, gathered under the searching gaze of the psychiatrist. In modern psychiatry there are attempts to make the cause visible in functional magnetic resonance imaging techniques and in representations – in popularised short-hand terminology to persuade sceptics – of the gene for mental disorder as if it could actually be seen through a microscope (e.g. Fonagy 2004).

The emergence of psychology as a discipline is characterised by a shift in focus so that what is observed is sometimes mistaken for the stuff of science itself – empiricism encourages psychology to measure regularities in behaviour and bypass the attempt to delve deep into their objects of study – or it sometimes becomes a function of an implicit model of its objects that is concerned with what is accomplished by observable behaviour rather than with its antecedent causes. This second approach is more in line with US American pragmatism than with English empiricism, and the discipline of psychology in the English-speaking world – the form of the discipline that is now spreading around the globe and displacing local traditions of research – oscillates between these two epistemological frames. So, here the object of study is treated as if it were directly visible, and then there is sometimes some disappointment that these objects, individuals who absorb the knowledge psychology provides, complain that crucial features of human existence seem to disappear in this knowledge. The object of study is produced and almost immediately lost as an alienated divided subject still in thrall to their own objects, to object a.

There is a subtle psychotherapeutic distortion of psychoanalytic accounts of the place of the object which is a function of how the analysand is encouraged to relate to the figure of the therapist who incarnates it. Psychotherapy values transparency and hopes to bring this about through empathic open communication, sometimes through clarity about the nature of the behavioural or cognitive procedures that will take place in therapy and sometimes through resolving communicational failures (cf. Goldiamond 1974). For those forms of psychotherapy that take psychoanalytic notions like transference seriously, for example, the client is inducted into a knowledge of what is going on so that they can recognise patterns they repeat in relation to others (White 2006). The upshot of this attention to communication in the therapeutic relationship – deceptively clear communication that Lacanians would avoid as that which runs along the line of the imaginary – is that the therapist attempts to overcome their opaque status and turns into an example, the exemplary therapeutised subject with which the client can identify and which they can use as a measure of what kind of person they should be.

Let us very briefly trace how this shift of emphasis from obscure object to exemplary subject is given ideological grounding by much larger-scale failures to overthrow capitalism in the twentieth century. This admittedly tendentious 'context' for the recent success of psychotherapy does throw some light on conceptions of otherness in psychotherapy. First, Marxism values collectivity, collective activity as the basis for participation in struggle which is not reduced to simple equality or equivalence of each individual's voice but subjects constituted in such a way as to be able to together understand and change the world through praxis as the intimate link between interpretation and intervention (Lukács 1923/1971). The bureaucracy in the Stalinist states replaced this collective activity with a cult of personality in which great leadership individualised resistance and subordinated it to party and state discipline. Second, Marxism is a form of internationalism, a self-consciously cosmopolitan movement which pits itself against the imperialist and globalising ambitions of capital to segregate the workforce. Against this, Stalinism revived nationalism through the motif of 'socialism in one country' and an appeal to national sentiment in each country where a variety of home-grown bureaucracy ruled (Mandel 1978).

Neoliberal capitalism feeds on a sense of revulsion at the self-contained individual, the 'personality' around whom a cult seems to operate, and revulsion against the division between 'us and them', but at the same time there is now even more intense individualisation of processes of production and consumption, and racism directed to those represented as themselves intolerant of others (Balibar and Wallerstein 1991). At the one moment there is a rise in psychologisation, the renewal of a model of individual responsibility that then also, of course, gives conspiratorial inflection to anti-capitalist critique that Marxists have had to pit themselves against as a form of ideology. At the same moment there is a rise in popularity of psychotherapy which accompanies and complements this psychologisation, of psychotherapeutic capital accumulated by those who feel they have come to know more about themselves within a certain vocabulary of the self which values 'relationships' between individuals.

What should be noticed here is that the psychoanalytic concept of 'extimacy' is replaced with a segregationist logic by which the very connection between individuals becomes an ideological motif, one which dissolves accounts of political-economic conflict into reparation that individuals make to each other. There is some sense of collectivity, one that extends to valuing all other human beings around the world, but this runs alongside a sense of personal self-worth that should be guarded against the intrusion of others. Something like 'glocalisation' with the spread of neoliberal capitalism also takes place at the level of the self in the local sub-cultural worlds where psychotherapeutic capital circulates and values diversity, but this neoliberal world order only thrives insofar as it can turn diversity into something from which surplus value can be extracted (Went 2000). There is a niche market here in which psychotherapeutic capital circulates around the diverse selves it values but which it then, in line with the worst of benevolent multiculturalist toleration of reified cultural differences, locks in place.

Conjunctions

There are many different forms of psychotherapy and, as an ideological complex concerned with the management of the self, it is an eclectic mixture of different elements that are weighted differently in cognitive, humanistic and psychodynamic schools. It is understandable that some of these forms should chime with popular images of psychology in such a way as to make the circulation of psychotherapeutic capital compatible with psychologisation. Psychotherapeutic conceptions of clinical practice as concerned with discovering hidden meanings correspond with commonsense understandings of the self, and they then sustain notions that are antithetical to psychoanalysis, notions of empathy, harmony, empirical truth, moral education, normalisation, pathologisation, predictive validity and rationality. Dominant forms of 'psychoanalysis' in the English-speaking world, when they are not busily attempting to ingratiate themselves with psychiatrists or psychologists, have also done exactly that, and have even attempted to press Lacan into that adaptationist project (e.g. Bailly 2009).

Some forms of 'psychotherapy' pretend to be part of a radical new alternative to old versions of treatment. This is all the more reason why therapeutic categories should be treated with suspicion by psychoanalysts, and that suspicion should be directed as much to the practice of psychotherapy when it operates as the soul of a spiritless condition under capitalism as to therapeutic ways of talking about the self; they reproduce the worst of popular cognitivist, humanist or spiritualised forms of ideological mystification. Lacanian psychoanalysis at its best refuses to adapt itself to psychotherapeutic categories, and it refuses all forms of bourgeois psychology in its search for something more progressive.

Lacanian psychoanalysis cuts against the commonsensical nostrums about the self that pretend to bypass representation but which simply lock the subject all the more tightly into late capitalism. Psychotherapy has profited from the failure of attempts to overthrow capitalism, and it presents itself now as the most flexible and comforting democratic solution to what it pretends is an outdated revolutionary tradition. I have noted problems with psychotherapy in this chapter, and in the next will concentrate on some of the more insidious attempts to install a therapeutic notion of the self in each subject in the name of 'ethics'.

Chapter 6
Reflexive recuperation

This chapter focuses on differences between Lacanian psychoanalysis and psychotherapy in the field of ethics. Psychotherapists often adhere deliberately or by default to an ethical injunction to do and be good, an injunction that both complements and contradicts psychoanalytic practice. I explore with reference to clinical practice the affective underside of ostensibly 'correct' speech, and the difference between popular therapeutic assumptions about language and the distinctive Lacanian attention to it. These questions play out in relation to different clinical structures, including in consequences of taking these structures as given in analytic work, and I lay bare political consequence of working toward sexual and gender difference within a Lacanian theory of 'sexuation' and limitations of therapeutic transformations of sex into 'deep gender'. First there is an examination of the way differences between psychoanalysis and psychotherapy are blurred in psychotherapy training bodies, and this sets the scene for questions of structure anchored in the 'feelings' of the therapeutic analyst.

Distance

Lacanian psychoanalysis, in breaking from its roots in French psychiatry, has had to negotiate a tortuous path around forms of psychology to which mainstream psychoanalysis in the English-speaking world has often been reduced, and forms of psychotherapy as the more flexible and popular modality of self-help in contemporary capitalism (Kovel 1978). The attempt by Lacanian analysts to distance themselves from the rather antiquated pathological categories inherited from psychiatry and sedimented into commonsensical usage propagated by psychology then risks appearing to endorse a humanised, if not humanistic version of those disciplines. Motifs of discourse, recognition and otherness seem more palatable than old mechanistic models of the human being, and recent interest in Lacan's work could be its undoing precisely because it is then easier to incorporate a humanised version of it into psychotherapy. There are powerful ideological processes at work here which are relayed through cultural representations of what psychoanalysis should be and through institutional mechanisms that distort and adapt Lacanian psychoanalysis while it is being transmitted.

Cultural representations of psychoanalysis include the well-known hydraulic model attributed to Freud as an element of the conceptual machinery against which emerge more ostensibly progressive phenomenological approaches (Schwarz 1999). Here psychotherapeutic discourse feeds on an image of what is to be avoided and then suffuses the English-speaking world before then being rapidly globalised to anticipate and neutralise responses by the old Freudians. The new therapeutic argot seeds into now commonsensical images of the self notions of 'subconscious' stuff that is 'repressed' or 'projected' and an image of the person as being 'defensive' if they do not show they are 'attuned' to others, if they do not 'identify' with good others or with what is good about themselves and, of course, if they do not identify with this therapeutic vocabulary itself. Resistance to this psychotherapeutic reinterpretation of psychoanalysis is then sometimes voiced in the French-, Italian-, Portuguese- and Spanish-speaking world in terms of defence against Americanisation (e.g. Dufour 2008). This reaction tends to draw attention to the threat posed by cognitive behavioural imports, a too convenient target that plays on the psychological adaptation of psychoanalysis in the United States and Britain, and it thereby neglects the force of a deeper more insidious wave of therapeutisation in culture (Pupavac 2005).

This therapeutic mutation of psychoanalysis is in some ways a repetition of notions that Lacan set himself against after his first break with the IPA, and it revives themes concerned with intersubjectivity and countertransference that once went under the misleading rubric of 'two body' psychology (Hanly and Nichols 2001). Lacan (1975/1991: 11) argued then that actually 'there is no two-body psychology without the intervention of a third element'. In the two-body perspective developed by those concerned with the importance of 'object relations' as a description of what goes on between mother and child and then between analyst and analysand, there is a failure to recognise this third element, the symbolic register: 'In fact, this register disappears completely in the object relation, and by the same token the imaginary register as well' (ibid.: 206). In this way the analyst (and here Balint was the main target of Lacan's critique) was '*entangled in a dual relation, and denying it*' (ibid.: 205). Lacan (1964/1973: 198) underscored this emphasis on the symbolic register later in his work through close attention to the way a signifier represents the subject for another signifier and to the way a subject is supposed to know by the analysand in transference.

A new version of 'two-body' psychology is now present in therapeutic reframing of psychoanalysis, and it leads the analyst to the idea that they can get underneath the symbolic to the real, a real of 'affect' which both partners in therapeutic interaction experience but which the therapist is in a position to attend to and work with as part of their 'countertransference'

(Heimann 1950; cf. Malone 2008: 190). The conception of the real that is operative here is therefore very different from a Lacanian view of it. This 'real' that the therapeutic analyst leads the analysand towards (and which a supervisor leads the analyst towards) is a supposedly objective view of reality and so an abstracted alienated image of the patient's internal processes is conjured into being, processes that are assumed to be distorted by the transference. The aim of stripping away the effects of transference and countertransference in order to arrive at a purified 'intersubjective relation' between two individuals (and so also to arrive at a parallel relationship of mutual recognition between analyst and supervisor) leads the analyst towards a celebration of the imaginary, if they but knew it. The line of the imaginary, which is characterised by systematic misrecognition, may lead to some beneficial psychotherapy but it leads away from psychoanalysis.

These cultural representations of psychoanalysis are given currency as professionals and networks of devotees accumulate psychotherapeutic capital through which a career can be constructed or more precarious lifestyles sustained. Here the notion that the citizen should be a kind of therapist of the world also orients political activity in an attempt to make it more compatible with a feminist sensibility, and then critics of therapeutic culture are susceptible to accusations of being macho, a potent charge (Samuels 1993). Here we need to maintain a distinction between feminism – a political force which challenges patriarchy and, according to its own particular logic of resistance and prefiguration, capitalism too – and feminisation which is the necessary complement of present-day therapeutisation. The harnessing of quasi-feminist motifs to a therapeutic mode of being complements the incorporation of this political force into little islands of femocracy where it is the sovereign power of women which is supposed to bring about a balance of the sexes (Eisenstein 1996). In therapeutic circles the balance is resolved through the conceit that men can be powerless too, so this feminisation is thus interwoven with therapy in the clinic. Psychotherapeutic capital condenses around particular personnel who determine who is being 'defensive' and who is not, and it is when they configure themselves as exemplary in their duty of care that we are in the realm of contemporary therapeutic ethics.

The characteristic configuration of subjectivity that psychotherapeutic capital accomplishes as it circulates and encloses the care of the self in contemporary capitalism is evident in training organisations that model themselves on what they imagine to be 'academic' knowledge. What should be noticed about academic institutions and organisations patterned upon them today is that there has been a reflexive transformation that makes them compatible with the practice of psychotherapy. We are then faced with a very different problem from that described by Lacan (1991/2007) in his warnings about the role of the 'university' in the provision of bureaucratised knowledge that would make it seem as if certificates in psychoanalysis could be dispensed as if they were driving licences.

Universities provided an influential home for the discipline of psychology, but the internal privatisation of academic institutions and globalisation of a reflexive attention to the self in teaching and learning have led to a mutation of knowledge and forms of agency sustained by it (Ecclestone and Hayes 2008). Academic institutions have become places that are now more congenial than ever to psychotherapy and so to psychotherapeutic education, but therefore by the same token even more dangerous places for Lacanian psychoanalysts. The question here is not whether Lacanians should take up university or college positions and use the material resources of the university. Many leading figures have done so. One of the advantages of an academic environment is that the reflexivity it promotes can be worked with as a space for exploring limits and possibilities for doing something different. The real question is how we deal with the symbolic and imaginary effects of the new therapeutic academic ethos when it is used as a template for training everywhere else.

The reflexive imperative at work in psychotherapy draws on a particular conception of ethics that is at odds with the ethos of Lacanian psychoanalytic practice. As with the versions of ethics promoted by psychiatry and psychology, psychotherapeutic ethics is most pernicious when it turns into a system of rules and a way of life to which all should conform, when it turns from being ethics as such into a kind of morality. Knowledge about what people are like and what makes them happy and unhappy is then turned into prescriptions for what is good for people. It may not at all be necessary to formulate these ideas explicitly as little homilies that are slipped into the session. There are many ways a therapist can convey a moral position to the client, and sighs and silences may be just as effective ways of moralising, sending a message to them about what is right and what is wrong. The therapist often does this because they have been inducted into training that itself crystallises and makes explicit commonsense nostrums about the self. So, we now focus on institutional practices that are incompatible with Lacanian psychoanalysis, practices compatible with psychotherapy that draw on contemporary academic discourse (De Vos 2009b).

Reflexive identity

When a university confers the title of 'psychotherapist' or 'counsellor' on someone, they do more than simply tell them what they can do to others. The conferment of a title also sends a message about what kind of activity therapy is; that it is something that is sedimented in a kind of person who possesses the identity of therapist. This reflexive identity, which encourages the therapist to believe that they have arrived at a closer, more authentic and immediate connection with who they really are, then encourages identification and idealisation of the therapist by the client (Safouan 1983/2000).

This reflexive identity might be compatible with some psychoanalytic traditions, those that encourage identification between the ego of the patient and the ego of the analyst, but it is one that Lacanian psychoanalysis refuses. There is also, of course, a danger that the analytic work becomes turned into an educational procedure, and the training that the therapist has received from the academic institution may inform how they think other people should learn about themselves.

A therapist who has taken on board the message that they have the identity of therapist by virtue of a title they have obtained from an academic institution is liable to turn the therapy itself into machinery for manufacturing others like themselves, in conformity with the 'ethics' that flows from the contemporary neoliberal university. Let us take the instance of class, which is now often also reduced to being an identity. Academic institutions have historically reproduced the middle class, and the class character of therapy as a profession tends to mirror the class character of the academic institutions (Bourdieu and Passeron 1977; Burman 2001). Psychotherapy trainings portray their host organisations as flexible, inclusive and innovative, but this itself is a cynical expression of the marketisation of higher education. The changing relationship between the social class composition of academic institutions and the free-market economy can be mapped onto the current landscape of therapy. The emergence of a layer of therapists working 'independently' (as a euphemism for private practice) has also created a new market niche for academic courses. And in the process the class character of both the academic and the new trainee group is mutually reinforcing.

Provision of therapy in social welfare services is already structured against working-class clients, and the classic criteria used to determine whether someone is suitable for psychotherapy serve to exclude many people from ethnic minorities who do not buy into the dominant culture. As we have noted, the criterion of 'psychological mindedness' is sometimes interpreted in a narrow way to mean that the potential client should have some notion that they have an unconscious (Coltart 1988). Even in its broader sense 'psychological mindedness' is often equated with the way the client speaks using an elaborated code which the middle-class professional can recognise as being like their own. The internal class structure of therapy is also reproduced by the internal class structure of academic provision. The traditional pecking order between psychoanalysts, psychotherapists and counsellors in many countries is stratified according to class, and academic institutions keep alive hierarchies that sit uneasily with the egalitarian liberal project of therapy itself (Richards 1995; cf. Jacobs 2002).

Tracks

The academic world is tailored to forms of representation organised to accord with logical sequences. It is a place where anomalies in experience are neatly rationalised and where the elaboration of theory often operates as a form of defence. At the same time, and as a reflexive reaction to this form of rationality, there is often hostility to theory because it is felt to be 'alienating' (in the reduced experiential meaning of the term). This contradictory deployment of rationality and theory opens up a split between the realm of the cognitive and the realm of affect. The cognitive aspect is privileged when course tutors write documents for circulation to academic committees and have to frame what they are doing in terms that trace a sequence of aims and outcomes. The translation of therapeutic phenomena into transferable skills, by virtue of which they are already turned into abilities abstracted from context, does not only occur in the production of written documents. This translation process also happens when tutors have to defend what they are doing to outsiders brought in for validation panels, for reviews of programmes or for 'teaching quality' inspections (Strathern 2000; House 2005).

It is tempting to see this process as itself ensuring that therapeutic knowledge stays at the level of what Freud (1915a) called conscious 'word presentations' combined with 'thing presentations'. When it is kept at that level, it is quite possible to talk about all the things that are important in such a way as to avoid real engagement, to avoid engagement with the stuff of the unconscious which is organised by 'thing presentations' alone. A 'cognitive' explication of what is going on then assumes privilege over the unconscious in such a way that a domain of 'emotion' is constituted as its other, and this is the way that a focus on 'defence mechanisms' also often operates (Vaillant 1971). This does more than simply make it difficult to engage with what we imagine to be the affective level of experience, the feelings we have about topics being studied and our subjective engagement with research. Not only are these affective aspects avoided, but they are replaced by something else, the 'emotions' as things that are then treated as if they can be grasped in and of themselves.

Therapy is organised around direct immediate connection with the unconscious, and so the temptation to stay at a conscious cognitive level in academic work itself invites a search for authentic engagement with something underneath. The refashioning of theoretical discussion of psychoanalysis into cognitive terminology leads to the re-emergence of what has been defended against, now as things that are numinous, mysterious, as not being susceptible to any kind of rational explanation. We then see appeals to 'intuition' or talk of countertransference as if it operated as a kind of telepathic communication between the analyst and analysand. The academic not only privileges a cognitive account in the documents and accounts for committees, then, but incites an undergrowth of appeals to 'emotions' that resists theoretical examination (Burman 2001).

This cognitive sequential conception of knowledge is locked into and reinforced by a predictable temporal shape that may be appropriate for some kinds of therapy, but is certainly not for psychoanalysis. This temporal shape is given by the structure of academic courses, and it can then all too easily frame analytic practice. Academic institutions run along a particular temporal track, the 'academic year', and courses have a certain structure because they must fit into that kind of time frame. The trajectory of a student is also characterised by a definite beginning, middle and end, and this means that things such as 'deferred entry', 'intercalation' and 'extensions' are defined as deviations from a normative route through the course. There is a serious danger, then, that the set period of an academic course will come to define what the prescribed length of a psychoanalytic training should be. Different kinds of engagement with analysis, different rhythms of life, and even some kind of 'readiness' to practise must then in some explicit or implicit way be subordinated to what the normal trajectory of a student is expected to be (e.g. Mace 2002).

There are two consequences for practice. One is that a training governed by the academic calendar may well lead to therapy which is less sensitive to what Lacan calls 'logical time', and less sensitive to the way that our understanding of things is elaborated after the event, as being *'Nachträglich'*, deferred (Lacan 1946b). A second consequence is that because our notions of linear time are culturally-bounded, courses that operate according to these notions will also be culturally-loaded. One way of understanding norms of punctuality and deadlines in different cultures is to measure how late someone might be expected to be for an appointment. The linearity of academic training is of a piece with linear time that structures our sense of history today (Brennan 1993); it then has consequences for conceptual and cultural issues that may be antithetical to genuine analytic practice (Moncayo 1998).

Standards

A student in an academic environment learns that knowledge must be anchored in existing knowledge. Referencing conventions repeat the conventional wisdom in academic institutions that therapeutic knowledge is something that can be represented in written text. This means, along the way, that one of the key qualities of psychoanalysis, that it is an oral tradition of apprenticeship and practical work, must be avoided or misrepresented (Bakan 1958/1990). Norms of practice in an academic setting are then transformed from being shaped by discussion and the crafting of rhetoric – qualities compatible with the nature of psychoanalysis as a 'talking cure' – into norms that can be put into written form. Needless to say, the written form that is required in modern academic institutions is particularly bureaucratised. When 'competencies' and 'skills' are specified by academic institutions as part of an attempt to recognise qualities that do not always involve writing the effect is to turn those competencies and skills into techniques that must be reshaped by writing, often as clearly delimited bullet points in course documents, before they are handed back to the students to be 'applied'.

It is then entirely understandable that the state regulation of therapy is taken up with gusto by academic institutions. Those who would like to regulate psychotherapy and tie it down into a clearly defined profession are keen to turn to the academic institutions to back them up. There is, of course, a requirement that academic institutions observe and regulate students through various forms of assessment, and this assessment process is a little more relaxed now with respect to final year and course examinations. However, greater emphasis on course-work and other forms of more open flexible assessment actually increases the degree to which the student is tracked in their progress through the course, and it increases the reflexive commitment of the student to a particular form of knowledge (Mace et al. 2009).

A further effect is that psychotherapy and counselling become crystallised into layers of experts who are expected to have knowledge and skills about the domain of subjectivity. This knowledge and skill, it is hoped by some, will then be ratified by the state, backing up the registration bodies so that only those who have been through recognised training procedures will be able to use the label 'psychotherapist' or 'counsellor'. The definition of different identities currently proposed in UK legislation on the regulation of psychotherapists, for example, has psychotherapy as concerned with 'treatment of the disordered mind' and counselling as concerned with mental health and 'well-being' (Low 2009). Therapy is in this way being distorted while being professionalised (House 2002). Many psychoanalytic trainings, then, are searching for respectable institutions to validate what they do, and academic institutions are keen to do more than simply give a stamp of approval; this structural deference and dependence on the academic world then opens the way for already existing 'professionals' to determine how others should be admitted, fashioned and judged.

The role of the academic institution in monitoring and evaluating professional training and practice fits quite neatly with broader processes of observation and control. The academic institutions in this way effectively become part of the apparatus of the psy complex, and they search for the causes of potential deviation deep inside each individual subject. And there is a twist, which is that the therapist also comes to crave regulation as a means to identity, security and a guarantee that others are also dutiful followers of the law (Mowbray 1995; House and Totton 1997).

Mastering meaning

The contemporary academic world operates on deep-grained assumptions about what criteria should be used to evaluate subjects taught. Psychoanalysis is under pressure to account for what it does and why it works in academic settings, and is susceptible to a distortion of important underlying clinical principles. Academic programmes are now designed to enable tutors to monitor and assess the progress of the student, with much of the burden of the assessment resting on verification that the work is indeed the student's own. Various provisions are made for 'accrediting' the prior learning of students so that there is no unnecessary duplication of material to be covered, and such accreditation itself rests on the assumption that the knowledge that potential students have been exposed to in the past may be functionally the same, equivalent to, the knowledge they may be offered on the course. That is, the relation to knowledge is not seen as contextual but as empirical, contained and replicable. The 'accreditation of prior experiential learning' repeats the same assumption, but this time with respect to other aspects of the work. These other 'experiential' aspects are then differentiated from academic knowledge but are also treated by the academic as reified and repeatable.

There is a series of assumptions built into this process that is, unfortunately, entirely compatible with recent attempts to make psychoanalysis subject to the imperatives of 'evidence-based medicine'. Evidence-based medicine works on the premise that only those treatments that have demonstrable measurable outcomes in randomised controlled trials should be funded. The notion of medicine that it operates on is one that looks to evidence in the natural sciences, usually a particular distorted version of the natural sciences (Schwarz 1999; Goldacre 2008).

There is a further respect in which the appeal to 'evidence' skews psychoanalysis. The message conveyed to students undergoing training in academic institutions is that it is possible to distinguish between reality, which can be empirically studied, and fantasy. This is one reason why 'infant observation' has become popular as an empirical guarantee that analysis is grounded in something that can be rendered visible (Miller et al. 1989). The way is then open for a shift from an attention in analytic work to the distinctive personal truth that a client will find a way to speak, to the presumption that there is such a thing as objective truth that the client might better be brought in line with. Certain notions about what reality is and what counts as truth are thus reinforced by academic trainings (Heaton 2001).

Ethics is one of the most uncertain and contested issues in academic research, and is addressed in different ways in different disciplines. The attempt to make any one of these ways of thinking about ethics in the academic world compatible with discussions of ethics in Lacanian psychoanalysis is fraught with problems. The slide from ethics to moralising, and the incitement of an equally problematic reverse discourse which defends the 'rights' of the individual free from any interference, is evident in the way that academic institutions have tried to implement policies on ethics. The ethics committee attracts and sustains those who are either driven by an anxiety that others will do something wrong, and the committee will be held responsible, or who gain such satisfaction from regulating what other people do that their own ethical judgement is systematically distorted. The ethics committee in an academic institution usually operates on the basis that harm is likely to occur if it is not prevented and that the way to prevent it is through the stipulation of correct behaviour (Badiou 1998/2001).

This kind of committee, which is also the dominant model in social welfare organisations, then serves as a model for the formation of ethics committees in psychoanalytic training organisations, but it knows that it will be able to exercise its bureaucratic function much more efficiently if it can draw the psychoanalytic trainings into the academic frame. Some models of therapy are compatible with a view of ethics as the calculation of harms and benefits and rules for practice that distinguishes right from wrong. The 'internalisation' of a supervisor could, in this model, also be seen as the internalisation in the course of the training of a moral code (e.g. Casement 1985). However, compartmentalisation of ethics in this kind of way in academic-based trainings is, as has also been pointed out inside the IPA, antithetical to the ethics of psychoanalysis (Haas 2001).

Affect

We are now tangled in a retroactive looping back in culturally-dominant notions of ethical behaviour, back from the rather mechanistic cost-benefit model adapted from Jeremy Bentham that is so dear to psychology (and that interested Lacan as the source of an internally-contradictory antipsychology), back to an approach to ethics that preceded Bentham's but which attends to something deeper in the core of the subject to which it pertains. That chronologically earlier Kantian ethics resonates with a psychoanalytic conception of the subject, but it ripens into a form of ideology when psychoanalysis mutates into psychotherapy. We might say, following Kant, that unconscious knowledge that we suppose to function in the individual subject is operating at a completely different level of representation, even of the things in themselves that exist as if they were 'noumena' beneath the phenomena that fill our experiential life-world (Zupančič 2000).

Kant foregrounds an imperative to follow the right course of action, which we assume, he says, to be potentially if not actually present in each other individual human being. This 'categorical imperative', in which we are asked to assess our action according to the maxim that we should imagine it to be carried out by all other human beings, applicable to them, is a maxim designed to bring some measure of universality directly into the moral decision-making of any particular individual. This is an ethical paradigm that we can imagine certain traditions in psychology adopting with ease. The image of the person as containing within themselves a conscience by virtue of which they are able to participate in society as a civilised enlightened human being can then even be translated into certain psychoanalytic models of the personality that are included in psychology. Freud (1923: 35) himself argues, for example, that the super-ego 'in the form of conscience or perhaps of an unconscious sense of guilt' has a 'compulsive character which manifests itself in the form of a categorical imperative'. The problem with this paradigm, which operates according to a notion of the existence of conscience under law, is that some people who carry out the most horrific actions do feel themselves to be following some version of a moral injunction and to be in conformity with what human nature is like (Lacan 1963; Rajchman 1991). This is why Lacan (1986/1992: 77) argues that the Kantian imperative might be expressed as '"Never act except in such a way that your action may be programmed"'.

The problem here as one version of Kantian ethics comes to fruition in psychotherapy today is not only that the therapist follows the command to be an exemplar of good conduct which they then wish all others to adhere to, but that they also follow the command to reflexively position themselves in relation to those they wish good for, that is, their clients. There are a number of consequences for conceptions of what is normal and what is pathological in the clinic. The most important consequence is that the reflexive inclusion of the therapist in the relationship with their client insinuates a version of 'countertransference' into their sense of that relationship which is used as a compass for understanding what is going on between the two of them – as if it is a two-body psychology – and what is going on inside the client. This then gives a peculiar twist to how 'clinical structure' might be conceptualised, conceptualised in a particular way because it has been experienced first by the therapist. A therapeutic imperative is at work in specifications of forms of pathology, even in the way that Lacanian conceptions of 'clinical structure' might be understood, and it is most powerfully expressed in the way the therapist comes to believe in the reality of such structures (cf. Johnstone and Dallos 2006).

One might read this concern as but another take on the danger of reifying clinical structures, something at work in the psychiatric framing of psychoanalytic practice and in the embedding of notions of character types in culture with the spread of psychology. This reification includes a form of subjectification compatible with pathological positions opened up by the development of capitalism such that the analysand configures themselves in these ways when they come to speak to an analyst. But more is at stake now. Here we are concerned with the way the psychoanalyst who attends to their relationship with the analysand – the analyst who follows the therapeutic injunction to delve into their countertransference as reflexive source of knowledge of others – comes to believe in the reality of such structures because they have *experienced* them for themselves.

One way of tackling this problem is to map the production of therapeutic subjectivity in the analytic relationship by taking each of the clinical structures and noting how each is the manifestation of a particular kind of relation the analyst has to their analysand. So, I will now trace in more detail how psychotherapeutic reason structures the analytic relationship in order to constitute 'clinical structures' of the analyst, particular forms of affect conditioned by the way the clinic takes shape today. This does not mean that the production of this version of 'clinical structure' is really 'inside' the therapist any more than an unreconstructed psychiatric Lacanian would treat clinical structure as inside the analysand. An examination of the constitution of clinical structure *as if* it were 'inside' the therapist will help us rethink what the clinic as such is and then what the relation between clinical and political change might be.

Extending the argument in this way does not mean either that the production of clinical structure through therapeutic attention to countertransference in an imaginary two-body relationship is accidental or that there is thereby random allocation of structure by the therapist to different clients. Dramatising one's distress, warding off possible reminders of one's complicity with the conditions that evoke it, treating anxiety in the other as access to enjoyment or shutting out what others want are already in a psychiatrised culture, likely to attract psychiatric labels. The psychologisation of identities makes it even more likely that such strategies will turn responses to alienation under capitalism into modes of being embedded in interpretations oneself makes before the therapist reiterates them as categories and confirms that, yes, they are discrete modes of being (Miller 2008).

It is precisely the different ascribed identities of the client that provoke in the therapist the sense that there is someone speaking to them who could be defined as hysteric, obsessional, pervert or psychotic, defined in these ways even if the therapist does not deliberately, consciously want to subscribe to those pathological categories. Therapeutic modes of subjectivity operate with such power precisely because they catch those they recruit by surprise; therapeutic discourse makes explicit underlying assumptions about self and other that are at work even before its subjects consciously subscribe to those assumptions. This recruitment of the subject in such a way that their awareness of who they are and what their position is becomes layered upon underlying ideological presuppositions is 'interpellation' (Althusser 1971); the subject is interpellated into a meaning system in which their own 'secondary elaboration' is a form of intelligibility which itself operates as a kind of facade. The 'fascinating result of secondary elaboration is that *the intelligibility blocks the understanding*' (Močnik 1993: 148); in consequence '[t]he active part played by the interpellated individual consists precisely in her/his helping to establish a "facade" – an ideological effect of coherence' (ibid.: 150). Attention to countertransference, what the therapist experiences in the relationship as if it consisted of their 'feelings' that are treated as clues to what is really going on, thus leads to a reflexive recuperation of psychoanalysis by psychotherapy (e.g. Rustin 2003).

Here we are concerned with the organisation of affect – anticipated, solicited, suspected or feared – constituted in various ways as if it were an emotion experienced by the analyst, as if the patient will emote according to therapeutic precepts. The conceptual resources that we draw upon to bring this to light are sometimes counterposed to psychoanalysis. However, Deleuze as a key early theorist of such resources marks a distance from the therapeutisation of psychoanalysis, and was once close enough to Lacan to be invited into his circle with the words 'I could use someone like you' (cited in Smith 2006: 39); well, now maybe we can (see also Tamboukou 2003; Ahmed 2004; Clough with Halley 2007).

The hysterical analyst

We already know that gender suffuses psychoanalytic images of hysteria, but Lacanians radicalise the construction of these images beyond 'gender', beyond an experientially-grounded commitment to what are then believed to be mere cultural correlates of underlying biological sex differences. In Lacan's (1975/1998) 'formulae of sexuation' there is a disjunction between the side of 'man' organised around the fantasy that there is an exception to the rule that all men are subject to castration, a cut in power by the signifier, and the side of 'woman' in which there is no exception but instead inclusion of all the women in the symbolic as 'not-all'. The woman does not 'exist' because there is no signifier that will entirely capture and define what she is, while man's subjection to the symbolic gives benefits aplenty in compensation for this subjection even though he is haunted by the idea that while there is a way out it is for one other lucky bastard, not for him.

These late Lacanian formulae cannot be mapped directly onto hysteria as stereotypically 'feminine' and obsessional neuroses as stereotypically 'masculine'; this even if these two aspects of neurotic clinical structure are sometimes portrayed as if they simply concern gender, as if they are a new way of comprehending what gender really is (e.g. Kotsko 2008; Pound 2008). Lacan is here refusing the category of gender as a comforting shell of symbolic and imaginary sexual identity to which we might retreat in the face of sex as something real, and he treats that 'real' difference as something that is itself constituted, that cannot be taken for granted as 'man' and 'woman' underneath gender.

The Lacanian psychoanalyst therefore acts in line with an ethical commitment to difference, but a difference as that which is symbolically constituted rather than a difference which is romanticised as if it could be reduced to two complementary identities or substances, places from which each putatively heterosexual subject could admire the other (Neill 2009). When the analyst 'hystericises' the analysand, this is in order to bring the analysand to a point from which they can call into question how they have been brought into being, and although this does play into stereotypical femininity – one in which she, slave, accuses the other conceived of as her master to be dethroned – it is a tactical manoeuvre that we might even liken to the 'strategic essentialism' of postcolonial feminist debate (Spivak 1990). It plays into received images of gender but deepens the critique and auto-critique which is thereby set in motion, deepens the critique so that what she is as slave and what he is as her master are thrown into question, reduced to nonsensical signifiers of sexual difference. The analyst is therefore, among other things, a witness who guides the subject to the real so that this real – sexuation in place of gender – can be traversed, reinterpreted, turned into a different kind of ground on which she can stand and face others.

A therapeutic ethos, on the other hand, is directed to an idea of what is good for the client and is governed by a duty to conform to a rule of law, to underlying presuppositions about what is being withheld and what should be released. The exemplary subject of this law is the therapist themselves, and they are driven to find some way of reducing the encounter between analyst and analysand – a real encounter that Lacanians treat as structured by sexuation, whatever the 'sex' of the analyst and analysand may appear to be – to a relation between two bodies (cf. Samuels 2009). The therapeutic subject aims directly at affect; those who appear to manifest that affect, perhaps by virtue of what they have learnt of their femininity, are idealised, given substance and given a name 'hysteric'. This experience of the other who is expected to emote in therapy, and is such a delightfully perfect human subject when she does so, is constituted through a 'clinical structure' which is configured by the therapist. The therapist identifies with this kind of client and wants to be their partner.

A Lacanian psychoanalytic intervention hystericises the analysand, the master against whom the hystericised subject rebels is thereby at some moments 'masculinised', and so the analyst needs to take responsibility for the effects this position produces. In contrast, the therapist who wants to be the partner of their client, and who thereby organises affect in the clinic around a hysterical clinical structure that they experience as a cluster of emotions they already anticipated before they appeared, is feminised. This therapist is feminised as part of the process of therapeutisation which they feel they must participate in as a command to be a self open to this emotion and have others be like them, hysteric.

The obsessional analyst

The work of a psychoanalyst is defined by enough elaborate procedures of time and record-keeping to turn the practice into something obsessional. The intuitive interpersonal aspects of the work – the encounter with the analysand – are rendered in the popular imagination into something stereotypically feminine even if the analyst does not want to subscribe to those characterisations of the relation that is formed in the clinic. And, around and against this feminine enclosed space even the most Lacanian of psychoanalysts, even when they operate with a theory of sexuation in place of gender, are caught in the minutiae of an apparatus of surveillance and control that is stereotypically masculine. Gender, then, already enters into the definition of what an obsessional dialect of hysterical neurosis is like, of what the obsessional is and what the analyst is who attempts to hystericise the obsessional so that they will start to speak to another instead of attempting to blot the existence of the other out. Lacan's account of sexuation sidesteps this gendered aspect to the man-to-man talk that blocks free association, keeps the analysand locked into their little maze of problems and possible self-made solutions.

Lacan's (1975/1998) 'diagram of sexuation' that accompanies his formulae cues the analyst into curious reversals of difference between 'man' and 'woman' that occur in the clinic. The diagram specifies what 'man' aims at as that which lies at the other side of the divide, woman; the way in which he is something castrated, subject to a cut in power under the rule of the signifier is as a divided, 'barred' subject tied to an object of fantasy, the object a. This interlocking of the barred subject with the object a is, for Lacan, the very formula for fantasy, and so the 'man' in this equation traces the internal shape of a quintessential psychoanalytic subject. If the hysteric is sometimes seen in psychoanalysis as closer to what it is to be a subject as such, this is because she is 'not-all' of psychoanalytic discourse itself but opens the way to something beyond it. The 'woman' who does not 'exist' because she is eccentric to the symbolic order that cannot wholly define what she is has, in Lacan's diagram, two vectors through which she channels her desire: one vector reaches across to the side of the man, to something of the power that he does not even possess himself, phallic jouissance; the other vector takes her to something else, a signifier of the lack in the Other, a place of feminine jouissance.

One direction, toward the man, takes her to an enclosed stereotypically masculine kind of jouissance that an obsessional neurotic would himself like to possess, while the other direction takes her to a more mystical dimension beyond enjoyment that escapes, even as it is conditioned by the symbolic (that which we need to also conceptualise here as heteropatriarchy). This means that when the analyst hystericises what he takes to be an obsessional neurotic he configures himself as semblant of object a, as object of desire that is not actually on the side of the man. There is therefore an ambiguity of sexual position, an ethics of difference at work in the figure of the analyst at this moment which would be sabotaged if it were to be mapped directly onto what we think we know of sex or gender. And indeed it is sabotaged by the therapeutic mutation of psychoanalysis.

We have noted reasons why the analyst might come to adopt the position of the obsessional neurotic, but we are concerned here with why that analyst could then come to experience their analysand as being obsessional, why a therapeutic mutation of analysis would encourage the analyst to attribute that clinical structure to some of those they treat. The therapist is sometimes faced with a client who does not emote as they have come to believe that subjects should, will not anticipate emotion as something that will be readily accessible, as they think it should be; they will do their best, driven by the command to enable all others to be in contact with their feelings, to solicit emotion. In this process the therapist is drawn into rivalry with their client, a rivalry that intensifies the sense the therapist has that they are in the presence of 'resistance', defensiveness that can only indicate that they are faced with what they will come to call an obsessional neurotic.

There is, in feminised therapeutic practice, a retreat to an ideological notion of deep gender, in which stereotypical characteristics of masculinity and femininity are assumed to operate as universal, perhaps complementary 'archetypal' forms of being (Samuels 1985; Austin 2005). When this notion is mobilised in the clinic the stereotypically masculine resistance to therapy comes to be mirrored in a just as intransigent insistence on the part of the therapist that this kind of subject should find their own necessarily imperfect way of being in touch with their feelings. There is then also resistance on the side of the therapist, resistance which configures them as experiential site if not source of the clinical structure of obsessional neurosis.

The psychotic analyst

For Lacan the absence of anchoring points in a discourse considered to be psychotic would be filled by the Name-of-the-Father, and so already the nature of these anchoring points in the discourse is sexed (Sharpe 2006). The Name-of-the-Father provides relief from the mother's 'ravage', an overwhelming suffocating presence in which the subject has no room to breathe, to become a subject as such with their own unconscious. Lacan (1981/1993) broke from Freud's (1911) argument that paranoia was a function of repressed homosexuality, and argued instead that the ego itself was paranoiac in its structure. However, Lacanian descriptions of psychosis are still riddled with culturally-historically negative images of female sex, with the assumption, for example, that there may be an attempt by a subject with psychotic structure to cross the boundary between the sexes in a 'push to the woman' by psychotics of whatever sex (Brousse 2003). It is as if, on the one hand, there is a kind of madness into which the hysteric falls and, on the other, another kind of madness given by an excess of reason, masculine reason.

Lacan (1981/1993: 208) argues that there is a kind of subject, that with psychotic structure, who is 'certain', that 'the unconscious is present but not functioning', that psychosis is a name for 'madness', that this structure manifests itself in language disturbances that include neologisms (cf. Georgaca and Gordo-López 1995). Then there may be what he calls a *'passage à l'acte'* as an act in which the Other is not present to the subject, and here the symbolic is reduced to the imaginary as the realm in which the subject can fabricate an image of what it is to be a normal subject by borrowing and copying from others. So, the question that concerns us now is how a therapist who works with the to and fro of a dialogue, balanced reason in as open and transparent language as possible, a performance of one partner for the other as they try to make each other understood and a clear allocation of roles in the clinic, how this therapist might be made anxious when their assumptions about how things should proceed fall apart. This grounds the claim that the unconscious interprets, 'and especially so in psychosis, since psychosis more than neurosis highlights the structure of the locus of the Other' (Laurent 2008: 90).

There is, first, an assumption at work in therapy that the client is in some way like the therapist, and that the existence of the unconscious gives to dialogue an ambiguous character that can then be reflected upon. For the normal neurotic subject, we are told, there is doubt about what things might mean, and this doubt becomes a fruitful resource for the therapy, it is a kind of doubt in which the therapist feels at home. This assumption then poses a question for a therapist who is faced with certainty, especially so in a therapeutic culture in which there is a moral injunction to reflexively question ideas about the world, and this is one of the defining characteristics of politically-correct speech in the clinic. There is, second, an assumption that this doubt should be managed in a reasonable way, that there are limits which one respects in one's encounters with others. This conception of reason within limits is maintained in the institutional practice of the clinic, especially in a clinic with clear and tidy rules about the beginning and ending of sessions. This assumption poses a question for a therapist who is faced with excess, madness which carries with it hosts of publicly circulating images of barbarism and chaos (cf. Cantin 2009).

Third, there is an assumption that what is said by the client will be understood, and that if there are neologisms, there should not be too many of them, just enough to take the therapist into the realm where they feel they are learning something when the neologism is explained. This assumption poses a question when a therapist is faced with someone whose speech they cannot comprehend, with a subject who does not seem to make sense. Fourth, there is an assumption that the client is a partner who is speaking or acting for another, for the therapist, and an attention to transference will make all speech and action into something directed to them. An attention to countertransference, to the therapist's feelings about the client, will then give access to aspects of the transference that have not already been noticed. This assumption is questioned when they are faced with a client who neither 'acts out', which the therapist understands to be a displaced performance for them, nor 'acts in', where they can see and feel things being enacted for them in the clinic. And, fifth, there is an assumption that therapist and client roles in the clinic are defined such that one does good for the other and the other receives help from their benefactor, even if they pay for it. This assumption is questioned when the client seems to mimic, to replicate, to mirror the way the therapist behaves.

The therapist who feels threatened – threatened by excessive certainty, by excess beyond reason, by a discourse they do not understand, by activity that is not addressed to them or by a client who tries to take their place – might well be driven mad. Then there is indeed a clinical structure to the encounter that is unhelpful for the therapist or for a psychoanalyst who turns into a therapist in the face of something that seems to fall out of the frame of analysis, a clinical structure that we might call psychotic.

The perverted analyst

Lacanian psychoanalysis at one moment opens the way to therapeutic appropriations of the clinic (offering a less judgemental approach than psychiatry and psychology) and at the next draws a clear line between itself and therapeutic culture. This tension, an ambiguity about where our psychoanalysis stands, is nowhere more potent than in the case of 'perversion'. This should not be surprising because this clinical structure is one that leads the subject to disturb and transgress boundaries, including boundaries maintained by the notion of structure itself. We find an ambiguity of position at work in Lacan's insistence that perversion should not be defined by way of particular sexual behaviours, as Freud (1905) would have it, but by way of the subject's orientation to oedipal norms set in place as a precondition for entry to the symbolic. Lacan (1964/1973: 185) defines the pervert as 'the subject who determines himself as object, in his encounter with the division of subjectivity'. A perverted orientation to the law is one that overcomes a normal neurotic conflict with norms, and turns to enjoyment in enactment of the law itself; in this the subject makes himself 'the instrument of the Other's jouissance' (Lacan 2006: 697). Lacan follows Lévi-Strauss (1958/1972) here in seeing Oedipus as the site in which nature is transformed into culture, a structural transformation that makes the human subject into a being that operates at the dialectically-mediated interface of the biological and social, neither one nor the other, ambiguously positioned in 'second nature'.

There is ambiguity in Lacan's position because, unlike the pervert, the analyst will not attempt to enforce norms and bring the analysand to conform to them. To do so would bring the analyst closer to a version of Kantian ethics that all too quickly folds into something more sadistic, which is precisely what attracts a pervert to dutiful implementation of the law (Lacan 1963). So, on the one hand, Lacan saw homosexuality as a perversion insofar as it defied the normative structure laid down by the Oedipus complex; it remains mired in narcissism in which, Freud (1910: 100) argued, the subject 'loves in the way in which his mother loved him when he was a child'. The diagnosis of 'narcissism' is then used within a moral standard to evaluate what is taken to be normal sexuality in the clinic and in the supposed degeneration of contemporary culture (Lasch 1978; cf. Žižek 1986). On the other hand, Lacan accepted analysands he took to be 'homosexual', including into psychoanalytic training, unlike most other orthodox Freudian organisations (O'Connor and Ryan 1993). Lacan's later reformulation of sexual position around sexuation, a real of sexual difference inscribed in the symbolic, rather than in a 'natural' or 'cultural' notion of sex or gender, allows him to circumvent such moral-ideological notions.

The direction of the treatment is more convoluted when the analyst cannot hystericise the analysand by configuring themselves as semblant of object a because the analysand is already attempting to embody that object themselves, when the analysand takes the formula for fantasy – barred subject with object a – and reverses it so that the other is made into a barred subject, one who may then feel anxious at their inability to make sense of what is going on. This reversal, this enactment of fantasy – when the subject becomes the instrument of the Other's jouissance – is the hidden underside of obsessional neurosis; perversion itself is a fantasy of the obsessional against which the normal neurotic defines themselves, a reversal neatly anticipated by Freud's (1905: 165) comment that neuroses are '*the negative of perversions*'. In such cases – instances defined by the direction of the treatment, not by the label attached to a category of analysand – the Lacanian analyst positions themselves, a position prescribed for the analyst in Lacan's early writing, as Other, Other as site of symbolic law for the analysand.

One of the hinge-points between Lacanian psychoanalysis and psychotherapy is where Lacan intimates that the pervert produces anxiety, anxiety in the analyst. This can be treated as a function of the place of the object a – anxiety for Lacan appears with the approach of the object a – and so of the ambiguous place of that object on the side of the analyst at one moment and on the side of the analysand at the next. Lacan (1961–1962), in *Seminar IX* on 'identification', likens the approach of object a to the anxiety felt when one is faced with the desire of the Other (and here he employs the image of the male praying mantis faced with a female who will eat him up after sex). It is an image worth pondering when thinking about why the analyst may be anxious. However, anxiety really becomes important when the psychoanalysis turns into psychotherapy.

It is when there is a slippage back from sexuation to gender that we find ourselves in the Kantian moral universe of psychotherapy, and we can then see why certain kinds of client cause the therapist anxiety so that they then might conclude that they are in the presence of a pervert. Again, we need to keep in mind that many therapists, more so than rather old-fashioned psychoanalysts in this respect, will want to refuse to acknowledge that there is such a thing as a pervert as such. This refusal is precisely where they may be caught unawares, caught when an underlying assumption they have made about perversion captures them, interpellates them as unwitting, even unwilling, converts to the idea that there really is such a thing as a pervert. Notice again the ideological process by which the subject who imagines they are outside ideology is all the more ripe for interpellation by it (Žižek 1989). There are two aspects to this reflexive mutation of psychoanalysis that leads a therapist to be anxious in the face of a certain kind of subject. This is when the emotion displayed by a client seems merely to make instrumental use of the affect the therapist values so much.

The first aspect flows from the therapist's ideological subscription to either 'culture' or 'nature' as that which grounds what they understand gender to be; they often start with a belief that gender is cultural but end up with the assumption that there is a 'deep gender' defined by nature. Clients who disturb that boundary between culture and nature, who seem to want bad things that are uncivilised or unnatural, are liable to cause the therapist anxiety. The second aspect to the therapeutic reflexive mutation of psychoanalysis is a function of the ambiguity of position that the therapist must live with, a function of clinical practice rather than of their own gender identity. As we have noted, on the one hand the therapist is positioned as stereotypically-masculine obsessional manager of their practice and on the other hand as stereotypically-feminine voyager into relationships with clients, and so a client who plays on that ambiguity is likely to cause anxiety. It is little wonder that perversion leads the therapist to make the silent assumption that perversion is the name for something wrong with sex, and they are then – in striking contrast to the Lacanian position of the analyst as Other, as site of symbolic law – positioned as a victim. If the obsessional's fantasy is perverse, the presence of something that is perverse in the clinic then feminises this poor victimised therapist; they must be victimised because they feel themselves to be so.

An ambiguity in Lacan's own discussion of perverse clinical structure makes psychoanalysis susceptible to the contemporary therapeutic inversion of its practice, but there is one respect in which Lacanian psychoanalysis sets itself against any kind of moral endorsement of good conduct in capitalist society. Here we turn to two further reasons why certain kinds of client will make a therapist anxious. While Lacanian psychoanalysis requires a disjunction between the clinic and the outside world, psychotherapy attempts to run the two worlds together. One way of conceptualising this difference between analysis and therapy is to say that the Lacanian clinic is in capitalism but operates as a space *extimate* to it while the therapeutic clinic is a space of capitalism infused by its contemporary forms of subjectification. The therapeutic clinic is enmeshed not only in a moral-political context, one in which there is a duty to reflexively work upon oneself and make all others do the same, but also in a political-economic context in which the labour of the analyst and the analysand gives rise to a surplus – surplus labour which is the source of the therapist's livelihood – labour which structures the therapeutic relation as a class relation.

We are confronted again with a series of ambiguities, and we can note two manifestations here. One ambiguity flows from the nature of class in the clinic, class as a process in which the client works upon themselves but pays another for the privilege, in which a subject who does not want to be alienated addresses a subject who does not seem to be so bothered by it. This is how things look in the clinic with those then viewed as normal neurotics, but the picture is less clear when the client does not seem to resort to accusatory or guilty strategies in response to their alienation. The therapist is then led to confuse class as a substantial identity with class as a process, and when they are faced with a client who does seem to be alienated but without any such identity they are liable to feel anxious. Their name for that kind of client is 'pervert'.

A second ambiguity flows from the class position of the therapist, in which they obey the laws of the market to make a living if they are in private practice, or, in a vicarious but all the more insidious way, if they obey the internal market of a health service but still try to take a distance from the excesses of that particular replication of the economy inside their own institutional home. Because they are good reflexive subjects they adhere to the liberal ethos of neoliberal capitalism and, at the same time, worry about the machinery of exploitation that makes it possible. Some good subjects of capitalism, however, have no such qualms, and seem to obey the injunction to enjoy with relish, seem to enact in their own every-day relationships a version of the fetishism of commodities that defines capitalism as such. And this is also liable to make a therapist anxious, for it brings to the surface their own complicity with a clinical structure they inhabit that is already perverse.

Disjunctions

The psychotherapeutic torsion in contemporary subjectivity invites a form of reflexivity which at one moment opens a space for Lacanian psychoanalysis and at the very next transforms psychoanalytic work into an ideological moralising force compatible with capitalism. Our task, then, is to open that space, and one way to do it is to insist on the importance of *disjunction*. This approach will need to insist upon a disjunction between signifiers and affect, so that we are able to conceptualise how 'feelings' operate by virtue of the names that shape and carry them and are organised into systems of emotion that are culturally-mediated historically-local forms of understanding the self. It will include a disjunction between the individual and the social that is suspicious of psychotherapeutic projects aiming to bring about emotional literacy which then enforce a homogeneous view of what subjectivity is. This theoretical and clinical work must also attend to a disjunction between the clinic and politics so that therapeutic reasoning does not operate in a closed ideological loop to confirm a particular model of the subject. And it will include a disjunction between views of the world so that psychotherapy cannot posit itself as an all-encompassing worldview, as a metalanguage which heals the divisions between different accounts of the world and the subject.

Therapeutic representations of psychoanalysis even (as we saw in the previous chapter) render it into something that seems to be complicit with Marxism, but this supposed complicity is an ideological representation of both psychoanalysis and Marxism that rests on a double-error. The first error is to think that the connection between the two domains of practice – clinical and political – should be broken because each in its own way is authoritarian or inauthentic, and the second error is to believe that psychoanalysis and Marxism are homologous and so descriptions of phenomena in one domain should, if the description is conceptualised correctly, be extrapolated to the other. The first error is one that needs to be addressed in a detailed historical analysis of the way each practice has become captured and caricatured by institutional processes that reiterate what each is actually attempting to unravel. The second error should be addressed as a real political problem, not by simply reclaiming as a virtue what psychotherapeutic reasoning assumes to be true.

We need to conceptualise how psychoanalysis functions as one of the names of peculiar conceptual capsules of the subject produced by capitalism. Marxism does indeed have an interest in the contradictoriness of this subjectivity as a site of ideology and a site of resistance to capitalism, and it is precisely for this reason that there is also a necessary disjunction between the clinic and politics. While the clinic does refract political questions, clinical phenomena cannot be extrapolated to political activity. The question now is whether psychotherapy will triumph as a reaction against a caricature of psychoanalysis or whether psychoanalysis can redeem that connection with Marxism as a revolution in subjectivity that breaks from capitalism.

Chapter 7

Mapping lack in the spirit

Now we explore cultural-spiritual contexts for the development of psychoanalytic conceptions of knowledge, agency and truth. The term 'spirituality' – a potent pre-capitalist conceptual capsule of the subject reactivated today – here describes holistic and redemptive conceptions of religion, the particular formation of individual subjectivity and yearning for personal and social change provoked and blocked by a political-economic system characterised by alienation. The role of Lacanian psychoanalysis as a response to spiritless conditions is critically reviewed, as is the way this version of psychoanalysis enables us to conceptualise 'lack' that spirituality today promises to fill. This account of institutional contexts for the development of psychoanalysis is grounded in clinical practice and in implications of theological conceptions of subjectivity. The appeal of a systematic alternative 'worldview' for psychoanalytic notions of self and other in contemporary culture is condensed in the popularised notion of the repetition of relationships under the sign of 'generalised transference'.

Alienation

In previous chapters we tracked the accumulation of expertise about individual subjectivity, technologies of the self provided by psychiatry, psychology and psychotherapy, and we saw how psychoanalysis re-energised by Lacan's work has tried to disentangle itself from such technologies. It is necessary for Lacanian psychoanalysis as a clinical practice to distance itself from expertise that defines what subjectivity is and closes down the space for it to be something different. As we have seen, each of those specific technologies correspond to particular political-economic arrangements, to historical moments that saw the emergence of capitalism, its flowering and its mutation into forms of neoliberal globalisation in which it often seems as if there is no alternative. It is all the more tempting now for psychoanalysis to bid for a place in the sprawling apparatus of the psy complex that governs even those with apparent expertise about how we should live and love, and sometimes it does indeed do so, unfortunately with some success. Lacanian psychoanalysts are then faced it seems with a forced choice between recuperation, the neutralisation and absorption of their critical energies into contemporary commonsense about the self, and steadfast defiance of representations of the self supposed to be healthy and happy.

While 'subversion' of the subject in the clinic does not release us all from alienated labour under capitalism it does enable us to refuse to adapt to the system that entails alienation. Lacanian work is informed by an ethics of psychoanalysis that is very different from moral ideals, dutiful behaviour or piecemeal redistribution. However, at the same time psychoanalysis is repetitively sucked into ideological processes, and even Lacanian psychoanalysis can be drawn into an endorsement of this world and pathologisation of those who argue that another world is possible. Here the danger is that Lacan's narrative about 'alienation' of the subject which is redoubled and intensified in the trajectory of each of us through imaginary attachments and symbolic bonds that hold families and societies together – alienation that is preserved and transformed in our separation from those who are first other to us – is treated as the end of the story.

This chapter opens out instead to a historical account of the way that alienation of the subject under the rule of the signifier can be mapped into quite distinct forms of exploitation under capitalism, alienation in relation to commodification. There is 'lack' in the subject as a function of alienation and separation at the level of individual subjectivity as Lacan claims, but we have to ask how that 'individual' aspect of subjectivity comes to assume importance under capitalism and how individuals attempt to fill in that lack with different ideological contents such that ideology itself comes to work as the *process* of filling in with these contents rather than being defined with reference to the stuffing itself (Lacan 1986/1992; Žižek 1989).

Lacan shows us that the 'subject' is not a pre-existing complete entity that can be retrieved if all the bad ideological stuff is scraped away, and 'barred subject' is his evocative term that imperfectly renders the empty space we inhabit as we try and fail to represent ourselves to others. The barred subject often appears to non-Lacanians to obscure something that would otherwise be substantial in this empty space and it invites the fantasy that we can find something to complete ourselves, an invitation Lacan describes in the formula of fantasy, barred subject with object a (Benvenuto 1996). There have been a variety of names for the subject under capitalism, names as 'conceptual capsules' of the subject that seem to give it some substance and in which the individual might accomplish at least the illusion of integrity and freedom, a consolation for alienation layered upon alienation. Psychiatry as a first 'scientific' approach to the individual provided names for this conceptual capsule and especially for the possible deviant forms that it might take, and psychology progressively adapted itself to capitalism in its most triumphant and then fragile moments with a constellation of descriptions that promise more 'positive' productive names.

Psychotherapy in recent years has operated as a place in which the names for conceptual capsules of the subject have included 'attachment', 'intersubjectivity' and 'relation', and these themes have chimed with feminist critiques so that a progressive political agenda in therapeutic work at the one moment is sceptical about mainstream psychiatry and psychology and, at the very next, is searching for alternative modes of being and ways of describing it. Psychotherapy suits a conservative normalising agenda for the subject in contemporary capitalism, but it is contradictory, and it is psychoanalysis, specifically Lacanian psychoanalysis, that can attend to those contradictions. This is because Freud names conceptual capsules of the subject in such a way as to intensify contradiction, to enable an intensification of contradiction that is already apparent in the attention to 'ambivalence' beloved of the most adaptable forms of psychoanalysis. The division between consciousness and the unconscious, division in the unconscious and then the naming of the barred subject gives us a conception of 'lack' which is itself unstable, not amenable to the promise of harmonising social relations let alone harmonious self-understanding. This contradictoriness operates in psychoanalysis that circulates in culture in an otherwise ideological way, and this contradictoriness of psychoanalysis that serves to frame how the psychoanalyst works is the main concern of this chapter. This contradictoriness also operates in the clinic and between the clinic and its host culture (matters that I will focus on in Chapter 8).

These different competing names for conceptual capsules of the subject have always pitted themselves against other notions that have at times been characterised as pre-scientific, notions which have survived outside the 'civilised' world, outside the class milieu of 'experts' or as a reservoir of alternative terms for grasping and transcending alienation, notions which we will group together here as 'spiritual' in nature (Kovel 1991). Scientific psychiatry and psychology managed to keep this religious dimension of human experience at bay most of the time, while psychotherapy has been more congenial to an expanded version of what 'religion' amounts to. Feminist interventions in psychotherapy have often drawn on a spiritual sensibility that is in tune with traditionally feminine qualities of embodiment, intuition and transcendence. The politicisation of psychotherapy has often taken place through a combination of spiritual resources and a feminisation of subjectivity that is sometimes also given a feminist slant which is then subversive of psychiatry, psychology and psychoanalysis that operates in a stereotypical masculine manner (Totton 2006).

Spirituality thus provides a different name, the revival of a name for conceptual capsules of the subject which has a double function. On the one side this spirituality conforms to contemporary commonsense, with conceptions of the subject that are ostensibly 'alternative' to those dominant in the psy complex. This spirituality is present not only in the institutional apparatus of mainstream religions and New Age paganism, shamanism,

Wicca and angel therapies, but also in the insurgent redemptive religious movements that have taken the place once occupied by radical political movements (Micklethwait and Wooldridge 2009). To this extent there is contradictoriness to spirituality that is at work even in those forms of it that are now dominant in some communities, and this contradictoriness should already itself be of interest to psychoanalysis concerned with social change (Roberts 2008a). I will focus in a little more detail on the connection between this form of spirituality and feminisation in the second half of this chapter.

On the other side there is spirituality as a call to the subject that is from way outside taken-for-granted reality, a call that assumes form as something traumatic to the subject that is quite close to what Lacanians might conceptualise as 'real'. At the very least, this oppositional spirituality breaks from the symbolic coordinates of capitalist society and the imaginary networks through which the subject is rendered understandable to others. This oppositional spirituality then provides a resource not only for quite different names of the subject but for the process of distancing, refusing, engaging in what Lacan on a few occasions called an 'act' (Neill 2005a, 2005b).

So, now we have two questions. One concerns the way 'lack' comes to operate, increasingly it would seem today, as lack in the spirit. The resurgence of old religious movements and the arrival of some new ones on the scene poses this quite new question to psychoanalysis, one that Lacanians are in a position to answer. It is clearly no longer sufficient to resort to Freud's (1930) wishful historical sequence of the development of civilisation from animism through religion and then to science. The way lack is configured now as lack in spirit calls for historical analysis of the development of forms of subjectivity, of the emergence of psychoanalysis and of how psychoanalysis sensitive to contradiction might intersect with the appeal to something spiritual as salvation, escape from alienation. Speaking of the empty space that sublimation as a process aims to fill, Lacan (1986/1992: 130) points out that '[r]eligion in all its forms consists of avoiding this emptiness'. The other question concerns the extent to which Lacanian psychoanalysis needs to come to terms with its own history with a quite particular dominant notion of spirituality, with Christianity, to disentangle itself from a series of assumptions about the subject that surreptitiously subscribe to ideological conceptions of the social and of subversion of the subject.

The complicity between Lacanian psychoanalysis and Christianity operates through the composition of the apparatus of the school formed after the break with the IPA, in its appeal to particular conceptual lines of work, in the imagery deployed to convey its meaning, in the formal structures elaborated to transmit it, and then by way of the frames retroactively mobilised by some of its supporters. These five aspects – personnel, reference, semiotics, form and devotion – constitute the background against which we might grasp the logic of Lacan's own comments about rival traditions, comments that cannot simply be dismissed as accidental or spiteful side-effects of the split with the IPA (Roudinesco 1990). Hostility to Lacan from inside that organisation for over half a century has been vehement and the sustained personalised attacks on him have sometimes included tendentious suggestions that this form of psychoanalysis is beyond the pale of what Freud and his followers invented as what was once part of a secular Judaic tradition (cf. Wallerstein 1988; Lander 2006). The complaint that Lacan Christianised psychoanalysis has been made before (Green 1995), and adaptation to Christian culture has not, of course, been confined to Lacan's work. Apart from the most obvious early collusion of Jungians with the Christian tradition, one which led Freud (cited in Gay 1988: 241) to be overjoyed when rid of 'the brutal holy Jung and his pious parrots', there have been a number of attempts by analysts inside the IPA to make of the future of illusion an 'illusion for the future', these sometimes taking avowedly Roman Catholic form (e.g. Symington 1990; cf. Coltart 2000).

We need to take seriously the consequences of the Christianisation of psychoanalysis if we are to combat the revival of different kinds of religious fundamentalism and engage with the spiritual yearning through which people express their discontent with contemporary capitalism (including, perhaps, even in Christian liberation theology). That spiritual yearning operates at the fault-line of the subject but simultaneously sutures, seals over the very gap that it symptomatically draws attention to. Psychoanalysis will only be able to break from capitalism if it explicitly breaks, renews its break, with Christianity and for that matter traverses any appeal to divinity as consolation for the subject.

Persons and texts

The first two aspects of this problematic history of Lacanian practice concern the incipient Christianisation of psychoanalysis in France in the 1950s and can be found in the personal composition of Lacan's group and the points of reference mobilised there to 'return' to Freud.

Let us take this question of personnel first, starting with Lacan himself who had his children baptised and dedicated his doctoral thesis on self-punishment paranoia to his Benedictine brother, inscribing it to Marc-François as 'my brother in religion' (Roazen 1996: 324; Pound 2007: 24). Too much might be made of Lacan's own request of his brother that he should arrange an audience with the Pope; he was also keen to meet Mao on his abortive trip to China and had sent his Rome report to the leader of the French Communist Party (Roudinesco 1990: 205). However, the circles Lacan moved in and drew around him as he formed his own school included a good number of priests. Louis Beirnaert, Michel de Certeau and

François Roustang, for example, were three Jesuit Fathers who joined Lacan to create the École freudienne de Paris in 1964, and while the theological predilection of these three is fairly obvious, other key figures in the school were also devout Catholics.

Françoise Dolto who was specifically proscribed by the IPA in 1963 along with Lacan – eventually, after some internal manoeuvring the IPA only named these two as not being permitted to train analysts – turned to the Christian Gospels during her own analysis and thenceforth insisted that the commandment 'love thy neighbour as thyself' indicated a Samaritan ethic through which one comes to help others, this because, she writes in *The Jesus of Psychoanalysis: A Freudian Interpretation of the Gospel*, '[i]t is to oneself, narcissistically projected, that one brings aid' (cited in Slattery 2002: 369). Alienation, for Dolto, consisted of poverty, violence and false regard given by significant others; it blocked compassion for others, for the spirit of 'total openness' (ibid.). This conception of human desire as born from the love of God the creator issues in a psychoanalytic ethics that is underpinned by a sense of the lack of others rather than a moral commandment to do good deeds, and it is possible to divine a logic to Dolto's argument that takes forward Lacan's own exploration of ethics (ibid.: 371).

This does overlook, as does Lacan, that Freud's suspicion of the 'neighbour' to whom the Christian wants us to show love probably has something to do with that neighbour actually at the time Freud was writing being a Christian anti-Semite; why, Freud (1930: 110) asks, should one love one's neighbour when 'he thinks nothing of jeering at me, insulting me, slandering me and showing his superior power'? As he points out a few pages later, 'When once the Apostle Paul had posited universal love between men as the foundation of his Christian community, extreme intolerance on the part of Christendom towards those who remained outside it became the inevitable consequence' (Freud 1930: 114). This neighbour, Lacan (1986/1992: 76) argues, is 'the foundation of the thing' (a pathological disturbing object which Lacan indexes to the mother but later re-elaborates as object a). However, a conception of human desire grounded in a substantial Other is harvested in Catholic fundamentalist readings of Lacan in which love of our neighbour is grounded in the fact that 'our very being is constantly discovered to be mediated through the Other in mutual participation in God's love' (Pound 2007: 99–100).

One can quibble over whether or not Dolto herself is properly Lacanian, even though she was for many years the acceptable and popular face of Lacanian psychoanalysis on French radio, feeding psychoanalytic ideas into the culture (Slattery 2002: 363). In this respect Dolto played a similar role to that of the (Methodist and then Anglican Christian convert) paediatrician Winnicott (1957) in England, whose radio broadcasts re-educated young mothers about what they already knew but with an additional layer of psychoanalytic terminology. Winnicott interviewed Dolto for the IPA panel of investigation into the Lacanian heresy, and judgement on her by the panel seemed to have been less harsh because she was, like Winnicott, a child analyst (Roudinesco 1990). The point is that the Lacanian break with the IPA was to some extent a break that gave voice to a Roman Catholic current inside French psychoanalysis, and the 'return to Freud' can be seen in the wider cultural context of the Jesuit and Dominican *'ressourcement'* – a 'return to sources' – which was, exactly at that same moment of Lacan's formation as a psychoanalyst and formation of his school, seeking to anchor theology back in Catholic Church tradition (Pound 2008: 75; Žižek and Milbank 2009).

This brings us to the second aspect of Christianisation, conceptual reference points Lacan used to return to Freud, and here this return does indeed seem compatible with the *ressourcement* undertaken by Catholic theologians. Aside from the many references to St Thomas Aquinas, St Augustine and St John the Baptist in Lacan's writing, one finds a number of references to the Scholastics (Glejzer 1997). Lacan's characterisation of the attempt by the IPA to prohibit him from teaching as a *'kherem'*, as expulsion from the synagogue just as Baruch Spinoza had suffered three centuries before in Amsterdam, already provides some coordinates for how the work of his new school should be understood. And then Lacan (1964/1973: 3–4) immediately adds another layer of meaning upon this image, one repeated by generations of Lacanian psychoanalysts who refer to this exclusion as an 'excommunication'. This ecclesiastical term evocative of Christian institutional practice also cues us into the fact that Spinoza himself then joined a Christian community, if a fairly liberal one, and so even if the grounds on which he was excluded for heresy are unclear at the time, they did at least become interpretable to the Jewish community after the event.

Lacan's choice of theoretical reference points does not, of course, mean that there is a deliberate mobilisation of a theological apparatus of any kind, let alone an appeal to Christianity as such. However, every choice signals something of the tradition in which Lacan is read whether or not he wanted this to be so. The use of Hegel, for example, does not mean that Lacan really was a Hegelian, though it is possible to read him in that way, and the use of motifs from Hegel like the master–slave dialectic does not in itself mean that Lacan subscribes to Hegel's view that Christianity is the only revealed religion, that in it absolute spirit is revealed to consciousness such that the truth of Christianity can be sublated into absolute knowledge (Vogt 2006).

Kierkegaard's distinction between repetition and recollection is employed by Lacan to embed the emergence of the human subject in the transition from 'the Pagan world' and 'the world of grace, which Christianity introduces' (Pound 2007: 68–69). Even before the emergence of Western science, which forms the subject upon which psychoanalysis operates, there is thus, it is said, another earlier precondition for the practice to be able to work, which is the emergence of Christianity; this is the basis for the claim that 'it is only subsequent to the Incarnation that there can be analysis at all' (ibid.: 153).

Signification and form

We are already straying into the later appropriation of Lacanian psychoanalysis by Christians, but we do need to reflect on why such appropriation should be so plausible, and we can get more of a sense of why Lacan should appeal to this audience if we turn to the next two Christianising aspects of his work: how it is rendered into something meaningful, and the particular arrangement of formal elements.

So, the third aspect concerns imagery that serves to transmit Lacanian psychoanalysis, the semiotic stuff that is transmitted along with the psychoanalysis as such. Biblical imagery is present in Freud's writing, though there is a difference of tone between Freud's rather scathing accounts of religious illusion and his history of monotheism, on the one hand, and Lacan's appeal to biblical motifs ranging from Abraham to St Paul on the other. There is in Freud's (1930) writing what might now be seen as a 'supersessionist' account of the development of civilisation – there is animism before religion and then there is science as the nearest thing that psychoanalysis comes to as a worldview – and this classical Freudian account provides the bare bones which Christians can then flesh out, and, it would seem, Lacan does. In some of his earliest writings on the decline of the paternal imago and the resulting problem of suffocating ravage at the hands of the mother, Lacan provides an account of the figure of the father which plays into Christian imagery. This provides grounds for the claim that even in Freudian psychoanalysis before Lacan there is a 'truth of Christianity (and not Judaism)', that 'to enter social life one must pass through the dead father' (Pound 2007: 2). This is before the 'Name-of-the-Father' is erected as a principle which the subject must encounter as they enter the symbolic, a principle that is more redolent of the New Testament than the Old (cf. Reinhard and Lupton 2003: 82).

The entry into language is then configured as castration of a very different kind than that described by Freud. It is no longer the threat or fear of actual castration – one which, Freud points out, is potent in Christian anti-Semitic responses to circumcision – but castration as cut into illusory fullness, plenitude of the subject, perhaps even the plenitude of God's love (Pound 2007). Then there is a quite different relation to the flesh as an ethical question, and the stance the subject takes to their castration under the rule of the signifier is configured in terms of a suffering that accords well with that of suffering Christ on the Cross. This imagery plays out in at least three ways in Lacanian psychoanalysis. First there is a conception of passion under the cut of the signifier, in which the lack of being in language is a fall, if not a fall from original grace then a fall from a condition of non-being as such (Shingu 1995/2004). The psychotic is then viewed as suffering in a different way, as seeking redemption through delusional constructions, and becomes paradigmatic of the subject who makes of their symptom a '*Sinthome*', for which one of the homonyms is 'saintly man' (Thurston 2002). Second, there are images of the analyst as a saintly figure, one whose desire is purified, as the one who pays with their body for the form of martyrdom that comes with being used by the other. Elsewhere, Lacan described the analyst as a monk, 'a solitary being, who in past times ventured out into the desert' (cited in Roazen 1996: 328; cf. Pound 2007: 24). At the end of analysis, one Christian account of Lacanian practice by an Episcopal priest has it, 'the analyst as saviour dies; the saviour dies, often crucified on the bitter invective of the frightened, disappointed analysand who had come seeking salvation and found only another human being who shares his or her very fate' (Hackett 1982: 191).

Third, there is introduced into psychoanalysis mysticism adverted to as site of jouissance beyond phallic enjoyment for those on the side of woman in Lacan's diagram of sexuation. To say that this jouissance is sexual, that St Teresa portrayed by Bernini is 'coming', actually shifts the emphasis from a classical pre-Lacanian Freudian account of religious desire fuelled by dissatisfaction of the drive to an account of sexual enjoyment as itself in some way arriving at mystical pleasure in pain, something beyond the subject. That this imagery should also connect with what is supposed of 'feminine enjoyment' grounds this peculiarly Christian account in a patriarchal society which distributes masculinity and femininity between mind and flesh – Adam's mastery of reason as phallic in contrast to Eve's subversive feminine concupiscence – and then, in an ideological reversal of this opposition which operates in tandem with it, between body and spirit where manly focused phallic jouissance is transcended by feminine encounters with the divine (Barnard and Fink 2002).

This gives to hysteria a double-function: as that which refuses inscription into the symbolic and sends a message to the Other directly from the body – the task of analysis being to put this bodily communication into words – and as that which refuses to dirty itself with what is required of the woman in sex in favour of more refined pursuits. Psychoanalysis has traditionally responded by seeing its aim as restoring to the woman what the analyst imagines to be a happy and fulfilling sexual relationship. In one Lacanian Christian argument by a Marist priest 'only males – like Jesus – can represent God's active paternity in the world' (Dalzell 2004: 12; cf. Watson 2009). The notion that there is some other place, another world that is possible for the subject in her mode of enjoyment, then gives way to struggles for liberation as encounter with alienation that would refuse the way it is materially instituted in capitalist society; these would be struggles which invite a connection between femininity and redemption. This is in some ways, it is true, subversive but at the same time it replicates stereotypical representations of femininity and masculinity (and we will return to these matters of the cultural inscription of psychoanalytic knowledge in the second part of this chapter).

There is Christian stuff aplenty in the imagery mobilised by Lacan, but it is worth spending a moment taking account of the fourth aspect of Christianisation in his work, which is to be found in formal elements upon which this stuff is fleshed. The arrangement of formal elements in Lacanian theory, particularly when it starts to operate as a worldview rather than as a guide to clinical practice, is actually more insidiously Christian, and has encouraged theological readings of Lacan which work on the assumption that his is a hermeneutic psychoanalysis, which it is not (Laplanche 1996; cf. Ricoeur 1965/1970).

We can trace this through three popular motifs in Lacan's work, and then see how it plays out in attempts to reinterpret his return to Freud as also giving the good news about Christ. It has been noted, first, that there is an evocation of the Trinity of Father, Son and Holy Ghost in the triad of symbolic, imaginary and real, three registers held together by the Borromean knot as a formal structure (Ragland and Milovanovic 2004). One could argue that Freud too employed such tripartite models, but this formal structure resonates with Christian imagery through its intersection with other elements in Lacan's work. So, this Borromean linking of the three registers needs to be set in relation to Lacan's account of the Other, of that in whose gaze and for whom one is a subject, the Subject supposed to know, and that in whom other subjects are supposed to believe (Shingu 1995/2004). The place of the subject that this formal arrangement of elements evokes is not then directly filled with content – God as Other, for example – but is suggestive of the answer each subject may give to the question they are posed by a symbolic already suffused with Christian imagery, 'Christian good news, the incarnation, real presence or Eucharist, the passion, the resurrection', which is incited in the televisual globalisation of religion which is 'at the same time a "globalatinization" of the very concept of religion' (Derrida 2001: 58–59); this Vogt (2006: 28) glosses as 'the fundamentally Christian character of mediatization'.

Third, there is a distinctive twist to Freud's (1933: 181–182) vision of psychoanalysis as attached to an enlightened scientific worldview, but as not providing a worldview itself as such, as 'too incomplete', making 'no claim to being self-contained'. There is a mutation in Lacanian writing of the place of psychoanalysis within the Western Enlightenment tradition into a warrant for a new form or a new gesture towards universality. Here, perhaps, there is again something of the influence of Hegel, for whom Christianity is the apogee of theological development in civilisation that provides the possibility for transcending religion as such in favour of absolute reason; 'what is revealed in Christianity is not just the entire content, but, more specifically, that *there is nothing* – no secret – *behind it to be revealed*' (Žižek 2003: 127). It is then not such a stretch to find in Lacan intimations of St Paul; the way Lacan constructs 'the human pilgrimage in the hermeneutical circle of psychoanalysis can be correlated with Paul's concepts of sin, law, gospel, and the Kingdom of God' (Hackett 1982: 189); and 'the inner life of God [is] revealed in the beautiful form of Christ' (Dalzell 2004: 4). Sin is seen as corresponding to the misrecognition that occurs during the mirror-stage and 'the anxiety of the imaginary corresponds to the anxiety of death'; though we are destined to live under the law it announces a wholeness that is quite unachievable, not at least until the arrival of the Kingdom of God. The Gospel then stands in 'correlation' with insight in analysis, 'that the Law can neither save nor can it be dispensed with, the insight that the fundamental fault is an unavoidable part of human existence' (Hackett 1982: 191).

Devotion and contestation

Overblown and wishful though such accounts of Lacanian psychoanalysis might be, they do draw attention to Christian elements of Lacan's work that are then mined further and elaborated by some later Lacanians. This brings us to the fifth aspect of Christianisation, a devotion to his work that emphasises and exaggerates spiritual motifs. This *ressourcement* is motivated and contested, and we need to know how this field of argument works if we are to find another secular path to the revolution in subjectivity that Lacanian psychoanalysis promises; there is an institutional aspect to this question that goes beyond, even despite the intentions of those involved; it is, for example, significant perhaps that one of the few psychology departments in the US to welcome Lacanian psychoanalysis – in which the translator of the English edition of Lacan's (2006) *Écrits* is based – is hosted by the Congregation of the Holy Ghost (Smith 2002).

In some cases the turn of the already spiritually-minded to Lacan is quite patently instrumental, and psychoanalysis is seen as a useful vehicle for spreading the good news. In self-styled 'radical orthodoxy' interventions, for example, Lacan is seen as providing a good opportunity for insinuating a Christian message into contemporary commonsense (Žižek and Milbank 2009). It is precisely because Lacan does now to some extent chime with dominant ideological motifs that his own return to Freud is seized upon by some fundamentalists. (In this itself there should be some grounds for caution in a simple 'application' of Lacanian psychoanalysis outside the clinic, in the hope that circulating Lacanian critique in popular culture will necessarily be subversive.) The argument there is that Lacan's 'postmodern' variation on psychoanalysis 'provides the most coherent language' to 'communicate the mystery of transubstantiation within our cultural milieu'

(Pound 2007: xiii); we therefore, it is said, need to appreciate how 'the liturgy of the Eucharist is analogous to analysis' because it facilitates 'subjective reflection upon the truth' (ibid.: 155).

A return to medieval roots of Christianity is designed to circumvent the Franciscan John Duns Scotus's false separation of the worlds of theology and science. We are then also back to the supersessionist motif that Catholic theologians wriggle around but eventually endorse, which is that there is a key progressive historical shift from Judaism to Christianity; one marked by Thomas Aquinas as the shift from a religious worldview in which the truth of God is as yet deficient – that is, Jewish 'old law' – to one in which it is superabundant, in which the sacrament must function as a kind of filter for those subject to 'new law' who would otherwise be blinded by the truth; 'Aquinas situates religion on the side of the symbolic and God on the side of the real' (Pound 2008: 63). In this line of argument there is always to be found a supersessionist narrative of the development of civilisation which privileges Christianity (but which stops short of Hegel's next step which would transcend religion itself) (Vogt 2006).

It is said in this line of work that 'only a Christian can be properly anxious', and that 'God's call is the very calling of our freedom' (Pound 2007: 99). God becomes the 'arch-analyst', and 'the Sacred Mass' is seen as 'a social form of analysis' (ibid.: 142). If Christ's death on the Cross is treated as the first unassimilated trauma, already a big 'if', the Eucharist can be seen as the second trauma that resonates with and reconfigures the first trauma; the shock of realising that one is actually eating the body and drinking the blood of Christ re-activates the full horror of the crucifixion, just as someone in analysis replays and relives in transference a traumatic encounter with significant others that enables them to repeat the experience in such a way as to receive everything back anew (Pound 2007: 164).

There is a surreptitious slippage here from the domain of psychoanalysis as a practice that takes place in a particular site, the clinic, to analogical processes of enlightenment that take place elsewhere and that can be understood or reframed in psychoanalytic terms. There is the little matter of the institutional site for this conception of the Christian liturgy, 'Church', as akin to psychoanalysis as quasi-Lacanian Christian devotees themselves point out; it is said that Freud failed, and that only Christianity is able 'to bring together the social and the private in the community' as 'the necessary precondition of real therapy' (Pound 2007: 170).

A slightly different line of argument in the retroactive Christianisation of Lacan aims not so much at the smuggling in of a Christian message – at the convenient fit between Christianity, Lacan and currents of popular culture – but at the radical division that Lacan as Christian might open in an 'act' that would disturb the symbolic coordinates of capitalist society. Here the end of analysis is seen as a moment of subjective destitution in which the subject is able to wipe the slate clean and begin again. This requires a reading of Lacan that replaces the negative moment in psychoanalysis – castration, cut of the signifier, retroactive constitution of a supposed original access to jouissance – with a real fullness of being from which we have fallen. Lacan's 'subject of the enunciation' is then characterised as corresponding to the real as if it were something of substance.

This shift from an adaptationist to a disruptive Christianisation of Lacan is to be found in its most striking form in Slavoj Žižek's interventions, and we need to keep distinct here two domains in which his interventions appear (Parker 2004). Žižek's (2002: xviii) Lacanian reading of Hegel is designed to connect with a conception of the 'act' as radical break and disturbance of symbolic coordinates, including the symbolic coordinates that are taken for granted in bourgeois democracy. This is still, even if it is revolutionary rather than adaptationist, aimed at the domain of culture, specifically at debates taking place in alternative intellectual and political movements. Although it is not merely instrumental in nature it does aim to key into current concerns, current debates, current levels of political consciousness and circulating motifs. It connects political change with transformation of the subject but it does not pretend to inform clinical practice, which is treated as a completely separate domain. It is right to restrict its intervention to this cultural sphere, but that intervention does then also have consequences for the way analysands and analysts engage in clinical work.

Christianity even so then provides an account of the kind of decision that must be taken to impel revolutionary politics forwards, to break with the old and open the way to the new, 'a militant, divisive position . . . that enthuses' (Žižek cited in Vogt 2006: 14). This break would then also repeat an earlier historical break marked by Pauline Christianity in relation to its Judaic origins, and the promise is that this Christianity 'effectively replaces truth in the All with a truth *for* the All'. Žižek thus participates in a messianic line of radical politics alongside Alain Badiou (2003) and Giorgio Agamben (2005) in which communism as a movement that abolishes the present state of society operates as 'a form of *suspensive revolutionary consciousness*' (Roberts 2008b: 97).

There are two assumptions at work in this argument, that Christianity fuels a Lacanian revolutionary 'act'. One assumption concerns the nature of a decision as something available to consciousness and as a model for political activity that can be extrapolated from the clinic or elaborated in such a way that it then informs how an act takes place in the clinic. The other assumption concerns the way 'truth' appears in the act in relation to 'all', as an exceptional but universalisable 'act'. With respect to the first assumption, we are in the domain of a rich and bitter seam of Lacanian commentary on the act which usually revolves around the refusal of Antigone to obey Creon's edict that she should not perform burial rites for her brother. One key question is whether this 'act' is a decision as such, and another is whether it functions as 'act' by virtue of what others will understand it to be (Pluth 2008). In either case, in either question, it is not clear that Lacan intended the notion of 'act' to extend beyond human action as such, even though he did refer to the analytic act later as something more specific and dramatic; Lacan's (1964/1973) middle-period comments on the 'act' are usually as human action, not as something especially dramatic, though later he does specify that a 'psychoanalytic act' turns analysand into analyst (Lacan 1967–1968). One cannot simply extract the notion from Lacan's clinical work, and to import an elaborated version of it into the clinic would entail the destruction of clinical space as concerned with formal elements rather than ideological contents.

With respect to the second assumption, we have to again separate ourselves from the domain of the clinic in which each act or decision of the analysand is taken subject by subject on a case-by-case basis. Whether or not the act is undertaken by an individual, there may or may not be a connection with the 'universal', that is, there is no necessary opposition between individuality and universality. Lacanian psychoanalysis opens the way to the emergence of a different kind of subject not bound by the norms of bourgeois democracy, a subject who is at one and the same moment engaged in a process of revelatory change that is simultaneously individual and universal. This possibility (which brings Hegel into the equation) again is actually one of the most progressive of Žižek's interventions, and there are clinical consequences; the enlightenment that the analysand attains is not characterised as atomised and peculiar to them, does not become crystallised in cynicism about the possibility that others may change too.

Lacan does provide some coordinates for this possibility, not directly in Hegelian terms, but in the formulae of sexuation in which the side of woman is not-All – she is included in the symbolic but something of her escapes it – and this in contrast to the side of man who operates as an 'exception', in the fantasy that there is one who escapes the symbolic – Freud's father of the primal horde exempt from the law and who enjoys all the woman – and with whom one may identify in consolation for one's castration. The logic of this masculinist exception is, of course, that revolutionary change in the clinic may be conceptualised as some kind of escape, and this plays into the most alluring of bourgeois fantasies that one can step outside ideology, an ideological fantasy *in extremis* (Žižek 1989).

This returns us to antinomies, irreconcilable oppositions in Lacan's account of the act in psychoanalysis and politics, and to the pretence that there can be a direct connection between those two domains. Lacan's examples of those characters who undertake an 'act' are invariably women, and insofar as they accomplish an act as an individual, against the polis, they stand at the one moment on the side of exception and at the next on the side of universality, at the one moment on the side of man and at the next on the side of woman (Copjec 1993; Hook 2009). Those who 'act' in

Lacanian psychoanalysis are intimately enmeshed in categories of gender, and the redemptive act of those seeking a way to challenge and change the symbolic may end up tying spirituality and femininity close together. The Christianisation of Lacanian psychoanalysis then becomes closely linked to the feminisation not only of psychotherapy as a dominant ideological form of contemporary capitalism but also of psychoanalysis that tries to step out of this capitalism and find a way to create another world; in one feminist Lacanian formulation which pertains to women *and* men, 'the assumption of one's own femininity implies, along with the recognition of sexual difference, the acknowledgement of the loss of mythical completeness, the assumption of that symbolic castration that . . . marks the culmination of the analytical treatment' (Mieli 2000: 274).

Secularism and the state

Lacan charged the IPA with turning psychoanalysis into an adaptationist mechanism, one suited to free-enterprise capitalism in the United States as a model for how each individual should be happy and healthy around the world. Adaptation to the state, becoming a good citizen, went hand in hand with adapting oneself to an image of the individual, with the consequence that even resistance to the state would be conducted in such a way as to ratify individuality as the ideal shape of subjectivity. Lacan's formulae of sexuation unravel this model of each ego as exception and they introduce the possibility that there is another form of subjectivity that is universal precisely because it is extimate to the symbolic, not-All of it. That this other form of subjectivity should be tied to prevalent images of femininity needs to be addressed if we are to disentangle ourselves from some powerful ideological motifs (and we will turn to that task in the second part of this chapter). There is, however, already another problem that we need to address first, which is the way that Lacanian psychoanalysis adapts itself at one moment to the dominant Christian culture and at the next to a form of secularism that reinforces the very Christianity it pretends to avoid. We can unpick the peculiar shape of this problem, a side-effect of the Christianisation of psychoanalysis we have traced so far, by considering the way psychoanalysis positions itself in relation to 'other' religions (including Christianity as other to itself under capitalism, divided into Catholic and Protestant forms that do not directly map onto progressive and reactionary political traditions).

Lacanian psychoanalysis around the world has often adapted itself to different religious systems, and the forms of argument used to frame clinical work range from Christianity in Ireland (e.g. Dalzell 2004) to Buddhism in Japan (e.g. Shingu and Funaki 2008) to versions of New Age spirituality in Israel (e.g. Golan 2006). There is some serious scholarship on the intersection between Lacanian theory and Judaism (e.g. Reinhard and Lupton

2003), but the supersessionist narrative that positions Christianity as historically more advanced is powerful and carries worse in its wake.

Despite the generous defences of Lacan against the charge of anti-Semitism, for example in terms of the argument that he was nasty about everyone and did not single out the Jews in particular for contempt (Roudinesco 1990), there are some unpleasant eruptions of spite against the IPA that are then condensed into complaints about Judaism by Lacan that are indicative if not symptomatic of a problem. Lacan's 'Proposition of 9 October 1967 on the psychoanalyst of the school', for example, includes the appalling factually incorrect claim that 'the I.P.A. of Mittel Europa has demonstrated its preadaptation to this trial [of "common markets" and "the process of segregation"] in not losing one single member in the said [concentration] camps' (Lacan 1967/1995: 12). Between the 1938 and 1949 IPA congresses there was a sizeable loss of members, mostly victims of the Nazis (Frosh 2005). Lacan's comment has been defended and reframed as an argument that 'the religion of the Jews' should be questioned in the analytic movement on three points: that the 'Jewish religion' stresses the unity of God the Father, that there is 'strong identification in its existence as community', and that it incarnates 'the place of segregation' (Bassols 2002: 120–121). An analysand with Lacan for thirteen years acknowledges that Lacan's argument in the first version of the 1967 proposition – that 'the religion of the Jews must be questioned within our hearts' – was a call for searching enquiry but 'came to be understood as an unbearable hostility towards Judaism', and even suggests that Lacan was pointing to deals that were made between the IPA and the Nazis in which it was agreed that the German Society be cleansed of the Jews; 'Lacan showed a great deal of courage regarding this affair, which probably resulted in his expulsion from the I.P.A.' (Haddad 1994: 211).

The intersection between representations of religious difference and gender then produces some surprising twists to the way Lacan is mobilised. For example, Catholic 'feminist' writing – which, in some variants, included warrant for anti-Semitism – has been tactically mobilised in a reading of Lacan's formulae of sexuation in order to set up an opposition between 'the Jewish God [which] conforms to the structure of masculinity' and Christianity as 'the religion of love' (Pound 2008: 114).

Contemporary French secularism tolerates Christianity and Judaism insofar as they confirm the character of French society, but now pits itself against Islam as threat. On occasion Islam is then seen as throwing up obstacles to psychoanalytic practice (e.g. Bennani 2008). In more open readings, this then seeps into characterisations of Islam as that in which 'the Cogito of Arab culture' is 'organised by Writing' and as that which operates through revelation that aims to open 'a window onto the real' (Maucade 2009: 6–7). While this characterisation evokes without directly spelling out what this might entail in terms of psychotic structure, it is of a piece with the claim that in this religious system God does not have a paternal function and it opens a window onto one of the most pervasive representations of Islam, the veiled woman (Benslama 2009a).

The veil, it is said, is 'that which makes woman into a sign', and this then poses a particular kind of enigma for man in which woman 'presents herself as already *knowing* the truth of the Other' such that 'man must pass through the feminine operation of veiling-unveiling in order to *re-cognise* the sign in itself, and thus to gain certitude of this Other' (Benslama 2009b: 19). This Lacanian exploration of Islam challenges French secularist Islamophobia for sure – it questions the attempt by secularists to stop women wearing the veil as enacting the 'prohibition of prohibitions' which is of a piece with 'the identitarian myth of the modern West' – but in doing so it once again idealises femininity; here, this assertion combined with citation of Lévi-Strauss's lament that Islam came between Christianity and Buddhism and so prevented a '"harmonious collaboration"' between West and East, and blocked Christianity from returning to its sources such that 'the West lost the opportunity of remaining female', is quite ambiguous (Benslama 2009b: 25). Lévi-Strauss's formulation is described as 'the most limpid utterance of the identitarian mytheme of the West', but it confirms at the very moment it displays – veils in stereotypical gender at the moment it unveils sexist imagery – the shape of the problem. The diagnosis of a predicament of the West then re-inscribes femininity as a way out, re-inscribes femininity within the problem as if it could be the solution to the problem.

Separation

Lacanian clinical practice has already been put to work to differentiate authentic Christian faith from inauthentic attachments to figures of authority or to religious ideals (Roudinesco 1990). In this work the stakes are, we may be tempted to say, 'transferential'; they are revealed in the production of transference neurosis and worked through so that the subject is able to clarify what their desire as desire of the Other amounts to, whether that desire of the Other is really that of God. In this endeavour Lacanian practice is not alone, and there have been attempts in other psychoanalytic traditions to discern whether religious belief is underpinned by a wish, whether it is operating as an illusion or not, and this then aims (here expressed in Winnicottian vein) to weed out 'the belief of the child or the theologically naïve' (Meissner 1990: 110–111). Those who are driven by wishes relating to infantile relationships are, if you take this seriously, those who turn to God for the wrong reasons, as in the case of 'the naïve believer, whose God-representation is determined in large measure by the transferential derivatives from parental figures' (ibid.).

It is then tempting to expand the remit of psychoanalysis to try to discover such 'transferential derivatives' in the circulation of religious ideas in culture, and then we are in the domain of psychoanalytic social theory which usually entails the application of psychoanalysis to cultural phenomena. It may be the case, say, that most religious worship is driven by the attempt to return to infantile relationships, and it is assumed that psychoanalysis might then have something useful to say about this problem, to clarify it and open the way to either authentic faith or authentic scientific belief.

However, Lacan had a distinctive theory of transference that precludes such interpretation of the attachments of believers, and here we can see one important reason why Lacanian psychoanalysis cannot and should not be 'applied' to social phenomena. We can also see why some other forms of psychoanalysis lend themselves to such an application, why they feed psychoanalytic motifs in culture and how they then carry with them ideological specifications of femininity and masculinity. Lacanians are not immune from the evangelistic fervour that seems to grip practitioners and followers seeking to apply their ideas and spread the good news about the unconscious, but we can find in Lacan's account of transference in the clinic a sharp separation between this peculiar space and social transformation, a separation that is also, among other conceptual reasons I rehearse here, necessary to prevent it from turning into a cult which pathologises dissent (Gellner 1985; Leitner 1999).

Transference of feeling

Freud (1915b) argued that transferences are 'facsimiles' of fantasies of the analysand given new life and new objects, and we have already noted in previous chapters that attention to these facsimiles was later complemented in some accounts by what were termed the 'countertransference' responses of the analyst (Heimann 1950). Debates over the nature of countertransference have revolved around whether it is just another name for the analyst's transference, whether it is what is provoked in the analyst by the analysand's transference, whether it is an aspect of the transference that includes analyst and analysand, or whether it provides a means for accessing the unconscious of analyst and analysand (Sandler *et al.* 1979).

Countertransference has come to assume immense importance in many psychoanalytic traditions, and for some it promises to level out the relationship between analyst and analysand, to democratise the relationship so that it is clear that both partners are subject to the effects of transference. Countertransference then gives to transference itself a particular hue, and it opens the way to a blurring of boundaries between analyst and analysand, to the sharing of what each 'feels' (Hinshelwood 1997; cf. Palomera 1997). The transference relationship then treats what the analyst feels as a source of knowledge and it encourages the analyst to be more open to the analysand so that the analysand will feel respected and, perhaps, empowered by the disclosure made by one human being to another. This is the course taken by 'interpersonal', 'intersubjective' and 'relational' currents in psychoanalysis which have grown in importance in recent years and (as we will see in the next chapter) have promised to connect the personal and the political domains in clinical practice (Layton *et al.* 2006).

There is a danger in the clinic that this conception would activate a fantasy of a relation between two bodies and this may even be one reason why therapists are so bothered by the importance of boundaries and then why they are susceptible to the lure of a 'dual relationship' by which they can break through those boundaries to something they think is more authentic. Psychoanalysis, in contrast, is an ethics of speech, and Lacan's formulae of sexuation drive home the fact that the task of symbolising what divides analyst from analysand is never-ending, impossible to bypass with some transient gratification of what one feels one wants of the other; '[t]he two of sexual difference is a metaphor for the two of the analytic situation, and the two of the analytic situation is a metaphor for the sexed couple (that is *not* necessarily hetero-sexed)' (Dhar 2009: 170).

It is not surprising that a relational conception has appealed to some feminist psychotherapists, for the connection with femininity expresses yearning for connection with others at a deep, apparently most fundamental level of the constitution of the subject under capitalism as a gendered subject. This subject is torn between, on the one side, the masculinised imperative to operate within a binary logic of domination and subordination with its experiential corollaries of obedience and guilt, and on the other side, the feminised collusion with or escape from society which reinstates its own particular forced choice between being and meaning. This separation into two categories of subject – those named 'obsessional' and 'hysteric' in psychoanalytic conceptual capsules of the subject present in capitalism since the beginning of the twentieth century – pathologises femininity as a site of feeling, and then this site can be re-valued and treated as a site of rebellion against patriarchy in the production of feminist counter-discourse (Mitchell 1974; Foucault 1977).

The emergence of a version of feminist discourse in psychotherapy, and to an extent in psychoanalysis, has accentuated attention to feeling and what can be known of it in countertransference, and this has also resonated with the sense that femininity is also a form of access to the divine. This quasi-spiritual sensitivity is not necessarily compatible with organised religion. Religions provide their own false solutions to the contradictions of capitalism, solutions that are 'falsely conscious' of the dominant or subaltern realities they subscribe to. That is, they mimic such realities and adapt the subject to a version of capitalism or to a version of it that operates as if it is the reverse of it, the mere obverse of it.

Lacanian critique of the concept of countertransference – that it is part of transference as a series of signifying operations rather than feelings underneath representation – avoids the appeal to something that is the mere obverse of transference, a fantasmatic lure into ideology masquerading as truth. This critique can actually bring us closer to feminism as a political practice at the very moment it leads us away from idealised femininity in the clinic.

Transference of signification

Lacanian psychoanalysis, as we have noted through the course of this book, concerns itself with the signifying operations through which human beings come to be positioned in relation to each other and through which they struggle to position themselves. For Lacan, transference is defined by the repetition of signifiers, those that will be of specific value to the analysand and which appear in their speech as they produce a representation of themselves to the analyst; those that appear and reappear in the language of the analysis and that include signifiers introduced into the analysis by the analyst as well as the analysand (cf. Lacan 1960–1961). The analyst of whatever stripe will unwittingly introduce their own signifiers into the matrix of each analysis, and the writing of case notes and discussion during supervision enable these signifiers and their function in the analysand's speech to be noticed and tracked. Take the rather unusual case of a psychoanalyst still in thrall to some kind of religious faith. Lacanian practice maps the way 'lack' is articulated in the signifying operations that constitute the session, including the way spiritual concerns arise in such a way as to fill that lack; our practice does not appeal to 'spirit' or any other numinous experience to plug the gaps in the matter of the practice, speech (Riha 2003).

We have noted that this approach to transference is materialist insofar as it attends only to the actual signifiers and their position in relation to the system of signifiers in the analysis, and this is why the analyst tries to avoid appeal to a domain of feelings hidden beneath the signifiers (or inside the analyst in a separate domain of countertransference). There is no recourse to a 'metanarrative' that would provide a point of escape from their effects (or a place from which the transference could be interpreted to the analysand who remains trapped within it) (e.g. Guéguen 1995; Soler 1996b).

This means that whatever ideological gloss has been layered upon psychoanalysis outside the clinic – and this gloss includes the Christianising of Lacanian psychoanalysis as well as any other attempt to reconfigure Freudian theory as part of a political 'worldview' – its practice questions and refuses any such metanarrative or their seductive surreptitious appearance as feelings about this or that ideological motif. This also means, of course, that the masculinised analyst of whatever sex – cast into a masculine position as master however much they also incarnate the semblance of object a to hystericise the analysand – does not either confuse their analytic knowledge with feminine intuition or imagine that they are feeling what their hystericised feminised analysand of whatever sex is feeling (Samuels 2009). We try not to fall into the ideological separation and sedimentation of gender categories, however much the 'feminine' seems to have been subjugated in patriarchal society and however radical it might seem to idealise and to identify with that feminine other as an act of political resistance; we do not do this inside, and should not do so outside, the clinic.

This radical disjunction between the sexes has something in common with Kantian antinomies as conceptual oppositions that cannot be dialectically resolved, transcended through a sexual rapport in which each sex recognises the other. It can be read in line with the performative account of sexual difference offered by 'queer' theorists and activists. That twist in third wave feminism outside the clinic can provide some inspiration and breathing space for Lacanian psychoanalysis inside it (Watson 2009; Worthington 2008).

Applications

Psychoanalytic vocabulary has seeped into psychiatrised, psychologised and then psychotherapeutised accounts of individual and social activity in everyday life. As far as the 'application' of psychoanalysis is concerned, we need to contend with the way contemporary psychologisation invites the researcher to interpret and touch a real world of their fantasy 'outside' their own enclosed institutional setting (De Vos 2008). Here appears what I term 'generalised transference' used by analysts positioned as academics, whether or not they are actually writing inside an academic institution, commenting upon the networks of relationships and investments in relationships, phenomena that they detect in others. This generalised transference operates as a pathologising account in which the position of the researcher is cunningly excluded, and so this psychoanalytic research is conducted as if it were a metalanguage. This is not to say that inclusion of the researcher or theorist in the account would necessarily be a better option, for 'counter-transference' also often functions as an alibi for reflexivity in academic work bewitched by transference (Frosh and Baraitser 2008).

In his few forays into the analysis of group processes and cultural phenomena, Lacan elaborates specific concepts – logical time and social bonds – without ever applying 'transference' to these extra-psychoanalytic phenomena (Lacan 1946b, 1991/2007). The most sophisticated Lacanian social theory utilises a number of concepts from the clinic, elaborates them as part of a generative reflexive Hegelian account of the production of subjective phenomena, without attempting to find 'transference' between social actors outside the clinical setting. Even the 'unconscious' need not be supposed to exist outside the clinic (Nasio 1998; Voruz 2007). We find in Žižek's work, for example, a reworking of certain Lacanian categories –

drive and desire, the subject supposed to know, the big Other – derived from a Lacanian reading of Hegel, but even these categories are not 'applied' as such, and are treated instead as determinative conceptual devices to open up cultural phenomena, usually to read them finally in Marxist terms (Žižek 1989, 2009). The case of clinical structures is a little more complex, and there are some suggestive possibilities in Žižek's (2000b) characterisation of different political systems in terms of such apparently mental structures; they are ideas that may even illuminate what we make of someone appearing to exemplify them when they walk into the consulting room (cf. Lindner 1955/ 1986; Kovel 1981). However, we should treat these as metaphorical elaborations of concepts that take a quite different form in the real world.

This real world is already inhabited and organised by the dimensions of subjectivity that those Freudian clinical structures name. So we need to attend to the way we, as analysts, are implicated in the structures we all too often think we simply name, that we also along the way inject with our own contents. Our own position as structured subject, as subject inhabiting discourse, is now configured in such a way as to make it amenable to a psychoanalytic reading. We have already drawn attention to the way that stereotypical representations of men and women already invite the application of 'obsessional' and 'hysteric'. In addition, we could say that psychotic is the discourse that tells us and the subject that there is only one response to 'trauma', so that the certainty of the subject replicates the certainty of the discourse (Scraton and Davis 2001; Bracken 2002). Perverted is the discourse that evokes a transgression of social and personal boundaries that makes the analyst anxious, and it provokes a puzzle about the cause of anxiety that can be solved by attaching the label to a specific body, also itself a perverse strategy.

The clinic

Psychoanalysis that comes to circulate outside the clinic as generalised transference – the extrapolation of clinical phenomena to every social relationship – includes and frames the place of the clinic in culture and, as part of this problematic, the place of the clinic for those seeking to 'apply' psychoanalytic concepts. There is a good deal of deference to psychoanalytic clinical work that actually does psychoanalysis few favours, even if it is a deference that may itself be cultivated by some practising psychoanalysts. The privilege given to the clinic is marked in a number of social practices. We can note three practices here, and note the function of a form of 'transference' within them.

The first social practice concerns a kind of 'pre-transference', and is to be found in a domain of discussions in clinical work that attempts to connect with social processes, that for good sound clinical reasons attempts to embed the actual clinical work in a network of pre-existing cultural processes and structures of power (e.g. Kareem and Littlewood 1999). It is sometimes noted, for example, that an analysand entering analysis for the first time already carries with them preconceptions that will determine how they will relate to the analyst. These preconceptions may even be conceptualised as a kind of 'cultural baggage' that will determine choices of analyst based on racial or ethnic characteristics or assumptions about the ways that an analyst of a certain type might treat them. The working assumption may be that there is already transference before the analysis starts. This transference or 'pre-transference' may be to the analysis itself, and may include a number of stereotypical representations of what analysis is and anticipation of the forms of repetition of patterns that will take place within it. In this case there is the risk of extrapolating from the transferential space of the clinic to other kinds of social space; it is only useful insofar as it is used *retroactively* to reconfigure how the actual transference works. The mistake would be to treat transference as operating in the abstract, independently of any psychoanalysis actually taking place. It is in this light that we must read Miller's (2008: 9) argument that at the beginning of analysis there is 'transference' rather than a 'demand for analysis'; this transference is there prior to the subject contacting the analyst, something we can conceptualise as 'the subject's pre-interpretation of his symptoms', and this because we live in an age of interpretation, in a culture saturated with psychoanalytic discourse (Parker 1997).

The second social practice concerns what can be termed 'shallow transference', and I employ this notion to characterise the particular attachment some social researchers have to clinical practice as a fund of concepts which they can draw upon in order to understand their own work or to understand the activities of their 'subjects' as their objects of enquiry (Wolfe 1989). There is a degree of idealisation of psychoanalysis and the clinic as a privileged site of interpretation in contemporary culture (Parker 2009). This site operates as an anchoring point around which psychoanalysis in the clinic as a particular form of representational practice coheres, and clinical sites provide, at some moments, illustrative accounts as to how psychoanalytic practice operates in the popularisation of striking case studies, for example. However, 'shallow transference' merely serves to mimic what is imagined to take place inside the clinic, and has its own distinctive characteristics that should not be confused with transference as such. To say that there is transference to transference does not solve the problem but compounds it, for it obscures the complicated procedures by which subjects are enrolled in academically-framed research practice, for example, and it reduces all of these procedures to psychoanalysis itself as a pre-existing taken-for-granted grid of knowledge.

The third social practice concerns what we could term 'hollow transference', and this characterises the enthusiasm of those who have themselves had some intimate engagement with psychoanalysis, in the form of Lacanian psychoanalysis perhaps or some other form of psychoanalysis or psychoanalytic psychotherapy, and use that as their reference point to make sense of social phenomena (cf. Laplanche 1999). The reference to personal experience in therapy then provides a distinctive problem for those of us trying to disentangle the clinic from political critique, and those who want to conceptualise the intersections between clinical and theoretical psychoanalysis. In this case there is not merely an attraction to psychoanalysis and an image of it as a form of knowledge – as is the case for those already rehearsing psychoanalytic notions in their own lives as 'shallow transference' – but an avid attachment to a transferential space that remains idealised after the event. It would be too simple to say that those enmeshed in such forms of 'hollow transference' have been insufficiently analysed, and such explanation would itself fall back into the idealisation of what we might imagine a full or genuine analysis to be. It is, rather, better mapped as a particular social practice that is reproduced in interpretations of organisational debates that refer to the effects of multiple transferences or of resentment and resistance on the part of subordinate members of organisations as being the manifestation of 'transferences'.

We should not take transference for granted and simply see the clinic as a source of wisdom, and there is also an issue here for clinical training organisations that use the notion of transference as an explanatory device and thereby incite something very like it in the identificatory processes that structure the way they work. Instead, it is the place of the clinic itself that needs to be analysed, needs to be conceptually and empirically examined so that its function as a specific apparatus for the construction and deconstruction of subjectivity can be better understood. If it is not, then psychoanalysis, even Lacanian psychoanalysis, will be transformed into a kind of faith which promises to explain anything and everything, reduced to a promise to plug lack in the spirit (Palmer 2008). The task today is to grasp how a renewed appeal to 'spirituality' takes form in and against conditions of generalised transference, in an age of interpretation which is saturated with psychoanalytic reasoning.

Secularisation

Psychoanalysis emerges with the triumph of capitalism in Europe, and operates upon the subject of Western Enlightenment science, and so it works on the split between mind and body that has inspired mystical attempts to heal that division and political interventions that have aimed to bring capitalism as such to an end. Those responses to the dualism that structures the relation between mental and manual labour and between men and women have on occasion fused the spiritual impulse with progressive anti-capitalist anti-patriarchal resistance. Feminism as a political movement sometimes confused with 'feminisation', but which operates as a theoretical and practical critique of the idealisation of 'woman', contests the separation between public and private realms. Here Lacanian psychoanalysis plays a dangerous but necessary game when it argues that there must be a separation between the clinic and public space if psychoanalysis is to operate, and that a blurring of the division between the two is an invitation for the ideological prescriptions for subjectivity to enter into the process by which a subject unravels how they have come to be who they are in capitalist society. The very fact that an ideological agenda of whatever kind is attended to as a problem means that the most radical aims of psychoanalysis can be kept intact.

This separation also gives a peculiar but necessarily secular cast to psychoanalysis. In some respects the enforced separation of public and private – separation of social space from that of the consulting room – does re-enact fantasies of Western bourgeois individualism, of a popularised 'anarchist' or 'queer' rejection of any interdependence with others that fuels contemporary obsessional masculinity (e.g. Halberstam 2008). It is also that very refusal to adhere to a worldview that enables Lacanian psychoanalysis to operate as a 'secular' practice without participating in ideological forms of secularism demanded by the state.

Lacanians who draw upon Buddhist precepts, for example, argue that it is possible to be both Buddhist and atheist – Buddhism presupposes neither deity nor religious worldview – and that in this respect it is possible to remain true to psychoanalysis itself as elaborated by Freud as necessarily atheist, suspicious of the consolation provided by illusions of the afterlife or of an otherworldly authority that can determine what is right and wrong (Shingu and Funaki 2008). Those who engage with authentic or syncretic forms of liberation theology can treat 'belief' in the clinic in exactly this spirit; clarification of spirituality entails the reduction of religious signifiers, including science functioning as a religious belief system, to nonsense. As Miller (2002b: 149) points out, if 'science assumes that there exists in the world the signifier which means nothing – and for nobody' – which is why psychoanalysis is the only practice that could truly be called atheist – then this takes us well away from the search for any intuitively-right harmonic unity of things. The world is out-of-kilter, and each analysand learns that there is no harmonious relationship between themselves and others or between who they are and imaginary or symbolic representations of them as subjects.

It is difficult not to inject content into the speech of the analysand, to imagine that one knows what is really meant when they speak and to convey to them that ostensibly hidden meaning. The difficulty is exacerbated by the claim that the feelings that are aroused in the encounter with the analysand are a source of knowledge, and that a democratic psychoanalysis would be one that shared that knowledge with them. This temptation to share what is felt in the encounter then becomes the setting for also sharing what is 'felt' as the ideological stuff of a culture that circulates and frames how each individual understands who they are, and then we are faced with the acute danger that what is injected into the analysand will be ideology itself. Lacanian psychoanalysis resists this temptation, and we could say that here is one valuable instance where resistance must be on the side of the analyst.

Chapter 8
A clinic in the real

This last chapter focuses on the disjunction between clinical and political change, and on the specific nature of psychoanalytic speech that opens the space for revolutions in subjectivity. This enables us to tackle the supposed unity of knowledge and unity of self in versions of clinical practice informed by theological conceptions of ethics. An emphasis on the disjunction between the clinic and politics enables us to approach in a properly Lacanian manner the construction of transference, 'clinical structure' and the direction of the treatment in such a way as to treat each 'structure' as an instance of subjectivity rather than as 'pathological' deviation from capitalist society. The chapter engages with the 'relational' turn in psychoanalysis as an approach that does attend to political change, and I outline overlapping aspects of the 'relation' that is posited in that approach. Here an explicit connection is made with feminist explorations of the link between the personal and the political, and there is discussion of the often reactionary but potentially progressive – ambiguous, ambivalent, paradoxical – political role of Lacanian psychoanalysis.

Antagonisms

There is a crucial difference between psychoanalysis and other forms of 'psy' practice that accumulate in complexity and intensity as capitalism and contemporary neoliberalism become layered on old feudalism, a crucial difference that Lacan's work exacerbates and turns into a revolution in subjectivity. Psychiatry, psychology and psychotherapy, as was the case for the spiritualised conceptual capsules of the subject that preceded those modern psy practices, assumed that it would be possible to connect change in the clinic with social change. Their ethical prescriptions for arriving at the good, distributing the good of all or being dutiful in order to be good were part and parcel of an attempt to make clinical work part of a seamless web of moral comportment so that integration of the subject into society would eventually arrive at a point where adaptation would necessarily be to the best of possible worlds. This is why so many psychiatrists, psychologists and psychotherapists, again in keeping with well-meaning priests before them, have been tempted to intervene in the domain of the social, to intervene in the name of their professional identity in the belief that their knowledge could be beneficial to all.

This is the mode in which 'progressive' psychiatrists hoped to bring order to the world and embed their own medical treatment of individuals within positive programmes of education and moral improvement. Even today the motif of the 'democratic therapeutic community' signals, as one telling example, the adaptation of the patient to a social milieu in which they will get better and the endorsement of democracy as such as the healthy space in which individuals may flourish (Spandler 2006). Here psychiatry is infused with psychoanalytic themes of attachment and containment, with psychoanalysis of the kind that once fed on medical and then scientific psychological authority. The category of 'borderline personality disorder', for example, then comes to supplant Freudian clinical structures and focuses instead on cognitive failures that result from developmental abnormalities; 'chronic stress in children' is said to lead to 'highly dysfunctional and maladaptive brain activities' (De Zulueta and Mark 2000: 488). The 'therapeutic alliance' that is thereby forged between doctors and those with 'personality disorder' is then designed to bring the benefits of 'the healing power of the group' to those suffering 'severe attachment failure' (Campling 1999: 139).

Psychiatry, psychology and psychotherapy have come to operate at different historical periods, have their own 'surfaces of emergence' and forms of power; this gives rise to the temptation to assume that history of the cure culminates in the best of all worlds, turns into a kind of therapeutic alliance that attempts to put accumulating knowledge about the individual subject to work (Foucault 1977). The therapeutic community then becomes but one significant point of connection between individual and the social, a place where the therapist may use his 'cognitive and intellectual abilities' to alleviate anxiety by giving 'sensible advice' to a 'borderline patient' and in which, for example, a nurse may confess that 'she was regressively re-experiencing a moment of her earlier development' (Bateman 1995: 10–11).

The therapeutic community is a domain that exemplifies the double-intervention that progressive psy professionals aim at; it combines the two aspects of treatment and reform, amelioration of personal distress and improved social administration (Miller and Rose 1988). It is exactly at this point that Lacanian psychoanalysis breaks, where it must break, from other forms of psychoanalysis, must resist the temptation to run together clinical work with political activity. There is a question here that concerns the ethics of psychoanalysis and a political analysis of the place of psychoanalysis in relation to the social. We find this question at work most immediately in conceptions of the law and harmonisation of individual wishes with those of others. It is at work in the different conceptions of 'democracy' assumed by liberals and Lacanians, but it is also a question that appears in different conceptions of the clinic itself (Stavrakakis 2007b).

This brings us to three kinds of antagonism that bear on work in the clinic. The first is antagonism that lies at the heart of every social bond, the impossibility of a single harmonious vision of society that would be shared by all or of a confluence of different perspectives mediated by one vision. For Lacan, this impossibility is a function not only of a real that resists symbolisation and disrupts attempts to suture together different vantage points from which subjects attempt to grasp it, to bring it into the domain of 'reality'; this real impossibility also operates inside the symbolic itself as a function of the peculiar idiosyncratic knotting of the real, imaginary and symbolic for each subject and as a function of the nature of the symbolic as such. Insofar as it is possible to find a 'social theory' in Lacan it appears in an analysis of social bonds and then of the real operating in symbolisation itself, and this is productively elaborated by Lacanian psychoanalysts retrieving a conception of 'negativity' from Hegel in order to question and re-energise Marxism (e.g. Žižek 1989).

This is, in some respects, Lacanian analysis 'outside' the clinic. It presupposes a concept of 'deflected progress' to power an 'anti-historicist historical materialism' that looks to a 'messianic event' which forces a question as to what a psychoanalyst might anticipate to occur at a moment of revolutionary change inside the clinic (Roberts 2008a: 77). There is a break in this analysis from forms of historical understanding that are hegemonic in contemporary culture or in remaining fractions of the left demoralised by the triumph of neoliberal capitalism at the end of the twentieth century and beginning of the twenty-first; a break from time conceived of as homogeneous, regressive or recurrent – a break from comforting teleological narratives of progress or even of dialectical interruptions of historical narrative – is given a new shape when there is a sense of direction in history. Here, where a 'messianic event' becomes constitutive of revolutionary agency, it is possible to grasp theoretical interventions situated within a renewed engagement with spirituality that are congruent with Lacan and, even if they are not all Marxist, with revolutionary Marxism. Suffering today is often mediated by a spiritual impulse, yearning for something beyond the coordinates of this wretched world, and so revolutionaries, including revolutionary Lacanians, must engage with that. A revolutionary Lacanian articulation with Marxism is thereby re-energised by the Marxist tradition (as opposed to spiritualising that tradition).

As I have already indicated, this antagonism at the level of political interpretation and intervention outside the clinic begs a series of questions about clinical work, in the space where we find a second kind of antagonism, antagonism in the clinic. Antagonism structures, sometimes sabotages but sometimes productively so, the course of clinical work in Lacanian psychoanalysis from the commencement of the clinic, when it proves impossible to develop a 'therapeutic alliance' much-beloved of other therapeutic orientations, to the point where it is unthinkable that we may ever arrive at identification between analysand and analyst in which they both inhabit the same reality. It would be far easier for our task – articulation of a revolutionary standpoint outside the clinic with change inside it – if we could insist that the signifiers that circulate outside were matters that concerned the content of ideological systems and that psychoanalysis as such bears on *formal* structures including the reduction of signifiers to nonsense, to their operation in systems of terms for the speaking subject (Nobus and Quinn 2005). However, content also takes its imaginary and symbolic shape through the formal systems of meaning.

Fantasy itself is formally structured as a relation between the barred subject and object a, but is inhabited by a series of images, of the identity of the subject and semblances of the object, by many peculiar contents, some of which it may be possible to trace to culturally-potent signifiers, but which the analyst most-times refrains from so doing for fear of injecting their own ideas into the analysis. The most potent of the signifiers is what Lacan calls the phallus, and the key antagonism into which a variety of social categories are plotted by the subject is that of sexual difference, a 'non-relation' which charges certain other signifiers with meaning when they are articulated into a formal structure which divides 'man' from 'woman'.

We will return to social categories and sexual difference, and what the analyst may need and need not to know about them presently, but it is only possible to adequately mark those particular kinds of antagonism inside the clinic if we locate them in a third kind of antagonism, the disjunction between the clinic and its circumambient culture (Malone and Kelly 2004; Llorens 2009). Here I spell out in more detail points briefly reviewed in previous chapters concerning the peculiarity of interaction in the clinic as 'transferential space'. Now it is possible to flesh out some of the key theoretical elements of Lacanian psychoanalysis I skirted over in the introduction to this book to emphasise the point that psychoanalytic phenomena are constituted by and operate inside the clinic as a cultural-historical apparatus (Lichtman 1982; Dunker 2010).

Asymmetry

First, the clinic breaks from the etiquette of everyday interaction with respect to the role of money and with respect to the quite different positions accorded to those who speak. Let us take these two facets of the peculiar asymmetry constructed by the clinic in turn.

One facet is that the demand for analysis is sustained by a commitment to speak that is marked by monetary exchange. A peculiarity of transferential space is that the analysand should make a request for analysis, and pay to speak to the analyst. There have been exceptions to this rule – that it is necessary for the analysand to give something to the one they speak to – but the very fact that they are exceptions serves to prove the rule. That psychoanalysis requires commodity exchange does, of course, draw attention to psychoanalytic practice as intimately bound up with capitalism. This was, in fact, one of the grounds for prohibiting analysis in Eastern Europe before the fall of the Wall, for it was seen as a form of private entrepreneurship that ran against the ethos of public health provision (M. Miller 1998). The question of how the demand for analysis would be marked if not by the usual fee was one that exercised those involved in the public clinics run by psychoanalysts in the early years in Vienna (Danto 2005). We find great variation in practice over the years, and there are accounts of Freud waiving fees, lending his patients money in times of hardship, and there were even arrangements made by psychoanalytic institutions to give financial support to well-known patients, the Wolf Man for example (Gardiner 1972).

Disputes over how much should be paid, when exactly the time starts and finishes, and whether payment includes sessions missed by the analysand or holidays taken by the analyst, are grist to the mill of transference. The transference does, to some extent, revolve around such matters, but the point here is that this material exchange – money for not many words in return – is one of the material conditions for transference. Surveys of therapists working in private practice have shown that such therapists do, rather unsurprisingly, see payment as more important to the work than those working in public health settings, but even this motif of the self-interested therapist rationalising an aspect of their practice is the least of it (Power and Pilgrim 1990). The analysand makes an investment, a material investment in the analytic process, and it is in the tracks of this investment that many other kinds of transferential investment in the analyst will be constructed and revealed.

The second facet is that analytic speech is asymmetrical, and constructs unusual and distinctive positions of addressor and addressee. There are quite precise formal properties of the speech, for there is an explicit rule which the analysand, who speaks most of the time, is expected to attempt to follow, as well as implicit rules that the analyst follows in their own interventions.

The analysand does not follow the normal rules of conversation, but is invited to attempt the impossible, to follow the fundamental technical rule of free association by which they should say everything that comes to mind however irrelevant, ridiculous or unpleasant. Meandering indirect superfluous speech is sometimes tolerated in everyday life, of those to be humoured because they are pitied or because they are in positions of power, but this game is over in analysis. Not only do hesitations, blockages and failures of speech sabotage the attempt to speak, but the satisfaction of speaking is disrupted as the analysand comes to realise that their difficulty in saying everything is localised, organised around certain symptomatic points (Lacan 1964/1973: 232).

The content of analytic speech is important insofar as some things are circled around, and some things will be treated as extraneous, only of interest insofar as they are understood to be opportunities for circling around something else, which is the real core of the analysis. And the analyst will be attending to those moments where the speech stumbles and stops, taking absence as much as any positive content as a sign that at some level the analysand is aware of who they are talking to, or unaware of who they are not talking to, caught in transference not as something immediately present to awareness but as something that structures what appears and disappears in their speech unbeknownst to them.

What appears in analysis is not only an intimation of what is unconscious, and always only the contours of it rather than the stuff itself, but that there is knowledge of it. The divided subject who speaks in analysis, and whose division becomes more apparent as they fail to follow the rule of free association, conjures into the place where the empathic active listener should be another undivided subject who knows what it is that they are really trying to say. The analyst does not fill in that place, and if they were to do so it would be highly unlikely that this 'subject supposed to know' whose appearance defines the transference would appear. The sometimes bare, cryptic allusive interventions of the analyst in this necessarily asymmetrical relationship do not produce transference as a positive definable phenomenon but an absent cause of the speech itself whose clarification – the kind of clarification of meaning and substance that drives much normal interaction – is usually avoided (Klotz 1995).

Content

A second peculiarity of transferential space is that there are requirements that each party, analysand and analyst, speak in a certain kind of way, that one would expect there to be content to the speech of the analysand, but weird content or lack of content in the speech of the analyst. Let us take the side of the analysand and analyst in turn here.

On the side of the analysand, there are potent cues, extrinsic and intrinsic, about what should be included in the content of analytic speech. There is some expectation that certain things be spoken about, and a stereotypical list will include childhood, dreams and sexual fantasies. The content of the speech provides a series of opportunities for staging and reflecting upon relationships to others, and the combination of the different aspects of the speech produces a reorganisation of the speech around the one it is addressed to. It is not absolutely necessary, for example, that the analysand talks about their childhood, and there is a series of little traps for those who look to accurate representation of childhood events as the aim of analysis (Burman 1998). In both classical and Lacanian psychoanalysis, it is the representation of childhood that is of concern, not what actually happened there and then. It is precisely the attention to representations of childhood relationships that cues analysand and analyst into how such relationships are replayed and resignified in the present.

Dreams may then be indexed to the past, with childhood providing the most potent of the scenes to be rediscovered not only in the dream itself but in the retelling of the dream to another. And this figure as other, addressee of the speech of the analysand, becomes the one who may be the only one to hear of sexual fantasies or perhaps even of the lack of such fantasies and associated threads of guilt and shame at their appearance or non-appearance in the life of the analysand. Not every analytic session revolves around childhood memories or dreams or sexual fantasy, and rarer still will there be sessions that combine those topics in such a way as to draw attention to where the speech is coming from and to what point it may be directed. However, the very circling around those connections and their points of address is the stuff of analysis and so also, in a way very different from everyday conversation, the stuff of transference.

For the analyst, there are specific performative effects of analytic speech that frame, guide and elicit certain phenomena. The transferential space of analysis depends on the activity of the analyst, who adopts a rather strange position from the beginning of the interaction, and whose function is to intensify and manage the analytic work through specific kinds of intervention. Apart from the distinctive form of silence the analyst constructs around the words of the analysand, their actual interventions have a performative quality. The analyst does not direct the analysand to speak about particular things but, as we have seen, 'directs the treatment' (Lacan 1958). The contrast between quite different conceptions of how the course of the analysis will be framed and guided has consequences for how interpretation, including occasionally interpretation of the transference, will be made. Interpretation does not aim to excavate particular contents or to produce a certain kind of knowledge; rather than being descriptive it aims to bring about certain effects, it is performative (cf. Butler 1990).

One of the problems faced by the analyst is that an increasing number of analysands are themselves schooled in psychoanalytic theory, and ready to anticipate the kinds of interpretations that might be produced in the space of analysis. Thus interpretation of the transference 'has the effect of restricting the development of the transference: after a while, the analysand will say only what the analyst wants to hear in order to "interpret the transference"' (Rodríguez and Rodríguez 1989: 184). The aim of an intervention is therefore directed to the 'cutting' and disruption of the self-satisfied interpretative speech of the analysand, rather than the feeding of the unconscious and so the feeding of forms of defence against the drive (Miller 1999a).

Interpretation of transference, when it is made, does not then serve to locate analysand and analyst in a certain relationship, conceived as the repetition of a past relationship, but to disrupt what may be understood to be occurring between the two of them (Cottet 1993). Interpretation does not, in any case, aim to produce better understanding but to disturb that understanding. One of the consequences of such interventions is to throw into question all the more so than before the kind of knowledge that would be expected from analysis. This serves to emphasise Lacan's (1964/1973) argument that signifiers be reduced to nonsense in analysis rather than filled with meaning or form of understanding that could then be given to the analysand. It is the *relation* to knowledge, we have said, that comes to assume more importance than any knowledge as such, and so we are in the realm of performative effects rather than the production of new ideas or moral prescriptions.

Disjunction

A third peculiarity of the space of the clinic that operates as a condition of possibility for there to be transference is a spatial and temporal disjunction between the speakers, spatial and temporal matters which we can address in turn.

There is, first, a spatial disjunction in the analytic frame that magnifies the subjective implications of speech. Transferential space is engineered by the use of an apparatus, the couch, and this apparatus frames the relationship between analysand and analyst in such a way as to frustrate attempts at open, direct and transparent communication between the two of them. The apparatus itself takes slightly different forms in different kinds of practice, and we have seen in previous chapters that Lacanians are notoriously cautious about moving from face-to-face sessions to use of the couch, and they may extend the period of what are known as the 'preliminary meetings' to many months or even years. This is because such a speaking position for the analysand is so peculiar and productive of paranoiac phenomena that not every subject is able to bear or make use of it.

There is actually very little theoretical rationale for the use of the couch in Freud's own writing, and he is reported to have said that he started to put his analysands on the couch because he was sick of being stared at for so many hours a day (Mangabeira 1999). In this complaint there is, of course, a clue as to what is operating as something reassuring for the analysand when speaking directly to the analyst and observing their reactions to what they say. That form of communication has the effect of prioritising the line of the imaginary – in which the other is empathic partner or rivalrous counterpart in dialogue – over the symbolic. It is the symbolic through which the subject travels as they become other to themselves and which the speaking subject in analysis now attends to as they hear themselves borrow from it and repeat the signifiers that compose it.

The couch itself has been an object of psychoanalytic enquiry, with some discussion of how analysands make use of it, whether they may go to sleep on it for instance, or whether they might fall off it (Waugaman 1987). Particular interpretations might be made of such things, but the risk here is that the apparatus itself is being concretised, rather than attention being directed to the strange relationship between speaker and listener that is facilitated by it, and the quite different forms the couch takes in different cultures (Hartnack 2003). The strangeness of that relationship is what is aimed at by most analysts, including Lacanians, when they discuss, for example, the degree to which analysis over the telephone might or might not serve the same purpose, or whether the embodied presence, absent to sight, of the analyst is necessary to produce a space that is more than imaginary, that is distinctively psychoanalytic, condition of transference (Fink 2007).

Speech in analysis has a counter-intuitive temporality designed to question everyday conversational procedures. Transferential space is marked by its disturbing temporal quality, and it is by virtue of this quality that another dimension of thought is opened up which breaks from consciousness, typically structured by way of obedience to rational linear and predictable clock-time (Lacan 1946b; Brennan 1993). Not only will the speaking subject speak about things outside any contract, beyond what they have given their permission to be included, they will not know when they will say it or what it may mean until it is too late. Lacanians return to some of the earliest procedures of psychoanalysis, before the advent of the tidy fifty-minute hour (which was perhaps originally a function of Freud's wife watering the plants in the consulting room every hour) (Schmideberg 1971). Psychoanalysis breaks from clock-time to more closely track the time of the unconscious, and it is for this reason that Lacanians interfere with the temporal space of analysis to open up the unconscious.

A neatly-structured analytic session that ends at a pre-determined time, for example, enables the analysand to predict and pace their speech according to a logic that is ordered by the clock and commanded by consciousness. Such conscious strategies of measured speech are sabotaged by the analyst who ends the session earlier, or perhaps sometimes later, than expected. The ending of such a session – the famous variable-length Lacanian session – may itself function as an interpretation, and such an interpretation which marks a point of some significance in the analysand's speech has the advantage of not spelling out what the exact meaning of that point may be. One may think of the end of this kind of session as setting in place an uncompleted task for the analysand, and the very ambiguity of the point of the ending may produce a question to be taken up in a later session (Burgoyne 1997).

Such tactics also bring into play a retroactive characteristic of analysis that repeats the retroactive character of traumatic events, and that retroactivity is a template for every other kind of experience in which the unconscious is at work. So, the organisation of the space for speech in analysis is designed to draw attention to the role of the unconscious, to make this space into a setting where the phenomenon of transference can appear, where it makes sense to feel that what is being repeated and reactivated after the event in the speech also repeats and reactivates something from the past of the speaker in relation to the one they are speaking to (Soler 1996c).

Presence

Now we come to a peculiarity of clinical space that appears as such when the first three strange defining characteristics of transference in the clinic are put to work, for analytic speech requires address to, and response from, another that is mediated by the terms of a defined social space. I hope I have established by now that by 'clinic' I mean a delimited space of work dedicated to the production of a certain kind of speech, and that means that this space is to some extent enclosed and private. It is not necessary that the one who speaks does this in an expensively decorated apartment or a hygienic hospital side-room, and we know that Freud, for example, sometimes conducted analyses while strolling along in the countryside. We have accounts of this 'clinic' structured in such unlikely locations as a South African township under apartheid (Straker 1994), even on long-distance phone lines (Fink 2007). This delimited space of work signifies to those speaking that psychoanalysis is taking place in such a way that transference can be activated. The characteristics of the psychoanalytic clinic conducive to transference cluster together in different ways, with different weighting depending on the distinctive tradition in which those who speak have been schooled.

It is here that we encounter the reflexive looping that positions the analysand in relation to the analyst as they speak but also that positions the analyst in relation to the subject who is speaking to them when they produce interpretations. This condition is actually the prerequisite for the others I have described so far because analysis must take place in a relationship – or we should say 'non-relationship' – between speaking beings (Wright 1999). Psychoanalytic interpretations are made to another subject for whom they function more by way of the response to the interpretation being made than with reference to its content. And, in many cases, the interpretations are made not by the analyst but by the analysand themselves, or they are interventions that come to take the form of interpretations as the analysand refuses or reconfigures what was said by the analyst, sometimes quite a while after the event. These are the stakes of theoretical discussions over the place of writing, and now email, within psychoanalysis. While it is true that there is sometimes an appeal to a metaphysics of presence of the speaking subject to another that we may already have detected in some of the other conditions, it is a condition that defines what psychoanalysis is and it makes possible a transformation in the subject's attachment to others; '[t]he signifier of transference allows . . . a loosening of "identifications"' (Laurent 2007: 13).

Speaking to another under transference is what defines psychoanalysis, is the most minimal single condition for there to be psychoanalysis. Transference is that *additional* element that turns all of the other specific elements into psychoanalysis in the clinic and only in the clinic. So now let us turn to a radical reworking of psychoanalysis growing in popularity that aims to bridge the gap between the clinic and the world, between personal and political change. Here we are faced with an account of transference that is actually rooted more in contemporary commonsense than in the clinic, and despite the good intentions of its practitioners is therefore not as radical as it first seems.

Relations

Relational psychoanalysis – a clinical and theoretical orientation that promises to connect the personal and the political – poses a particularly painful challenge to Left Lacanians, for it seems to force a choice between the 'Left' and 'Lacanian' sides of our practice. It rubs at a sore point in Lacanian work, at that point of uneasy alliance between radical political theory which runs the gamut of writing from Althusser to Žižek on the one hand and, on the other, the one-to-one frame of abstracted, individualised and limited horizons of change in the consulting room. One sees that uneasy alliance break at those moments when Lacanian psychoanalysis is adapted to the imperatives of brief therapy, the demand for evidence or social inclusion, and when it turns out that those strategic progressive interventions are designed to tempt potential analysands into making their own demand for the real thing (Jerry and Resnik 2003; Vicens 2009). And one sees it break at those moments when political theorists who are happy to employ Lacanian categories to interrogate ideology, power and violence shrink back from engaging with the clinic which then still functions as a sacrosanct space, one that the Left should still defer to as if it were the real thing. In this respect, this respect for the clinic, we actually have a worse record than many other psychoanalytic traditions, and it is not surprising, perhaps, that the 'relational' turn should now blossom in cultural contexts – object relations in the United States and the United Kingdom – that Lacanians have been scathing about, even if they have more recently promised to re-conquer the English-speaking world (J.-A. Miller 1998: 141).

There have also been attempts to maintain a separation between the clinic and activism in the English-speaking world, and that has entailed the following conclusions, sometimes linked, sometimes even embodied in the same individual or text: that a good psychoanalytic training regardless of its political orientation is a prerequisite for progressive interventions; that we should abandon psychoanalytic practice if we are to engage in politics; that we need to subordinate political analysis to categories derived from conservative psychoanalysis (Kovel 1988; Wolfenstein 1993; Orbach 2003). This is a first option, strict separation of different domains of practice, and so an influential strand of conceptual work clustered around the Frankfurt School has been radical, even Marxist in some variants, but has been chary of extrapolating from cultural analysis to what goes on in the clinic (e.g. Fromm 1932; Marcuse 1955/1974).

A second option is to use clinical work as an instrument to politicise subjectivity, and it turns psychoanalysis into something instrumental to social change, into an instrument of a particular kind, precisely because it turns against psychoanalysis as most-times being a practice intent on putting people in their place and leading them to cynicism or stoicism. This course of action also leads to an embrace of an ethics of the good in which some romantic image of natural forces replicates, only ostensibly in reverse, psychiatric prescriptions, or an ethics of the redistribution and balancing out of individual needs which conforms to a kind of psychology, or an ethics of duty to conform to the rule of enjoyment and a flourishing of pleasure that continues the line of psychotherapeutic exploration. Reich (1972) serves as an all too convenient warning here and his career pertains in different ways to each of these ethical pursuits, and, in addition, his adventures seem to indicate that politicised psychoanalysis would itself eventually adapt itself to some quite bizarre anti-psychoanalytic ideas (Chasseguet-Smirgel and Grunberger 1976/1986; cf. Kovel 1986).

But then there is a third option born of innovations in clinical practice that were just as problematic as the instrumental radicalisation of individuals or the attempt by social theorists to steer clear of the consulting room. One could say that Sándor Ferenczi's attempt to equalise the encounter between analyst and analysand involved boundary-breaking – 'active therapy', 'mutual analysis' and then sexual partnerships – that was taking seriously the relational aspect of psychoanalysis at the very same moment as it blurred again the boundaries between fantasy and reality. Perhaps there was a connection between a new understanding of relationships in childhood and relationships in analysis. On the one hand there was a turn back from analytic concern with sexual fantasies to what really happened to the child, a turn back from Freud's shift of attention to fantasy which inaugurated psychoanalysis as such and which surfaced again later in the concern with observable 'object relations'. On the other hand there was a turn back from abstinence on the part of the analyst to being present to the analysand, providing reassurance and disclosing what they made of reality or what they made of an internal reality that would give deeper insight into the analytic relationship.

Then the clinical interventions of Harry Stack Sullivan (who as a gay man had a different stake in challenging mainstream psychoanalytic pathologisation of sexual relationships in the name of what was known about their fantasy sub-structure) combined an emphasis on social context with the seduction of patients, clinical interventions now read as a precursor of what it might mean to queer psychoanalysis (Hegarty 2004; Wake 2008). The third option, then, is to introduce into the consulting room a *relational* sensitivity that would mirror conceptual work on the importance of relationships in child development and in processes of political change. Even if Sullivan was not a psychoanalytic gay rights activist he did prefigure what it might mean to connect how we might aim for social revolution – how we might aim for it rather than simply positing it as an ideal – and how we might aim for personal change in analysis. Inside psychoanalysis a trajectory from the interpersonal to the intersubjective to the relational is thereby set in train that will eventually connect with a renewal of feminist arguments inside the socialist movement, arguments that the personal is political and that the way we struggle for social change will prefigure what the outcome of that struggle will be. Relational psychoanalysis then draws together these two strands, though it has tended to be the journey through US American object relations to relational concepts and the subjectivity of the analyst that has been emphasised in the clinical debates (Mitchell 1997; Orbach 2007; cf. Benjamin 1988).

The question of countertransference, of what should be made of it as a resource for thinking about what is going on for the analyst and what should be disclosed of it in order to connect with and bring about mutative effects for the analysand, has taken centre-stage. However, in the background there are assumptions about actual relations that inform the development of object relations which are given form through use of the metaphor of 'attachment'. Actually, there is now sometimes a combination and sometimes an oscillation between two notions of transference and countertransference in relational psychoanalysis. In order to grasp the way transference is used in this approach we need to notice two different non-Lacanian conceptions of transference in psychoanalysis that are being mobilised.

There is, first, a tradition of work that views psychoanalysis as always having been concerned with some form of *attachment* between infant and mother, and then by implication between adult human beings, including those in psychoanalysis. The guiding motif of this model of development is that such early bonding is, in one way or another, evolutionarily wired-in to the formation of love relationships. The relationship between analysand and analyst then replays not only ontogenetic patterns but it also resonates with the phylogenetic account elaborated by Freud (1913) concerning events in the primal horde. This model of transference is of it as a special kind of glue holding people together, and it is of a piece with specifications of what the infant is presumed to already know of the world they are born into and with research using brain scans to discover which bits of the brain light up when attachment is activated (Fonagy and Target 2004; cf. Blass and Carmeli 2007). This overall covering explanation of transference, which treats it as a particular subset of the attachment of the subject to their objects, operates somewhere between the imaginary – complementary relationships which we all experience with our others – and the real. However, this 'real' is an imaginarised version of the real; rather than that which is resistant to representation and impossible to access – the Lacanian real – this real is conceived as something that can be observed or reconstructed by researchers (e.g. Fonagy *et al.* 2004).

The second tradition has come to value what is *intersubjective* in the psychoanalytic relationship, and focuses on what intuitive responses on the part of the analyst may tell the analyst, and potentially also the analysand, about what is going on between them. The guiding motif of this approach is that the relational dimension of human activity also operates as a kind of conduit for feelings that can be accessed by partners in the relationship. This means that what is intersubjective is given not only epistemological but also moral value, and so the analyst who is able to work with their own countertransference is therefore assumed to be actualising some of the deepest unconscious communication flowing from the analysand. This kind of communication also often bypasses the realm of representation to work directly with feelings. This tradition provides an overall covering account for transference that operates somewhere along a dimension running between the imaginary and the symbolic. Here, however, this symbolic is not a structured system of signifying processes that operates independently of the subject – the Lacanian symbolic – but is, instead, a realm of communicational material in which each subject is embedded and through which they might discover their shared humanity. This is the symbolic as the domain of commonsense, which gives a particular appeal to this account of transference and countertransference as a form of 'empathy' (e.g. Fairfield *et al.* 2002).

The signifier 'relation' in this tradition of work is what might be more accurately termed an 'empty signifier'. The unachievable 'fullness and universality of society' worried away at in Lacanian political theory is relevant here as still at work in an impulse for that fullness and universality that shows itself in 'the presence of its absence', which is manifested in an 'empty signifier' into which we pour different contents (Laclau 1996: 53; Howarth *et al.* 2000; cf. Močnik 1993). So we now find a terrain inside psychoanalysis where there is just such a yearning for 'fullness and universality', which is not to say that either an empty signifier, like emancipation, liberation or revolution, or the struggle over what would count as fullness or universality are necessarily bad objects, bad objectives.

As an *empty signifier*, 'relation' seems to connote at least the following kinds of relation: between analysand and analyst, between infant and caregiver, between self and other, between individual and collective, between body and mind, between material and spiritual, between personal and political, and between clinic and world. Let us try to disentangle the way these different binary oppositions are woven into each other, and so work out whether 'relation' might come to mean something altogether different. Along the way we will also encounter some different conceptions of ethics that have been worried away at in Lacanian work as an alternative to dominant notions of ethics that have tended to govern psychiatry, psychology and psychotherapy.

Ensembles of power

The relational turn in psychoanalysis raises a question about the end of analysis, and the extent to which it is possible to go beyond Freud's (1937: 252) rather pessimistic formulations about the interminable nature of the process, the impossibility of circumventing the rock of castration or the 'repudiation of femininity'. Shifting attention to the process itself rather than aiming for an idealised end point at which the analysand thinks they are completely free is something that is hinted at in Freud and taken further in quite different ways in relational psychoanalysis and Lacanian psychoanalysis.

There are four conceptual elements that need to be borne in mind here in this shift. The first is Marx's (1845/1888) characterisation of the human being as 'an ensemble of social relations', a characterisation that is given different inflection in the relational psychoanalytic attention to attachment and in Lacanian accounts of the necessity for the child to process inchoate bodily states through the mediating externalised form of the 'Other' (Verhaeghe 2004). The second element which is also present in Marxism, and which owes something to its working-through of its conceptual debt to Hegel, is 'negativity', and this force which powers dialectical logic expresses itself in psychoanalytic theory in accounts of the vicissitudes of the drive, sometimes conceived of as death drive, and 'aggression' or, the less biologically-loaded term, 'aggressivity'. These first two elements themselves operate dialectically, in an opposition of social relations and negativity that complicate how we think about social relations as such. So, a third conceptual element that we need to introduce here, and which has been named as such in relational psychoanalysis more than in Lacanian psychoanalysis, is power, the reproduction of power relations inside the clinic (Ullman 2007). It is only if we take power seriously that it makes sense to think through the possibilities of the fourth conceptual element, which is that there are 'prefigurative' aspects of analysis, the socialist feminist argument that oppositional analysis and practice should enact or 'prefigure' the social relations posited as an alternative (Gramsci 1971; Rowbotham *et al.* 1980). However, if power is taken seriously this also has limiting effects on what prefigurative work is possible inside the clinic.

In Lacanian terms we might think of prefigurative work as involving a shift from the register of the imaginary, that realm of idealised communication in which we think we understand each other, to the register of the symbolic in which we forge the kinds of social bond through which something like that understanding is grounded in practice. Power under heteropatriarchal capitalism, on the other hand, operates against this progressive political shift through a reduction, condensation, crystallising of given symbolic forms into how we conceptualise how we stand in relation to others, from a reduction of the register of the symbolic to the imaginary. Negativity – our debt to Hegel coming into play here – disrupts the easy flow of communication at each level and between them, operating as the 'real' which is resistant to symbolisation and which frustrates understanding. This invites us to think of the ensemble of social relations Marx describes as the linking of those three registers of symbolic, imaginary and real, a linking that Lacan describes using the curious figure of the Borromean knot through which each ring intersects with the others and holds them in place. My claim here is that the linking of the three realms by way of the fourth is not given substance in one particular signifier which would then have ideological weight (Ragland and Milovanovic 2004).

If the relationship between analysand and analyst is modelled on and rooted in the relationship between infant and care-giver, then there is already imported into the clinic a particular conception of power and an understanding of what the first most important ensemble of social relations is into which a human being takes form as a sentient being. The signifier 'attachment' links those two first kinds of relation – analysand and analyst, infant and care-giver – but then makes it difficult to prefigure another form of relating outside the frame of what attachment is understood to be.

This brings us to a conception of ethics explored in Lacanian psychoanalysis which is concerned with the uncertainty and indeterminacy of human action, an ethics which argues for the importance of coming to terms with uncertainty and indeterminacy as such. Discussion of the nature of 'democracy' and 'radical democracy' associated with the tradition of 'post-Marxist' theory initiated this conception of what we might aim for and how we need to keep open possibilities precisely because arrival at a finished end point would itself close down those possibilities (Laclau 1996; Stavrakakis 1999, 2007b).

We might then conceive of the end of analysis as the production of a kind of knowledge that is incomplete, that is evanescent, lost again soon after it appears in analysis as the truth of the subject, a kind of knowledge the relation to which repeats the subject's relation to their objects as always already lost. The connection between the first two relations – analysand

and analyst, infant and care-giver – therefore offers a kind of knowledge that Lacanian psychoanalysis, in stark contrast, aims to de-complete.

Dialectics of authority

Let us turn to two more intertwined aspects of the concern with 'relations' in the clinic in relational psychoanalysis, one aspect calling on the other in order to forge an alliance between this form of psychoanalysis and radical politics. One aspect is the attempt to connect the kinds of relations that are built in the clinic with those outside, and the other is the more ambitious hope that the kinds of relation we would aim for outside the clinic provide the best kind of context for therapeutic change; the way in which that therapeutic change takes place would thereby anticipate and enable the kinds of relations we are aiming for in the outside world. The connection between these two aspects – between self and other and between individual and collective as the third and fourth of the relations evoked in relational psychoanalysis – has been captured in the claim that the relational turn is 'democratizing psychoanalysis' (Orbach 2007), and there is some resonance here with the claim within the broad Lacanian tradition that democracy is the only context in which psychoanalysis is able to thrive (which also picks up the point rehearsed above that the ethics of psychoanalysis necessitates a democratic openness) (Roudinesco 2006; cf. Žižek 2008).

Leaving aside for a moment the question as to whether we should want to harmonise the kinds of relations that pertain outside and inside the clinic – a harmonisation that could either be seen as an illusory mirroring across the domains within the line of the imaginary or conceptualised as a mapping of symbolic coordinates – there is another implication of these two combined aspects of the relational turn which bears some comparison with Lacanian practice. The democratising impulse dethrones the analyst as master in the clinic, and it opens the way to think through how the clinic operates in structures of power that are then often relayed from a cultural-political level into the fabric of subjectivity, relayed from the outside world into the little world of analyst and analysand.

Lacanian psychoanalysis makes use of the master–slave dialectic through which subjectivity emerges in a battle for recognition with the other, as we have seen, but the conclusion of this dialectic in the clinic is very different from the humanist therapeutic readings of Hegel in which the happy outcome even for radicals is mutual recognition, a synthesis of two viewpoints so that both can thrive (Proctor *et al.* 2006). The battle that takes place in the most peculiar context of transference never ends, and, when the analysand 'de-supposes' the analyst as one who knows, this entails dropping any idealisation of them such that they are turned from gold into shit and then we have the place for analyst that Lacan (1987a) on occasion referred to as that of the martyr or saint (Regnault 2009).

Lacanians do not go all the way with the democratising impulse that would promise to overthrow the authority of the analyst, and one reason for this is that challenge to authority, the hysterical questioning of the master of whatever sex by analysand of whatever sex, is not designed to engineer the formation of the analysand as another little master, master in their own house. The outcome of this enclosed master–slave dialectic is no democratic synthesis of shared perspectives on the world nor is it triumphal emergence of the analysand as the one who knows. Instead, the analysand learns something about the relational aspect of subjectivity – they are who they are only by virtue of their difference with others – without actually enacting that relation as an ideal. That is, identity as such is dropped as an ideal, and so a 'relation' as such is also dropped. It is in this respect that it is possible to say that what has taken place is psychoanalysis rather than psychotherapy or communion.

The key concept that Lacan derives from a reading of Hegel, one which brings relations to the fore, is that of 'desire', and this desire is then sometimes used to ground Lacanian ethics. The formulation that Lacan (1986/1992: 319) gives in his seminar *The Ethics of Psychoanalysis* is that 'the only thing of which one can be guilty is of having given ground relative to one's desire'. This precise formulation does not stipulate that each individual should follow their desire. Lacan locates 'one's desire' as 'desire of the Other', and so the 'relation' between self and other is deconstructed; this deconstruction of the relation between self and other thereby reconfigures the relation between individual and collective such that the way one becomes a subject with an unconscious (which is itself, remember, the 'discourse of the Other') is by way of collective relational processes. If anything, the enactment of desire as something only individual is a betrayal of what that desire actually is. We are thereby able to unpack some ideological specifications of the 'individual' self as that which is pitted against the other as something 'collective'. So, the connection between the third and fourth relations – self and other, individual and collective – is, in Lacanian psychoanalysis in the clinic at least, dismantled.

Forms of agency

The clinic is itself a particular configuration of power relations; relational psychoanalysis has worried away at how these relations position analyst and analysand, however much the analyst might want to give up their power (Layton *et al.* 2006). This then gives to the revolt of the analysand, hysterical revolt that we incite, a particular character that is infused with representations of difference, dimensions of difference that are already mapped out in such a way as to fill the clinic with ideological content.

In some respects, for instance, the clinic is a white space, and this sets the terms on which analysts who are not themselves white engage with analysands. The history of psychoanalysis as a Jewish science and the analyst, Jewish or not, as extimate to mainstream medicine also makes it more amenable to reflection on the impact of racism on mental health, and to making some alliances between marginalised cultural groups that have coloured in this white space (Ernst and Maguire 1987). This sensitivity also invites attention to the spread of psychoanalysis as a form of cultural imperialism, but then the question is how the practice of psychoanalysis as that which disturbs and unravels all forms of identity can be maintained without adapting itself to each different culture and then turning into something other than psychoanalysis. Here is a case where use of psychoanalytic ideas to explore the role of whiteness as a privileged signifier then clears a different space for clinical work, but it does not thereby change the clinical work as such (Seshadri-Crooks 2000).

The clinic also operates as a classed space, one in which there is privilege given to those who can pay for the analysis – notwithstanding 'free clinic' initiatives, socialised health-care provision or attempts to widen insurance cover – and to those who can afford to train as an analyst. There are a host of class-laden assumptions that determine how the treatment is to be conducted, and a combination of benevolent intent and rationing of resources has led to the popularity of short-term versions of psychodynamic therapy provided by those who have been trained in briefer, cheaper programmes, programmes in which it is a next logical step to abandon the psychodynamic element altogether. It seems here as if the institutional space in which psychoanalysis can function is one which is geared to the reproduction of class relations.

So, rather than attempting to dissolve that problem into what we might hope for as a 'class-neutral' psychotherapy, the task is to treat the clinic as a site in which class antagonism is played out, not to be resolved in the clinic but worked on so it can be enacted again, including outside. Then we are once again posed with a choice. On the one hand, the analysand may sink deeper into the ideology they have interrogated in the clinic, an ideology facilitated by a therapeutic ethos of dialogue, reconciliation and transparent communication that renders class division into something invisible again. On the other hand, the ostensibly anti-therapeutic trajectory may be into open and more consciously undertaken class conflict, one stripped of the old ideals and one that would aim for a world in which this kind of clinic would be as anachronistic as psychoanalysis itself; 'psychoanalytic therapy [i.e. psychoanalysis] is necessary only where it is not possible, and possible only where it is no longer necessary' (Žižek 1994: 15).

The way we think about how this choice operates in relation to ideology entails a quite different notion of agency, of an agentic position inhabited by Lacan's barred subject, an agent very different from the rather macho model of it implicit in some versions of ego psychology and rife in some versions of Left politics. Here there is another connection between strands of Lacanian and relational psychoanalysis, but the conception that we have of femininity and feminism does need a little work if it is to have anything useful to say to our comrades. There is a paradox in the way the clinic operates in relation to gender, for even though the apparatus and procedures of the clinic may be understood as stereotypically masculine, the concern with feelings has reconfigured the clinic itself as a feminised space. This is so to the point that one could say that it is quite unnecessary for psychotherapeutic practice to be injected with feminist ideas, because good therapy is always already implicitly feminist. Again, however, this clinic opens a choice for the subject; they are enclosed within a conception of femininity as attuned to relationships and thereby reinforcing a moral ideal of intuition, negotiation and resolution of political differences, or they arrive at feminism as a critique of the way gender is allocated but in such a way as to cover over conflict so the oppressed stay silent and the oppressors simply learn to speak their language in order to maintain their power.

A therapeutic sensitivity tends to reduce feminism to idealised femininity, and this then reiterates a relation between the 'body' and the 'mind' in which countertransference becomes a motif for thinking about embodiment; embodiment is then realised through a channel of communication with language as a system of signifiers still in place as the albeit now disparaged site of the 'mastery of reason', an old patriarchal opposition that is sometimes infused with a quasi-feminist sensibility (Walkerdine 1988). This image of body and mind is given a twist in Lacanian theory that is, if anything, worse. An opposition between phallic jouissance and feminine jouissance, which is sometimes referred to as 'jouissance of the Other', seems to provide a critique of what masculinity as such is, but is still very much caught within the ideological coordinates of patriarchal reasoning about gender. This jouissance of the Other which takes the subject beyond themselves into a mystical dimension valorises quite traditional images of femininity and martyrdom (Lacan 1975/1998). When the analysand of whatever sex is 'hystericised' we are forced to work within available signifiers of femininity which then surreptitiously and problematically map the relation between body and mind – a fifth relation evoked in relational psychoanalysis – into a sixth relation between the material and the spiritual (Webb and Sells 1995; White 2006).

There is another aspect to this appeal to femininity in Lacanian psychoanalysis that configures the choice I have referred to as an ethical 'act', yet another Lacanian conception of ethics in which the subject remains true to their desire. That examples of such an act in Lacan's writings are drawn from literature is already an indication that we are playing with ideological material here, and even though Antigone, for example, is not supposed to be an 'example' at all, the fact that she is invoked by Lacan and then in endless Lacanian commentary on the ethics of the act mires us in an image of the feminine as idealised resistance to law and order (Zupančič 2000).

Perhaps one way through this is to take seriously the cultural-historical construction of femininity as Other (Beauvoir 1949/1968); then we can treat the attempt to leap into feminised spiritual transcendence as an indictment of the kind of masculinised material reality we inhabit today. This then introduces into the impossible relation between man and woman as they have been constructed and maintained in line with the imperatives of capital accumulation a connection with history and politics, a connection between past and future that also questions what we know of gender. In this respect, Lacanian psychoanalysis makes it possible for the barred subject to be queerer than it thinks (Butler 1990, 1993; Watson 2009). It may indeed be the case that 'the assumption of one's own femininity', and so a new engagement with feminism we might say, 'marks the culmination of the analytical treatment' (Mieli 2000: 274).

However, the only way to desubstantialise and queer this conception of the feminine is to disconnect the fifth and sixth relations – body and mind, material and spiritual – so that neither side of each of those relations is idealised or reified. This is particularly important today, at a time characterised by a powerful ideological appeal of 'embodiment' among academics and 'spirituality' among some radicals.

Politics of the personal

The way we think about the relation between the personal and the political then needs to be disconnected from the relation between the clinic and the world, disconnected from and then rearticulated with it. The ideological effect of psychotherapy as part of the therapeutisation of subjectivity and politics in contemporary capitalism feeds into the clinic in two ways. First, there is the well-meaning attempt to democratise psychoanalysis that takes place inside the clinic, to make it something that is itself more immediately therapeutic and compatible with the amelioration of heterosexism and racism, for example, in the outside world. Second, there is an ideological rendering of the space of the clinic as the space of personal change, and so the infusion of the clinic with a particular moral-political agenda ends up reducing the political to the personal.

The personal is already political, but the clinic can only operate as a place to unravel the ideological constitution of the individual subject if we insist on a radical *disjunction* between this site and the world. It is precisely because psychoanalysis breaks from everyday conversational procedures – because it refuses the 'relational' dimension of interaction and the attempt to forge an intersubjective space between speakers – that the analyst is able to provoke a questioning of what power is for the subject. What is at stake here is whether we should or should not map the seventh relation, personal and political, onto the eighth concerned with the clinic and world.

This question reframes the Lacanian conceptions of ethics that I have referred to so far – conceptions of indeterminacy, desire and act – so that the call not to give up on the uncertain desire which we inhabit, as that which is given through our relation to the Other, can be formulated as 'do not give up on that part of yourself that you do not know' (Badiou 1998/ 2001: 47). The concept that Lacan invents to name this part of the self that we do not know, and which causes the analysand to question the analyst about the desire that inhabits them as they rework that desire in the transference, is object a. It is in a disturbing, ungraspable way, he claims, 'real', and our clinic is therefore a clinic of the real that has an extimate and antagonistic relation with everyday reality.

Conclusions

To say that the clinic is 'real' is to extract it not only from taken-for-granted reality, reality that is suffused with fantasy, the place we retreat to in order to dream with our eyes open when we have encountered some traumatic point in our more obviously surreal dreams functioning as the guardians of sleep (Freud 1900/1999; Lacan 1964/1973). This real is disconnected for a crazy moment or two from the realm of the imaginary – communication between analysand and analyst that pretends to provide corrective emotional experience of communication between infant and caregiver – and even from the symbolic which grounds us in a link between self and other, between individual and collective. To speak of it as real marks the clinic as place of suffering as well as a space of reverie, a place of absolute difference rather than self-confirming similitude. The enigma that the clinic provokes in Lacanian psychoanalysis also opens again a space for desire and then a questioning of that desire itself, for which 'drive' might be the name (Žižek 2006: 63), but only if that drive is conceptualised as on the border of the physical and the psychical, as movement itself, that which propels us and which we try to make sense of after the event (Copjec 2006).

Here it is vital that we rework another ninth relation into this antagonistic process, that between psychoanalysis and psychotherapy. Psychoanalysis, as we have seen in the course of this book, has struggled to unhitch itself from psychiatry and disentangle itself from psychology. Lines of separation between 'psychoanalysis proper' and 'mere psychotherapy' have been blurred in recent years, and this has been a necessary and progressive effect of the emergence of new lines of conceptual and clinical work. Far from dissolving the choice between psychoanalysis and psychotherapy, however, it poses that choice in starker terms, now as a quite different choice at a different historical moment. Either we merge psychoanalysis into psychotherapy, and so also make it correspond with a thoroughly therapeutised sense of self that has become the sensible unit of reflexive accountability in contemporary neoliberal capitalism, or we insist on those psychoanalytic moments in *every* good therapeutic practice in which the clinic as real carves out a space for the subject to differentiate itself from an apparatus of control, prediction and anxious obedience. Lacanian psychoanalysis is not the only site of the clinic as real, but it does show us more clearly than other traditions in psychoanalysis what that clinic might look like and what the stakes are.

The clinic might operate as a crucible of revolutionary subjectivity. However, this claim must be tempered by the tendency for the 'end of analysis' to amount to nothing much more than an ironic distance from systems of meaning, from the dominant ideology perhaps but also from alternative political movements, and so the fantasy that one has escaped from ideology leads the subject deeper into it, into the very distance that ideology needs to confirm each subject as one who has made a free choice to participate in the social order. The most that can be hoped for is that the clinic as real operates as a space that is extimate to the society that encloses it; it provides a moment of separation from social relations so that a renewed encounter with them might be from another position, a moment that can be re-enacted, perhaps, outside the clinic too.

Refusal of relationship rather than a direct embrace of it brings us to a tenth kind of relation alongside the other nine we have plotted so far, the relation between interpreting and changing the world. Lacanian psychoanalysis reverses a popular commonsense understanding of what happens in the consulting room, one in which the analyst provides interpretations and thereby reinstates the clinic as a privileged site of interpretation in a culture that has become saturated with psychoanalytic vocabulary and imagery. This is one possible meaning of the argument that we now live in an age of interpretation in which the only radical response is to engage in 'interpretation in reverse'. For Lacan, we have said, it is not the analyst who interprets, but the analysand, and in recent Lacanian practice it is more often the case that the analyst 'cuts' interpretation rather than provides it. The 'cut' of interpretation that causes an enigma to appear in the session – the 'cut' of the session that ends it and marks a separation between this space and the outside – and the 'cut' of the relationship between analyst and analysand each introduce something of the 'real'.

Lacanian clinical psychoanalysis does not solve the riddle of whether the spirit of revolt can take the place of the revolt of spirit against capitalism today. However, Lacanian work can be taken forward in order to reflect on its own practice and on the limits to what it can claim to do. Theoretical advance in its therapeutic practice is predicated on a theory of revolution that occurs outside the clinic, even if the paradoxical point of connection is a point at which we learn about the necessary disjunction between the two spheres of action. The kind of revolution in subjectivity that occurs inside the clinic makes of the clinic a quite specific site of refusal – one that is extimate, implicated in the social at the moment it refuses it – but even then it is the site of refusal of the very capitalist world that made it possible. It gives birth to glimmering, fading, and glimmering again of a subject open to change, to subjectivity in revolution.

References

Adorno, T. W. and Horkheimer, M. (1944/1979) *Dialectic of Enlightenment*. London: Verso.
Agamben, G. (1998) *Homo Sacer: Sovereign Power and Bare Life*. Stanford, CA: Stanford University Press.
Agamben, G. (2005) *The Time That Remains: A Commentary on the Letter to the Romans*. Stanford, CA: Stanford University Press.
Ahmed, S. (2004) *The Cultural Politics of Emotion*. Edinburgh: Edinburgh University Press.
Alexander, F. and French, T. M. (1946) *Psychoanalytic Therapy*. New York: Ronald Press.
Althusser, L. (1971) *Lenin and Philosophy and Other Essays*. London: New Left Books.
Althusser, L. (1977) *For Marx*. London: New Left Books.
Anderson, P. (1979) *Lineages of the Absolutist State*. London: Verso.
Anderson, P. (1980) *Arguments within English Marxism*. London: Verso.
André, S. (1999) *What Does a Woman Want?* New York: Other Press.
Ansermet, F. and Magistretti, P. (2007) *Biology of Freedom: Neural Plasticity, Experience, and the Unconscious*. New York: Other Press.
APA Task Force on Appropriate Therapeutic Responses to Sexual Orientation (2009) *Report of the Task Force on Appropriate Therapeutic Responses to Sexual Orientation*. Washington, DC: American Psychological Association.
Appignanesi, L. and Forrester, J. (1993) *Freud's Women*. London: Virago.
Ariès, P. (1962) *Centuries of Childhood: A Social History of Family Life*. New York: Knopf.
Atkinson, D. R., Wampold, B. E. and Worthington, R. L. (2007) 'Our identity: how multiculturalism saved counseling psychology', *The Counselling Psychologist*, 35, 476–486.
Austin, S. (2005) *Women's Aggressive Fantasies: A Post-Jungian Exploration of Self-Hatred, Love and Agency*. London and New York: Routledge.
Badiou, A. (1998/2001) *Ethics: An Essay on the Understanding of Evil*. London: Verso.
Badiou, A. (2003) *Saint Paul: The Foundation of Universalism*. Stanford, CA: Stanford University Press.
Bailly, L. (2009) *Lacan: A Beginner's Guide*. Oxford: Oneworld.

Bakan, D. (1958/1990) *Sigmund Freud and the Jewish Mystical Tradition*. London: Free Association Books.
Balibar, E. and Wallerstein, I. (1991) *Race, Nation, Class: Ambiguous Identities*. London: Verso.
Balint, M. (1950) 'On the termination of analysis', *International Journal of Psycho-Analysis*, 31, 196–199.
Barnard, S. and Fink, B. (eds) (2002) *Reading Seminar XX: Lacan's Major Work on Love, Knowledge, and Feminine Sexuality*. New York: State University of New York Press.
Bassols, M. (2002) 'The analyst and his politics', *Psychoanalytical Notebooks of the London Circle*, 8, 107–123.
Bateman, A. (1995) 'The treatment of borderline patients in a day hospital setting', *Psychoanalytic Psychotherapy*, 9(1), 3–16.
Beauvoir, S. de (1949/1968) *The Second Sex*. London: Jonathan Cape.
Beck, A. and Ellis, A. (2000) 'New concepts in practice: on therapy – a dialogue with Aaron T. Beck and Albert Ellis', American Psychological Association 108th Convention Session 3309, http://www.fenichel.com/Beck-Ellis.shtml (accessed 29 September 2009).
Beechey, V. (1979) 'On patriarchy', *Feminist Review*, 3, 66–82.
Beloff, Z. (ed.) (2008) *The Somnambulists*. New York: Christine Burgin.
Benjamin, J. (1988) *The Bonds of Love: Psychoanalysis, Feminism and the Problems of Domination*. New York: Pantheon.
Benjamin, L. T. (2009) 'You too can be healthy, successful, and happy', *The Psychologist*, 22(5), 460–462.
Bennani, J. (2008) 'Psychoanalysis, women and Islam', *JCFAR: Journal of the Centre for Freudian Analysis and Research*, 18, 69–99.
Bensaïd, D. (2002) *Marx for our Times: Adventures and Misadventures of a Critique*. London: Verso.
Benslama, F. (2009a) *Psychoanalysis and the Challenge of Islam*. Minneapolis: University of Minnesota Press.
Benslama, F. (2009b) 'The veil of Islam', *S: Journal of the Jan Van Eyck Circle for Lacanian Ideology Critique*, 2, 14–26.
Bentall, R. P. (ed.) (1990) *Reconstructing Schizophrenia*. London and New York: Routledge.
Benvenuto, S. (1996) 'Lacan's dream', *Journal of European Psychoanalysis*, 2: 107–131.
Bettelheim, B. (1986) *Freud and Man's Soul*. Harmondsworth: Pelican.
Bick, E. (1968) 'The experience of the skin in early object relations', *International Journal of Psycho-Analysis*, 49, 484–486.
Billig, M. (2006) 'Lacan's misuse of psychology: Evidence, rhetoric and the mirror stage', *Theory, Culture and Society*, 23(4), 1–26.
Bisson, T. (2009) *The Crisis of the 12th Century: Power, Lordship and the Origins of European Government*. Princeton, NJ: Princeton University Press.
Blass, R. B. and Carmeli, Z. (2007) 'The case against neuropsychoanalysis: on fallacies underlying psychoanalysis' latest scientific trend and its negative impact on psychoanalytic discourse', *International Journal of Psycho-Analysis*, 88, 19–40.
Bourdieu, P. and Passeron, J.-C. (1977) *Reproduction in Education, Society and Culture*. London: Sage.

Bracken, P. (2002) *Trauma: Culture, Meaning and Philosophy*. Beckenham: Whurr.
Braverman, H. (1974) *Labor and Monopoly Capital*. New York: Monthly Review Press.
Brennan, T. (1993) *History After Lacan*. London and New York: Routledge.
Breuer, J. and Freud, S. (1895) 'Studies on hysteria', in S. Freud (1966–1974) *The Standard Edition of the Complete Psychological Works of Sigmund Freud* (translated by J. Strachey). London: Vintage, Hogarth Press and Institute of Psycho-Analysis, vol. II.
Britton, H. (2004) 'Contemporary symptoms and the challenge for psychoanalysis', *Journal for Lacanian Studies*, 2(1), 56–62.
Brousse, M.-H. (2003) 'The push-to-the-woman: a universal in psychosis?', *Psychoanalytical Notebooks*, 11, 79–98.
Budgen, S., Kouvelakis, S. and Žižek, S. (eds) (2007) *Lenin Reloaded: Toward a Politics of Truth*. Durham, NC: Duke University Press.
Burgoyne, B. (1997) 'Interpretation', in B. Burgoyne and M. Sullivan (eds) *The Klein–Lacan Dialogues*. London: Rebus Press.
Burgoyne, B. (2007) 'Socratic history', *JCFAR: Journal of the Centre for Freudian Analysis and Research*, 17, 108–133.
Burman, E. (1998) 'Children, false memories, and disciplinary alliances: tensions between developmental psychology and psychoanalysis', *Psychoanalysis and Contemporary Thought*, 31, 307–333.
Burman, E. (2001) 'Emotions in the classroom: and the institutional politics of knowledge', *Psychoanalytic Studies*, 3, 313–324.
Burman, E. (2007) *Deconstructing Developmental Psychology (2nd edn)*. London and New York: Routledge.
Burman, E. (2008) *Developments: Child, Image, Nation*. London and New York: Routledge.
Burston, D. (1996) *The Wing of Madness: The Life and Work of R. D. Laing*. Cambridge, MA: Harvard University Press.
Butler, J. (1990) *Gender Trouble: Feminism and the Subversion of Identity*. London and New York: Routledge.
Butler, J. (1993) *Bodies That Matter: On the Discursive Limits of 'Sex'*. London and New York: Routledge.
Butler, J. (1997) *The Psychic Life of Power: Theories in Subjection*. Stanford, CA: Stanford University Press.
Campling, P. (1999) 'Chaotic personalities: maintaining the therapeutic alliance', in P. Campling and R. Haigh (eds) *Therapeutic Communities: Past, Present and Future*. London: Jessica Kingsley.
Cantin, L. (2009) 'An effective treatment of psychosis with psychoanalysis in Québec City, since 1982', *Annual Review of Critical Psychology*, 7, 286–319.
Casement, P. (1985) *On Learning from the Patient*. London and New York: Routledge.
Chakrabarti, A. and Dhar, A. (2010) *Dislocation and Resettlement in Development: From Third World to the World of the Third*. London and New York: Routledge.
Chase, C. (1987) 'The witty butcher's wife: Freud, Lacan, and the conversion of resistance to theory', *Modern Language Notes*, 102, 989–1013.
Chasseguet-Smirgel, J. (1985) *Creativity and Perversion*. London: Free Association Books.

Chasseguet-Smirgel, J. and Grunberger, B. (1976/1986) *Freud or Reich? Psychoanalysis and Illusion*. London: Free Association Books.
Chiesa, L. (2007) *Subjectivity and Otherness: A Philosophical Reading of Lacan*. Cambridge, MA: MIT Press.
Clarkson, P. and Gilbert, M. C. (1991) 'The training of counsellor trainers and supervisors', in W. Dryden and B. Thorne (eds) *Training and Supervision for Counselling in Action*. London: Sage.
Clemens, J. and Grigg, R. (eds) (2006) *Jacques Lacan and the Other Side of Psychoanalysis*. Durham, NC: Duke University Press.
Clough, P. T. with Halley, J. (eds) (2007) *The Affective Turn: Theorizing the Social*. Durham, NC: Duke University Press.
Colletti, L. (1970) 'The question of Stalin', *New Left Review*, 61, 61–81.
Coltart, N. (1988) 'The assessment of psychological-mindedness in the diagnostic interview', *British Journal of Psychiatry*, 153, 819–820.
Coltart, N. (2000) *Slouching towards Bethlehem*. New York: Other Press.
Copjec, J. (1993) *Read My Desire: Lacan Against the Historicists*. Cambridge, MA: MIT Press.
Copjec, J. (2006) 'May '68, the emotional month', in S. Žižek (ed.) *Lacan: The Silent Partners*. London: Verso.
Corti, L. (2004) 'On the Freudian origins of jouissance: from the experience of satisfaction to beyond satisfaction', *JCFAR: Journal of the Centre for Freudian Analysis and Research*, 15, 66–98.
Cottet, S. (1993) 'Should we analyse the transference?' *JCFAR: Journal of the Centre for Freudian Analysis and Research*, 2, 3–10.
Craib, I. (1994) *The Importance of Disappointment*. London and New York: Routledge.
Cushman, P. (1991) 'Ideology obscured: political uses of the self in Daniel Stern's infant', *American Psychologist*, 46(3), 206–219.
Dalzell, T. (2004) 'Balthasar's theological aesthetics and Lacanian psychoanalysis', *Irish Theological Quarterly*, 69, 3–16.
Danto, E. A. (2005) *Freud's Free Clinics: Psychoanalysis and Social Justice, 1918–1938*. New York: Columbia University Press.
Danziger, K. (1997) *Naming the Mind: How Psychology Found its Language*. London: Sage.
De Shazer, S. (1985) *Keys to Solution in Brief Therapy*. New York: Norton.
De Vos, J. (2005) 'On psychology and other symptoms', *Journal for Lacanian Studies*, 3(2), 258–270.
De Vos, J. (2008) 'From panopticon to pan-psychologisation or, why do so many women study psychology', *International Journal of Žižek Studies*, 2(1), 1–18.
De Vos, J. (2009a) 'Now that you know, how do you feel? The Milgram experiment and psychologization', *Annual Review of Critical Psychology*, 7, 223–246.
De Vos, J. (2009b) 'The Academy of everyday life: psychology, hauntology, and psychoanalysis', *Educational Insights*. 13(4), http://www.ccfi.educ.ubc.ca/publication/insights/v13n04/articles/de_vos/index.html (accessed 25 March 2010).
De Zulueta, F. and Mark, P. (2000) 'Attachment and contained splitting: a combined approach of group and individual therapy to the treatment of patients suffering from borderline personality disorder', *Group Analysis*, 33(4), 486–500.

Declercq, F. (2006) 'Lacan on the capitalist discourse: its consequences for libidinal enjoyment and social bonds', *Psychoanalysis, Culture and Society*, 11, 74–83.
Deleuze, G. and Guattari, F. (1972/1977) *Anti-Oedipus: Capitalism and Schizophrenia*. New York: Viking.
Derrida, J. (1988) 'Geopsychoanalysis: ". . . and the rest of the world"', in C. Lane (ed.) *The Psychoanalysis of Race*. New York: Columbia University Press.
Derrida, J. (2001) '"Above all, no journalists"', in H. De Vries and S. Weber (eds) *Religion and Media*. Stanford, CA: Stanford University Press.
Descartes, R. (1641/1996) *Meditations on First Philosophy with Selections from the Objections and Replies*. Cambridge: Cambridge University Press.
Descombes, V. (1980) *Modern French Philosophy*. Cambridge: Cambridge University Press.
Dhar, A. (2009) 'Sexual difference: *encore*, yet again', *Annual Review of Critical Psychology*, 7, 168–186.
Dolar, M. (1998) 'Cogito as the subject of the unconscious', in S. Žižek (ed.) (1998) *Cogito and the Unconscious*. Durham, NC: Duke University Press.
Dufour, D.-R. (2008) *The Art of Shrinking Heads: On the New Servitude of the Liberated in the Age of Total Capitalism*. Cambridge: Polity Press.
Dunker, C. (2005a) 'Space, place and position: ethical operators in clinical work', in A. Gülerce, A. Hofmeister, I. Steauble, G. Saunders and J. Kaye (eds) *Contemporary Theorizing in Psychology: Global Perspectives*. Concord, Ont.: Captus Press Inc.
Dunker, C. (2005b) 'Truth structured like fiction: sexual theories of children viewed as narrative', *Journal for Lacanian Studies*, 2(2), 183–197.
Dunker, C. (2008) 'Psychology and psychoanalysis in Brazil: from cultural syncretism to the collapse of liberal individualism', *Theory and Psychology*, 18(2), 223–236.
Dunker, C. (2010) *The Structure and Constitution of the Psychoanalytic Clinic: Negativity and Conflict in Contemporary Practice*. London: Karnac.
Easthope, A. (1986) *What a Man's Gotta Do*. London: Paladin.
Ecclestone, K. and Hayes, D. (2008) *The Dangerous Rise of Therapeutic Education*. London and New York: Routledge.
Eisenstein, H. (1996) *Inside Agitators: Australian Femocrats and the State*. Philadelphia, PA: Temple University Press.
Eisenstein, Z. (1979) *Capitalist Patriarchy and the Case for Socialist Feminism*. New York: Monthly Review Press.
Ellenberger, H. (1970) *The Discovery of the Unconscious: The History and Evolution of Dynamic Psychiatry*. New York: Basic Books.
Ernst, S. and Maguire, M. (eds) (1987) *Living with the Sphinx: Papers from the Women's Therapy Centre*. London: Women's Press.
Esposito, R. (2008) *Bíos: Biopolitics and Philosophy*. Minneapolis: Minnesota University Press.
Ettinger, B. (2004) 'Weaving the woman artist with-in the matrixial encounter-event', *Theory, Culture and Society*, 21(1), 69–93.
Evans, J. (2007) 'Wellbeing and happiness as used by the UK Government', *Psychoanalytical Notebooks*, 16, 143–154.
Fairfield, S., Layton, L. and Stack, C. (eds) (2002) *Bringing the Plague: Toward a Postmodern Psychoanalysis*. New York: Other Press.

Fanon, F. (1967) *Black Skin, White Masks*. New York: Grove Press.
Fee, D. (ed.) (1999) *Pathology and the Postmodern: Mental Illness as Discourse and Experience*. London and Thousand Oaks, CA: Sage.
Feher-Gurewich, J., Tort, M. and Fairfield, S. (eds) (1999) *Lacan and the New Wave in American Psychoanalysis: The Subject and the Self*. New York: Other Press.
Ferenczi, S. (1909) 'Introjection and transference', in S. Ferenczi (1952) *First Contributions to Psycho-Analysis*. London: Hogarth Press and Institute of Psycho-Analysis.
Fernando, S. (2003) *Cultural Diversity, Mental Health and Psychiatry: The Struggle Against Racism*. London and New York: Routledge.
Fink, B. (1995) *The Lacanian Subject: Between Language and Jouissance*. Princeton, NJ: Princeton University Press.
Fink, B. (1997) *A Clinical Introduction to Lacanian Psychoanalysis: Theory and Technique*. Cambridge, MA: Harvard University Press.
Fink, B. (2004) *Lacan to the Letter: Reading Écrits Closely*. Minneapolis: University of Minnesota Press.
Fink, B. (2007) *Fundamentals of Psychoanalytic Technique: A Lacanian Approach for Practitioners*. New York: Norton.
Fonagy, P. (2004) 'Psychotherapy meets neuroscience: a more focused future for psychotherapy research', *Psychiatric Bulletin*, 28(10), 357–359.
Fonagy, P. and Target, M. (2004) 'What can developmental psychopathology tell psychoanalysts about the mind?', in A. Casement (ed.) *Who Owns Psychoanalysis?* London: Karnac.
Fonagy, P., Gergely, G., Jurist, E. L. and Target, M. (2004) *Affect Regulation, Mentalization, and the Development of Self*. London: Karnac.
Forrester, J. (1997) *Dispatches from the Freud Wars: Psychoanalysis and Its Passions*. Boston, MA: Harvard University Press.
Foster, J. B. (2005) 'The *Wall Street Journal* Meets Karl Marx', http://mrzine. monthlyreview.org/foster140705.html (accessed 8 September 2009).
Foucault, M. (1961/2009) *History of Madness*. London and New York: Routledge.
Foucault, M. (1975/1979) *Discipline and Punish: The Birth of the Prison*. Harmondsworth: Penguin.
Foucault, M. (1976/1981) *The History of Sexuality, Vol. I: An Introduction*. Harmondsworth: Pelican.
Foucault, M. (1977) *Language, Counter-Memory, Practice: Selected Essays and Interviews*. Oxford: Blackwell.
Foucault, M. (1984) 'What is Enlightenment?', http://foucault.info/documents/ whatIsEnlightenment/foucault.whatIsEnlightenment.en.html (accessed 7 September 2009).
Freeman, E. (1985) 'The importance of feedback in clinical supervision: implications for direct practice', *The Clinical Supervisor*, 3(1), 5–26.
Freud, S. (1894) 'The neuro-psychoses of defence', in S. Freud (1966–1974) *The Standard Edition of the Complete Psychological Works of Sigmund Freud* (translated by J. Strachey). London: Vintage, Hogarth Press and Institute of Psycho-Analysis, vol. III.
Freud, S. (1900/1999) *The Interpretation of Dreams* (translated by J. Crick). Oxford: Oxford University Press.
Freud, S. (1904) 'Freud's psycho-analytic procedure', in S. Freud (1966–1974) *The*

Standard Edition of the Complete Psychological Works of Sigmund Freud (translated by J. Strachey). London: Vintage, Hogarth Press and Institute of Psycho-Analysis, vol. VII.

Freud, S. (1905) 'Three essays on the theory of sexuality', in S. Freud (1966–1974) *The Standard Edition of the Complete Psychological Works of Sigmund Freud* (translated by J. Strachey). London: Vintage, Hogarth Press and Institute of Psycho-Analysis, vol. VII.

Freud, S. (1907) 'Obsessive actions and religious practices', in S. Freud (1966–1974) *The Standard Edition of the Complete Psychological Works of Sigmund Freud* (translated by J. Strachey). London: Vintage, Hogarth Press and Institute of Psycho-Analysis, vol. IX.

Freud, S. (1909a) 'Notes upon a case of obsessional neurosis', in S. Freud (1966–1974) *The Standard Edition of the Complete Psychological Works of Sigmund Freud* (translated by J. Strachey). London: Vintage, Hogarth Press and Institute of Psycho-Analysis, vol. X.

Freud, S. (1909b) 'Family romances', in S. Freud (1966–1974) *The Standard Edition of the Complete Psychological Works of Sigmund Freud* (translated by J. Strachey). London: Vintage, Hogarth Press and Institute of Psycho-Analysis, vol. IX.

Freud, S. (1910) 'Leonardo da Vinci and a memory of his childhood', in S. Freud (1966–1974) *The Standard Edition of the Complete Psychological Works of Sigmund Freud* (translated by J. Strachey). London: Vintage, Hogarth Press and Institute of Psycho-Analysis, vol. XI.

Freud, S. (1911) 'Psycho-analytic notes on an autobiographical account of a case of paranoia (dementia paranoides)', in S. Freud (1966–1974) *The Standard Edition of the Complete Psychological Works of Sigmund Freud* (translated by J. Strachey). London: Vintage, Hogarth Press and Institute of Psycho-Analysis, vol. XII.

Freud, S. (1912) 'Recommendations to physicians practising psycho-analysis', in S. Freud (1966–1974) *The Standard Edition of the Complete Psychological Works of Sigmund Freud* (translated by J. Strachey). London: Vintage, Hogarth Press and Institute of Psycho-Analysis, vol. XII.

Freud, S. (1913 [1912–1913]) 'Totem and taboo', in S. Freud (1966–1974) *The Standard Edition of the Complete Psychological Works of Sigmund Freud* (translated by J. Strachey). London: Vintage, Hogarth Press and Institute of Psycho-Analysis, vol. XIII.

Freud, S. (1914) 'On narcissism: an introduction', in S. Freud (1966–1974) *The Standard Edition of the Complete Psychological Works of Sigmund Freud* (translated by J. Strachey). London: Vintage, Hogarth Press and Institute of Psycho-Analysis, vol. XIV.

Freud, S. (1915a) 'The unconscious', in S. Freud (1966–1974) *The Standard Edition of the Complete Psychological Works of Sigmund Freud* (translated by J. Strachey). London: Vintage, Hogarth Press and Institute of Psycho-Analysis, vol. XIV.

Freud, S. (1915b) 'Observations on transference-love (further recommendations on the technique of psycho-analysis III)', in S. Freud (1966–1974) *The Standard Edition of the Complete Psychological Works of Sigmund Freud* (translated by

J. Strachey). London: Vintage, Hogarth Press and Institute of Psycho-Analysis, vol. XII.
Freud, S. (1920) 'Beyond the pleasure principle', in S. Freud (1966–1974) *The Standard Edition of the Complete Psychological Works of Sigmund Freud* (translated by J. Strachey). London: Vintage, Hogarth Press and Institute of Psycho-Analysis, vol. XVIII.
Freud, S. (1921) 'Group psychology and the analysis of the ego', in S. Freud (1966–1974) *The Standard Edition of the Complete Psychological Works of Sigmund Freud* (translated by J. Strachey). London: Vintage, Hogarth Press and Institute of Psycho-Analysis, vol. XVIII.
Freud, S. (1923) 'The ego and the id', in S. Freud (1966–1974) *The Standard Edition of the Complete Psychological Works of Sigmund Freud* (translated by J. Strachey). London: Vintage, Hogarth Press and Institute of Psycho-Analysis, vol. XIX.
Freud, S. (1925) 'Negation', in S. Freud (1966–1974) *The Standard Edition of the Complete Psychological Works of Sigmund Freud* (translated by J. Strachey). London: Vintage, Hogarth Press and Institute of Psycho-Analysis, vol. XIX.
Freud, S. (1926) 'The question of lay analysis: conversations with an impartial person', in S. Freud (1966–1974) *The Standard Edition of the Complete Psychological Works of Sigmund Freud* (translated by J. Strachey). London: Vintage, Hogarth Press and Institute of Psycho-Analysis, vol. XX.
Freud, S. (1927) 'Fetishism', in S. Freud (1966–1974) *The Standard Edition of the Complete Psychological Works of Sigmund Freud* (translated by J. Strachey). London: Vintage, Hogarth Press and Institute of Psycho-Analysis, vol. XXI.
Freud, S. (1930) 'Civilization and its discontents', in S. Freud (1966–1974) *The Standard Edition of the Complete Psychological Works of Sigmund Freud* (translated by J. Strachey). London: Vintage, Hogarth Press and Institute of Psycho-Analysis, vol. XXI.
Freud, S. (1933) 'New introductory lectures on psychoanalysis', in S. Freud (1966–1974) *The Standard Edition of the Complete Psychological Works of Sigmund Freud* (translated by J. Strachey). London: Vintage, Hogarth Press and Institute of Psycho-Analysis, vol. XXII.
Freud, S. (1937) 'Analysis terminable and interminable', in S. Freud (1966–1974) *The Standard Edition of the Complete Psychological Works of Sigmund Freud* (translated by J. Strachey). London: Vintage, Hogarth Press and Institute of Psycho-Analysis, vol. XXIII.
Freud, S. (1940) 'Splitting of the ego in the process of defence', in S. Freud (1966–1974) *The Standard Edition of the Complete Psychological Works of Sigmund Freud* (translated by J. Strachey). London: Vintage, Hogarth Press and Institute of Psycho-Analysis, vol. XXIII.
Freud, S. (1950) 'Project for a scientific psychology', in S. Freud (1966–1974) *The Standard Edition of the Complete Psychological Works of Sigmund Freud* (translated by J. Strachey). London: Vintage, Hogarth Press and Institute of Psycho-Analysis, vol. I.
Fromm, E. (1932) 'The method and function of an analytic social psychology: notes on psychoanalysis and historical materialism', in A. Arato and E. Gebhardt (eds) (1978) *The Essential Frankfurt School Reader*. Oxford: Blackwell.

Frosh, S. (1994) *Sexual Difference: Masculinity and Psychoanalysis*. London and New York: Routledge.
Frosh, S. (2003) 'Psychoanalysis in Britain', in D. Bradshaw (ed.) *A Concise Companion to Modernism*. Oxford: Blackwell.
Frosh, S. (2005) *Hate and the 'Jewish Science': Anti-Semitism, Nazism, and Psychoanalysis*. London: Palgrave.
Frosh, S. (2007) 'Disintegrating qualitative research', *Theory and Psychology*, 17(5), 635–653.
Frosh, S. (2008) 'Freud and Jewish identity', *Theory and Psychology*, 18(2), 167–178.
Frosh, S. and Baraitser, L. (2008) 'Psychoanalysis and psychosocial studies', *Psychoanalysis, Culture and Society*, 13, 346–365.
Furedi, F. (2003) *Therapy Culture: Cultivating Vulnerability in an Uncertain Age*. London and New York: Routledge.
Gardiner, M. (ed.) (1972) *The Wolf-Man and Sigmund Freud*. London: Hogarth Press.
Gay, P. (1988) *Freud: A Life for Our Time*. New York: Norton.
Gellner, E. (1985) *The Psychoanalytic Movement, or The Coming of Unreason*. London: Paladin.
Georgaca, E. and Gordo-López, A. J. (1995) 'Subjectivity and "psychotic" discourses: a preliminary study', in M. Sullivan (ed.) *Psychoanalytic Seminars, 1991–1994*. London: THERIP.
Gibson-Graham, J. K., Resnick, S. A. and Wolff, R. (eds) (2001) *Re{p}resenting Class: Essays in Postmodern Marxism*. Durham, NC: Duke University Press.
Giddens, A. (1992) *The Transformation of Intimacy: Sexuality, Love and Eroticism in Modern Society*. Cambridge: Polity Press.
Gilbert, M. C. and Evans, K. (2000) *Psychotherapy Supervision: An Integrative Relational Approach to Psychotherapy Supervision*. Buckingham: Open University Press.
Gilman, S. (1991) *The Jew's Body*. London and New York: Routledge.
Gilman, S. (1993) *The Case of Sigmund Freud: Medicine and Identity at the Fin de Siècle*. Baltimore, MD: Johns Hopkins University Press.
Gilman, S. (1996) *Seeing the Insane*. Lincoln, NE: Nebraska University Press.
Glejzer, R. (1997) 'Lacan with scholasticism: agencies of the letter', *American Imago*, 54(2), 105–122.
Glynos, J. (2001) 'The grip of ideology: a Lacanian approach to the theory of ideology', *Journal of Political Ideologies*, 6(2), 191–214.
Glynos, J. and Stavrakakis, A. (eds) (2002) *Lacan and Science*. London: Karnac.
Golan, R. (2006) *Loving Psychoanalysis: Looking at Culture with Freud and Lacan*. London: Karnac.
Goldacre, B. (2008) *Bad Science*. London: Fourth Estate.
Goldiamond, I. (1974) 'Toward a constructional approach to social problems', *Behaviourism*, 2, 1–84.
Gómez, C. (2009) 'Writing an algebra for the social sciences: Freud's and Lacan's mathemes', *Annual Review of Critical Psychology*, 7, 101–113.
Gramsci, A. (1971) *Selections from the Prison Notebooks*. London: Lawrence & Wishart.
Green, A. (1995) 'Against Lacanism: a conversation of André Green with Sergio

Benvenuto', *Journal of European Psychoanalysis*, 2, http://www.psychomedia.it/jep/number2/greenbenv.htm (accessed 11 September 2009).

Greenhalgh, T., Seyan, K. and Boynton, P. (2004) '"Not a university type": focus group study of social class, ethnic, and sex differences in school pupils' perceptions about medical school', *British Medical Journal*, http://www.bmj.com/cgi/content/full/328/7455/1541 (accessed 2 September 2009).

Grigg, R. (1998) 'From the mechanism of psychosis to the universal condition of the symptom: on foreclosure', in D. Nobus (ed.) *Key Concepts in Psychoanalysis*. London: Rebus Press.

Grigg, R., Hecq, D. and Smith, C. (eds) (1999) *Female Sexuality: The Early Psychoanalytic Controversies*. London: Rebus Press.

Groarke, S. (2008) 'Psychoanalytical infant observation: a critical assessment', *European Journal of Psychotherapy and Counselling*, 10(4), 299–321.

Guattari, F. (1984) *Molecular Revolution: Psychiatry and Politics*. Harmondsworth: Peregrine.

Guattari, F. and Rolnik, S. (2008) *Molecular Revolution in Brazil*. Los Angeles, CA: Semiotext(e).

Guéguen, P.-G. (1995) 'Transference as deception', in R. Feldstein, B. Fink and M. Jaanus (eds) *Reading Seminar XI: Lacan's Four Fundamental Concepts of Psychoanalysis*. New York: State University of New York Press.

Guéguen, P.-G. (2005) 'The battle of psychoanalysis in the twenty-first century', *Psychoanalytical Notebooks*, 14, 132–136.

Guéguen, P.-G. (2008) 'Lacanian interpretation', *Bulletin of the NLS*, 4, 65–68.

Haas, E. T. (2001) 'Does the IPA need a code of ethics? Ten arguments against', *International Psychoanalysis*, 10(2), 34–36.

Hackett, C. D. (1982) 'Psychoanalysis and theology: Jacques Lacan and Paul', *Journal of Religion and Health*, 21(3), 184–192.

Haddad, G. (1994) 'Judaism in the life and work of Jacques Lacan: A preliminary study', *Yale French Studies*, 85, 201–216.

Halberstam, J. (2008) 'The anti-social turn in queer studies', *Graduate Journal of Social Science*, 5(2), 140–156.

Hanly, C. and Nichols, C. (2001) 'A disturbance of psychoanalytic memory: the case of John Rickman's three-person psychology', *Philosophy of the Social Sciences*, 31(3), 279–301.

Haraway, D. J. (1989) *Primate Visions: Gender, Race, and Nature in the World of Modern Science*. London and New York: Routledge.

Hardt, J. (2006) 'Psychoanalytic and therapeutic training in Germany: "after" Freud', *European Journal of Psychotherapy and Counselling*, 8(4), 375–385.

Hardt, M. and Negri, A. (2000) *Empire*. Cambridge, MA: Harvard University Press.

Hardt, M. and Negri, A. (2004) *Multitude: War and Democracy in the Age of Empire*. New York: Penguin.

Harrington, R. (2003) 'On the tracks of trauma: railway spine reconsidered', *Social History of Medicine*, 16(2), 209–223.

Hartmann, H. (1939/1958) *Ego Psychology and the Problem of Adaptation*. New York: International Universities Press.

Hartnack, C. (2003) 'Freud on Garuda's wings', *International Institute for Asian Studies Newsletter*, 30, 10.

Healy, D. (2002) *The Creation of Psychopharmacology*. Cambridge, MA: Harvard University Press.
Healy, D. (2004) *Let Them Eat Prozac: The Unhealthy Relationship Between the Pharmaceutical Industry and Depression*. New York: New York University Press.
Healy, D. (2009) *Mania: A Short History of Bipolar Disorder*. Baltimore, MD: Johns Hopkins University Press.
Heaton, J. (2001) 'Evidence and psychotherapy', *European Journal of Psychotherapy, Counselling and Health*, 4(2), 237–248.
Hegarty, P. (2004) 'Was he queer . . . or just Irish? Reading ethnicity and sexuality in the biography of Harry Stack Sullivan', *Lesbian and Gay Psychology Review*, 5, 103–108.
Hegel, G. W. F. (1807/1977) *Philosophy of Spirit*. Oxford: Oxford University Press.
Heimann, P. (1950) 'On countertransference', *International Journal of Psycho-Analysis*, 31, 81–84.
Hinshelwood, R. (1997) 'Transference and counter-transference', in B. Burgoyne and M. Sullivan (eds) *The Klein–Lacan Dialogues*. London: Rebus Press.
Hinshelwood, R. D. (1995) 'Psychoanalysis in Britain: points of cultural access, 1893–1918', *International Journal of Psycho-Analysis*, 76, 135–151.
Hoens, D. (2006) 'Toward a new perversion: psychoanalysis', in J. Clemens and R. Grigg (eds) *Jacques Lacan and the Other Side of Psychoanalysis*. Durham, NC: Duke University Press.
Hook, D. (2007) *Foucault, Psychology and the Analytics of Power*. London: Palgrave.
Hook, D. (2008) 'Absolute Other: Lacan's "big Other" as adjunct to critical psychological analysis?', *Social and Personality Psychology Compass*, 2(1), 51–73.
Hook, D. (2009) 'Restoring universality to the subject: Lacan's Kantian logic of sexuation', *Annual Review of Critical Psychology*, 7, 151–167.
House, R. (2002) *Therapy Beyond Modernity: Deconstructing and Transcending Profession-Centred Therapy*. London: Karnac.
House, R. (2005) '"Audit culture", accreditation and the Academy: staying faithful to authentic educational quality', *New View*, 36, 59–64.
House, R. and Loewenthal, D. (eds) (2008) *Against and for CBT: Towards a Constructive Dialogue?* Hay-on-Wye: PCCS Books.
House, R. and Totton, N. (eds) (1997) *Implausible Professions: Arguments for Pluralism and Autonomy in Psychotherapy and Counselling*. Ross-on-Wye: PCCS.
Howarth, D. and Stavrakakis, Y. (2000) 'Introducing discourse theory and political analysis', in D. Howarth, A. Norval and Y. Stavrakakis (eds) *Discourse Theory and Political Analysis: Identities, Hegemonies and Social Change*. Manchester: Manchester University Press.
Howarth, D., Norval, A. and Stavrakakis Y. (eds) (2000) *Discourse Theory and Political Analysis: Identities, Hegemonies and Social Change*. Manchester: Manchester University Press.
Hyppolite, J. (1956) 'A spoken commentary on Freud's "Verneinung"', in J. Lacan (2006) *Écrits: The First Complete Edition in English* (translated with notes by B. Fink in collaboration with H. Fink and R. Grigg). New York: Norton.
Ingleby, D. (ed.) (1981) *Critical Psychiatry: The Politics of Mental Health*. Harmondsworth: Penguin.

Ingleby, D. (1985) 'Professionals as socializers: the "psy complex"', *Research in Law, Deviance and Social Control*, 7, 79–109.
Jacobs, M. (2002) '"That psychotherapy and counselling trainings should be based in universities"', *European Journal of Psychotherapy, Counselling and Health*, 5(4), 347–358.
Jacoby, R. (1983) *The Repression of Psychoanalysis*. New York: Basic Books.
Jakobson, R. (1975) 'Two aspects of language and two types of aphasic disturbances', in R. Jakobson and M. Halle, *Fundamentals of Language*. The Hague: Mouton.
Jerry, P. A. and Resnik, A. (2003) 'The tensions of the Brief Lacanian Psychotherapist: further work on the Brief Lacanian Therapy Project', *Journal for Lacanian Studies*, 1(2), 161–180.
Johnstone, L. and Dallos, R. (eds) (2006) *Formulation in Psychology and Psychotherapy: Making Sense of People's Problems*. London and New York: Routledge.
Kakar, S. (1974) *Frederick Taylor: A Study in Personality and Innovation*. Boston, MA: MIT Press.
Kant, I. (1784) 'An answer to the question: what is enlightenment?', available at www.english.upenn.edu/~mgamer/Etexts/kant.html (accessed 24 February 2003).
Kareem, J. and Littlewood, R. (1999) *Intercultural Therapy: Themes, Interpretations and Practice*. Oxford: Blackwell.
Kirk, S. A. and Kutchins, H. (1992) *The Selling of DSM: The Rhetoric of Science in Psychiatry*. New York: Aldine de Gruyter.
Kirsner, D. (2000) *Unfree Associations: Inside Psychoanalytic Institutes*. London: Process Press.
Klein, R. (2003) 'The birth of gender', *Psychoanalytical Notebooks of the London Circle*, 11, 51–60.
Klotz, J.-P. (1995) 'The passionate dimension of transference', in R. Feldstein, B. Fink and M. Jaanus (eds) *Reading Seminar XI: Lacan's Four Fundamental Concepts of Psychoanalysis*. New York: State University of New York Press.
Klotz, J.-P. (2009) 'Ordinary psychosis and modern symptoms', *Psychoanalytical Notebooks*, 19, 21–31.
Kojève, A. (1969) *Introduction to the Reading of Hegel: Lectures on the Phenomenology of Spirit*. New York: Basic Books.
Kotsko, A. (2008) *Žižek and Theology*. London: Continuum.
Kovel, J. (1978) *A Complete Guide to Therapy: From Psychoanalysis to Behaviour Modification*. Harmondsworth: Penguin.
Kovel, J. (1981) *The Age of Desire: Case Histories of a Radical Psychoanalyst*. New York: Pantheon.
Kovel, J. (1986) 'Why Freud or Reich?', *Free Associations*, 4, 80–99.
Kovel, J. (1988) *The Radical Spirit: Essays on Psychoanalysis and Society*. London: Free Association Books.
Kovel, J. (1991) *History and Spirit: An Inquiry into the Philosophy of Liberation*. Boston, MA: Beacon Press.
Kovel, J. (2007) *The Enemy of Nature: The End of Capitalism or the End of the World? (2nd rev. edn)*. London: Zed Books.
Kumar, M. (2009) 'Poverty and psychoanalysis: poverty of psychoanalysis', Paper presented at the annual meeting of the ISPP, 32nd Annual Scientific Meeting,

Trinity College, Dublin, Ireland, 14 July, http://www.allacademic.com/meta/p305202_index.html (accessed 2 October 2009).

Kutter, P. (ed.) (1991) *Psychoanalysis International: A Guide to Psychoanalysis Throughout the World, Vol. 1.* Stuttgart-Bad-Canstatt: Fromman-Holzboorg.

Kutter, P. (ed.) (1995) *Psychoanalysis International: A Guide to Psychoanalysis Throughout the World, Vol. 2.* Stuttgart-Bad-Canstatt: Fromman-Holzboorg.

Lacan, J. (1933) 'Motives of paranoiac crime: the crime of the Papin sisters', http://www.lacan.com/papin.htm (accessed 10 October 2001).

Lacan, J. (1938) 'Family complexes in the formation of the individual' (translated from French manuscripts by C. Gallagher; original published under the title 'La Famille' in *Encyclopédie francaise*, edited by A. de Monzie, vol. 8).

Lacan, J. (1946a) 'Presentation on psychical causality', in J. Lacan (2006) *Écrits: The First Complete Edition in English* (translated with notes by B. Fink in collaboration with H. Fink and R. Grigg). New York: Norton.

Lacan, J. (1946b) 'Logical time and the assertion of anticipated certainty: A new sophism', in J. Lacan (2006) *Écrits: The First Complete Edition in English* (translated with notes by B. Fink in collaboration with H. Fink and R. Grigg). New York: Norton.

Lacan, J. (1947/2000) 'British psychiatry and the war', *Psychoanalytical Notebooks of the London Circle*, 4, 9–34.

Lacan, J. (1953) 'The function and field of speech and language in psychoanalysis', in J. Lacan (2006) *Écrits: The First Complete Edition in English* (translated with notes by B. Fink in collaboration with H. Fink and R. Grigg). New York: Norton.

Lacan, J. (1956–1957) *The Seminar of Jacques Lacan, Book IV: The Object Relation* (unauthorised private translation from unedited French manuscripts).

Lacan, J. (1958) 'The direction of the treatment and the principles of its power', in J. Lacan (2006) *Écrits: The First Complete Edition in English* (translated with notes by B. Fink in collaboration with H. Fink and R. Grigg). New York: Norton.

Lacan, J. (1959) 'On a question prior to any possible treatment of psychosis', in J. Lacan (2006) *Écrits: The First Complete Edition in English* (translated with notes by B. Fink in collaboration with H. Fink and R. Grigg). New York: Norton.

Lacan, J. (1959/1977) 'Desire and the interpretation of desire in *Hamlet*', *Yale French Studies*, 55/56, 11–52.

Lacan, J. (1960) 'The subversion of the subject and the dialectic of desire in the Freudian unconscious', in J. Lacan (2006) *Écrits: The First Complete Edition in English* (translated with notes by B. Fink in collaboration with H. Fink and R. Grigg). New York: Norton.

Lacan, J. (1960–1961) *The Seminar of Jacques Lacan, Book VIII: Transference* (translated by C. Gallagher from unedited French manuscripts).

Lacan, J. (1961–1962) *The Seminar of Jacques Lacan, Book IX: Identification* (translated by C. Gallagher from unedited French manuscripts).

Lacan, J. (1963) 'Kant with Sade', in J. Lacan (2006) *Écrits: The First Complete Edition in English* (translated with notes by B. Fink in collaboration with H. Fink and R. Grigg). New York: Norton.

Lacan, J. (1964/1973) *The Four Fundamental Concepts of Psycho-Analysis: The Seminar of Jacques Lacan, Book XI* (translated by A. Sheridan). Harmondsworth: Penguin.

Lacan, J. (1965) 'Science and truth', in J. Lacan (2006) *Écrits: The First Complete Edition in English* (translated with notes by B. Fink in collaboration with H. Fink and R. Grigg). New York: Norton.
Lacan, J. (1966a) 'Position of the unconscious: remarks made at the 1960 Bonneval colloquium rewritten in 1964', in J. Lacan (2006) *Écrits: The First Complete Edition in English* (translated with notes by B. Fink in collaboration with H. Fink and R. Grigg). New York: Norton.
Lacan, J. (1966b) 'On my antecedents', in J. Lacan (2006) *Écrits: The First Complete Edition in English* (translated with notes by B. Fink in collaboration with H. Fink and R. Grigg). New York: Norton.
Lacan, J. (1967/1995) 'Proposition of 9 October 1967 on the psychoanalyst of the School', *Analysis*, 6, 1–13.
Lacan, J. (1967–1968) *The Seminar of Jacques Lacan, Book XV: The Psychoanalytic Act* (translated by C. Gallagher from unedited French manuscripts).
Lacan, J. (1975/1991) *The Seminar of Jacques Lacan, Book I: Freud's Papers on Technique, 1953–1954* (translated with notes by J. Forrester). New York: Norton.
Lacan, J. (1975/1998) *On Feminine Sexuality, The Limits of Love and Knowledge, 1972–1973: Encore, The Seminar of Jacques Lacan, Book XX* (translated by B. Fink). New York: Norton.
Lacan, J. (1976–1977) *The Seminar of Jacques Lacan Edited by Jacques-Alain Miller, Book 24: L'insu que sait de l'une bévue, s'aile à mourre* (translated by D. Collins, unpublished third corrected draft, 2008).
Lacan, J. (1978/1991) *The Seminar of Jacques Lacan, Book II: The Ego in Freud's Theory and in the Technique of Psychoanalysis, 1954–1955* (translated by S. Tomaselli, with notes by J. Forrester). New York: Norton.
Lacan, J. (1979) 'The neurotic's individual myth', *Psychoanalytic Quarterly*, 48, 405–425.
Lacan, J. (1980) 'A Lacanian psychosis: interview by Jacques Lacan', in S. Schneiderman (ed.) *Returning to Freud: Clinical Psychoanalysis in the School of Lacan*. New Haven, CT and London: Yale University Press.
Lacan, J. (1981/1993) *The Psychoses: The Seminar of Jacques Lacan, Book III: 1955–1956* (translated with notes by R. Grigg). London and New York: Routledge.
Lacan, J. (1986/1992) *The Ethics of Psychoanalysis 1959–1960: The Seminar of Jacques Lacan, Book VII* (translated with notes by D. Porter). London and New York: Routledge.
Lacan, J. (1987a) 'Television', *October*, 40, 7–50.
Lacan, J. (1987b) 'Introduction to the Names-of-the-Father seminar', *October*, 40, 81–95.
Lacan, J. (1987c) 'Founding act', *October*, 40, 96–105.
Lacan, J. (1991/2007) *The Other Side of Psychoanalysis: The Seminar of Jacques Lacan, Book XVII* (translated by R. Grigg). New York: Norton.
Lacan, J. (2006) *Écrits: The First Complete Edition in English* (translated with notes by B. Fink in collaboration with H. Fink and R. Grigg). New York: Norton.
Laclau, E. (1996) *Emancipation(s)*. London: Verso.
Laclau, E. (2000) 'Structure, history and the political', in J. Butler, E. Laclau and S. Žižek, *Contingency, Hegemony, Universality: Contemporary Dialogues on the Left*. London: Verso.

Laing, R. D. (1959/1965) *The Divided Self: An Existential Study in Sanity and Madness*. Harmondsworth: Penguin.
Lander, R. (2006) *Subjective Experience and the Logic of the Other*. New York: Other Press.
Laplanche, J. (1989) *New Foundations for Psychoanalysis*. Oxford: Blackwell.
Laplanche, J. (1996) 'Psychoanalysis as anti-hermeneutics', *Radical Philosophy*, 79, 7–12.
Laplanche, J. (1999) *Essays on Otherness*. London: Routledge.
Laplanche, J. (2003) 'Narrativity and hermeneutics: some propositions', *New Formations*, 48, 26–29.
Laqueur, T. (1990) *Making Sex: Body and Gender from the Greeks to Freud*. Cambridge, MA: Harvard University Press.
Lasch, C. (1978) *The Culture of Narcissism: American Life in an Age of Diminishing Expectations*. New York: Norton.
Laurent, É. (2002) 'The ethics of psychoanalysis, today', *Psychoanalytical Notebooks of the London Circle*, 8, 91–105.
Laurent, É. (2007) 'The birth of the subject supposed to know', *Bulletin of the NLS*, 2, 7–18.
Laurent, É. (2008) 'Interpreting psychosis from day to day', *Bulletin of the NLS*, 4, 83–97.
Layton, L., Hollander, N. C. and Gutwill, S. (eds) (2006) *Psychoanalysis, Class and Politics: Encounters in the Clinical Setting*. London and New York: Routledge.
Leader, D. (2000) *Freud's Footnotes*. London: Faber & Faber.
Lecourt, D. (1977) *Proletarian Science? The Case of Lysenko*. London: New Left Books.
Lefort, C. (1989) *Democracy and Political Theory*. Minneapolis: University of Minnesota Press.
Leitner, M. (1999) 'Pathologizing as a way of dealing with conflicts and dissent in the psychoanalytic movement', *Free Associations*, 7(3), 459–483.
Leon, A. (1946) *The Jewish Question: A Marxist Interpretation*, http://www.marxists.de/religion/leon/ (accessed 7 September 2009).
Lévi-Strauss, C. (1958/1972) *Structural Anthropology*. Harmondsworth: Penguin.
Libbrecht, K. (1998) 'The original sin of psychoanalysis: on the desire of the analyst', in D. Nobus (ed.) *Key Concepts in Psychoanalysis*. London: Rebus Press.
Lichtman, R. (1982) *The Production of Desire: The Integration of Psychoanalysis into Marxist Theory*. New York: Free Press.
Lindner, R. (1955/1986) *The Fifty-Minute Hour: A Collection of True Psychoanalytic Tales*. London: Free Association Books.
Litten, R. (2008) 'Responsibility and accountability in psychoanalysis', in I. Parker and S. Revelli (eds) *Psychoanalytic Practice and State Regulation*. London: Karnac.
Littlewood, R. and Lipsedge, M. (1993) *Aliens and Alienists: Ethnic Minorities and Psychiatry (3rd rev. edn)*. London and New York: Routledge.
Llorens, M. (2009) 'Psychotherapy, political resistance and intimacy: dilemmas, possibilities and limitations, part I', *Psychotherapy and Politics International*, 7(2), 122–131.
Loewenthal, D. and House, R. (eds) (2010) *Critically Engaging CBT in an Age of Happiness: Modality Perspectives*. Buckingham: Open University Press.

Loewenthal, D. and Snell, R. (eds) (2003) *Post-modernism for Psychotherapists: A Critical Reader*. London and New York: Routledge.

Lorde, A. (2007) *Sister Outsider: Essays and Speeches*. Freedom, CA: Crossing Press.

Low, J. (2009) 'The relation between the process and the appearance of the process: MHTP', http://hpcwatchdog.blogspot.com/2009/05/mhtp-thats-mad-hatters-tea-party-to-you.html (accessed 14 September 2009).

Lukács, G. (1923/1971) *History and Class Consciousness*. Cambridge, MA: MIT Press.

Lyotard, J.-F. (1979/1984) *The Postmodern Condition: A Report on Knowledge*. Manchester: Manchester University Press.

Mace, C. (2002) 'Research and the organization of knowledge: where do psychotherapy and counselling fit in?', *European Journal of Psychotherapy, Counselling and Health*, 5(4), 359–369.

Mace, C., Rowland, N., Evans, C., Schroder, T. and Halstead, J. (2009) 'Psychotherapy professionals in the UK: expansion and experiment', *European Journal of Psychotherapy and Counselling*, 11(2), 131–140.

Macey, D. (1988) *Lacan in Contexts*. London: Verso.

Macey, D. (1995) 'On the subject of Lacan', in A. Elliott and S. Frosh (eds) *Psychoanalysis in Contexts: Paths between Theory and Modern Culture*. London and New York: Routledge.

Machado, D. (1993) 'Phobia and perversion', *JCFAR: Journal of the Centre for Freudian Analysis and Research*, 2, 23–33.

Maleval, J.-C. (2000) 'Why so many "borderlines"?', *Psychoanalytical Notebooks of the London Circle*, 4, 111–127.

Malone, K. R. (2006) 'Regulation and standards for psychoanalysis: the place of the Other in psychoanalysis and its teaching', *European Journal of Psychotherapy and Counselling*, 8(3), 269–284.

Malone, K. R. (2008) 'Psychoanalysis: formalization and logic and the question of speaking and affect', *Theory and Psychology*, 18(2), 179–193.

Malone, K. R. and Friedlander, S. (eds) (1999) *The Subject of Lacan: A Lacanian Reader for Psychologists*. New York: State University of New York Press.

Malone, K. R. and Kelly, S. D. (2004) 'The transfer from the clinical to the social and back', *Psychoanalysis, Culture and Society*, 9, 23–32.

Mandel, E. (1971) *The Formation of the Economic Thought of Karl Marx*. London: New Left Books.

Mandel, E. (1974) *Late Capitalism*. London: New Left Books.

Mandel, E. (1978) *From Stalinism to Eurocommunism: The Bitter Fruits of 'Socialism in One Country'*. London: New Left Books.

Mandel, E. (1979) *Revolutionary Marxism Today*. London: New Left Books.

Mandel, E. (1986) *The Place of Marxism in History*. Amsterdam: Notebooks for Study and Research.

Mandel, E. (1990) *Karl Marx*, http://www.marxists.org/archive/mandel/19xx/marx/index.htm (accessed 5 September 2009).

Mandel, E. and Novack, G. (1970) *The Marxist Theory of Alienation*. New York: Pathfinder Press.

Mangabeira, W. C. (1999) 'On the textuality of objects in disciplinary practice: the couch in psychoanalysis', *Psychoanalytic Studies*, 1(3), 327–354.

Marcuse, H. (1955/1974) *Eros and Civilization: A Philosophical Inquiry into Freud*. Boston, MA: Beacon Press.

Marx, K. (1845/1888) 'Theses on Feuerbach', http://www.marxists.org/archive/marx/works/1845/theses/theses.htm (accessed 8 September 2009).

Marx, K. (1863) 'Theories of surplus-value [vol. IV of Capital]', http://www.marxists.org/archive/marx/works/1863/theories-surplus-value/ (accessed 5 September 2009).

Marx, K. and Engels, F. (1848/1965) *Manifesto of the Communist Party*. Beijing: Foreign Languages Press.

Maucade, J. (2009) 'Cogito and the subject of Arab culture', *S: Journal of the Jan Van Eyck Circle for Lacanian Ideology Critique*, 2, 6–9.

Mazin, V. (2007) 'Lacan and the cosmos', *Journal for Lacanian Studies*, 5(1), 97–122.

McCarney, J. (1990) *Social Theory and the Crisis of Marxism*. London: Verso.

McLaughlin, K. (2008) *Social Work, Politics and Society: From Radicalism to Orthodoxy*. Bristol: Policy Press.

Meissner, W. W. (1990) 'The role of transitional conceptualization in religious thought', in J. H. Smith and S. A. Handelman (eds) *Psychoanalysis and Religion*, Baltimore, MD: Johns Hopkins University Press.

Micklethwait, J. and Wooldridge, A. (2009) *God is Back: How the Global Rise of Faith is Changing the World*. London: Allen Lane.

Mieli, P. (2000) 'Femininity and the limits of theory', in K. R. Malone and S. Friedlander (eds) *The Subject of Lacan: A Lacanian Reader for Psychologists*. New York: State University of New York Press.

Miller, J.-A. (1977) 'Suture: elements of the logic of the signifier', *Screen*, 18(2), 24–34.

Miller, J.-A. (1980) 'Teachings of the case presentation', in S. Schneiderman (ed.) *Returning to Freud: Clinical Psychoanalysis in the School of Lacan*. New Haven, CT and London: Yale University Press.

Miller, J.-A. (1986) '*Extimité*', in M. Bracher, M. Alcorn, R. Corthell and F. Massardier-Kenney (eds) (1994) *Lacanian Theory of Discourse: Subject, Structure and Society*. New York: New York University Press.

Miller, J.-A. (1989) 'Michel Foucault and psychoanalysis', in T. J. Armstrong (ed.) (1992) *Michel Foucault: Philosopher*. New York: Harvester Wheatsheaf.

Miller, J.-A. (1998) 'Report for the General Assembly in Barcelona – 23 July 1998', *Psychoanalytical Notebooks of the London Circle*, 1, 117–152.

Miller, J.-A. (1999a) 'Interpretation in reverse', *Psychoanalytical Notebooks of the London Circle*, 2, 9–18.

Miller, J.-A. (1999b) 'Of semblants in the relation between sexes', *Psychoanalytical Notebooks of the London Circle*, 3, 9–25.

Miller, J.-A. (2000a) 'Paradigms of *Jouissance*', *Lacanian Ink*, 17, 10–47.

Miller, J.-A. (2000b) 'The Turin Theory of the subject of the school', http://www.londonsociety-nls.org.uk/pdfs/Turin.pdf (accessed 7 September 2009).

Miller, J.-A. (2001) 'Lacanian biology and the event of the body', *Lacanian Ink*, 18, 6–29.

Miller, J.-A. (2002a) 'Pure psychoanalysis, applied psychoanalysis and psychotherapy', *Lacanian Ink*, 20, 4–43.

Miller, J.-A. (2002b) 'Elements of epistemology', in J. Glynos and Y. Stavrakakis (eds) *Lacan and Science*. London: Karnac.
Miller, J.-A. (2003) 'Countertransference and intersubjectivity', *Lacanian Ink*, 22, 8–53.
Miller, J.-A. (2007a) 'Jacques Lacan and the voice', in V. Voruz and B. Wolf (eds) *The Later Lacan: An Introduction*. New York: State University of New York Press.
Miller, J.-A. (2007b) 'The era of the man without qualities', *Psychoanalytical Notebooks*, 16, 7–42.
Miller, J.-A. (2008) 'Clinic under transference', *Psychoanalytical Notebooks*, 17, 7–12.
Miller, J.-A. (2009) 'Ordinary psychosis revisited', *Psychoanalytical Notebooks*, 19, 139–167.
Miller, L., Rustin, M., Rustin, M. and Shuttleworth, J. (eds) (1989) *Closely Observed Infants*. London: Duckworth.
Miller, M. (1998) *Freud and the Bolsheviks: Psychoanalysis in Imperial Russia and the Soviet Union*. New Haven, CT: Yale University Press.
Miller, P. and Rose, N. (eds) (1986) *The Power of Psychiatry*. Cambridge: Polity Press.
Miller, P. and Rose, N. (1988) 'The Tavistock programme: governing subjectivity and social life', *Sociology*, 22, 171–192.
Millett, K. (1977) *Sexual Politics*. London: Virago.
Mitchell, J. (1974) *Psychoanalysis and Feminism*. Harmondsworth: Pelican.
Mitchell, J. (1984) *Women: The Longest Revolution: Essays on Feminism, Literature and Pyschoanalysis*. London: Virago.
Mitchell, S. (1997) *Influence and Autonomy in Psychoanalysis*. Hillsdale, NJ: Analytic Press.
Močnik, R. (1993) 'Ideology and fantasy', in E. Ann Kaplan (ed.) *The Althusserian Legacy*. London: Verso.
Moncayo, R. (1998) 'Cultural diversity and the cultural and epistemological structure of psychoanalysis: implications for psychotherapy with Latinos and other minorities', *Psychoanalytic Psychology*, 15(2), 262–286.
Moscovici, S. (1976/2008) *Psychoanalysis: Its Image and Its Public*. Cambridge: Polity Press.
Mowbray, R. (1995) *The Case Against Psychotherapy Registration: A Conservation Issue for the Human Potential Movement*. London: Transmarginal Press.
Muller, J. P. (1996) *Beyond the Psychoanalytic Dyad: Developmental Semiotics in Freud, Peirce and Lacan*. London and New York: Routledge.
Napoli, D. S. (1981) *Architects of Adjustment: The History of the Psychological Profession in the United States*. Port Washington, NJ: Kennikat Press.
Nasio, J.-D. (1998) *Five Lessons on the Psychoanalytic Theory of Jacques Lacan*. New York: State University of New York Press.
Neill, C. (2005a) 'The locus of judgement in Lacan's Ethics', *Journal for Lacanian Studies*, 3(1), 85–100.
Neill, C. (2005b) 'An idiotic act: on the non-example of Antigone', *The Letter: Lacanian Perspectives on Psychoanalysis*, 34, 1–28.
Neill, C. (2008) 'Severality: beyond the compression of the cogito', *Subjectivity*, 24, 325–339.

Neill, C. (2009) 'Who wants to be in rational love?', *Annual Review of Critical Psychology*, 7, 140–150.
Nobus, D. and Quinn, M. (2005) *Knowing Nothing, Staying Stupid: Elements for a Psychoanalytic Epistemology*. London and New York: Routledge.
O'Connor, N. and Ryan, J. (1993) *Wild Desires and Mistaken Identities: Lesbianism and Psychoanalysis*. London: Virago.
Oliver, B. (2005) 'Lacan and the question of the psychotherapist's ethical orientation', *South African Journal of Psychology*, 35(4), 657–683.
Orbach, S. (2003) 'Therapy from the left: interview with Susie Orbach', *European Journal of Psychotherapy, Counselling and Health*, 6(1), 75–85.
Orbach, S. (2007) 'Democratizing psychoanalysis', *European Journal of Psychotherapy and Counselling*, 9(1), 7–21.
Owens, C. (ed.) (2009) 'Lacan and Critical Psychology', *Annual Review of Critical Psychology (Special Issue)*, 7.
Palmer, S. (2008) 'Knowledge and mastery: is psychoanalysis a religion?', *JCFAR: Journal of the Centre for Freudian Analysis and Research*, 18, 100–121.
Palomera, V. (1997) 'On counter-transference', in B. Burgoyne and M. Sullivan (eds) *The Klein–Lacan Dialogues*. London: Rebus Press.
Parker, I. (1997) *Psychoanalytic Culture: Psychoanalytic Discourse in Western Society*. London: Sage.
Parker, I. (2004) *Slavoj Žižek: A Critical Introduction*. London: Pluto Press.
Parker, I. (2007) *Revolution in Psychology: Alienation to Emancipation*. London: Pluto Press.
Parker, I. (2008) *Japan in Analysis: Cultures of the Unconscious*. London: Palgrave.
Parker, I. (2009) *Psychoanalytic Mythologies*. London: Anthem Press.
Parker, I. and Revelli, S. (eds) (2008) *Psychoanalytic Practice and State Regulation*. London: Karnac.
Pavón Cuéllar, D. (2009) 'Untying Real, Imaginary and Symbolic: a Lacanian criticism of behavioural, cognitive and discursive psychologies', *Annual Review of Critical Psychology*, 7, 33–51.
Pavón Cuéllar, D. (2010) *From the Conscious Interior to an Exterior Unconscious: Lacan, Discourse Analysis and Social Psychology*. London: Karnac.
Pilgrim, D. (2008) 'Reading "Happiness": CBT and the Layard thesis', *European Journal of Psychotherapy and Counselling*, 10(3), 247–260.
Pluth, E. (2008) *Signifiers and Acts: Freedom in Lacan's Theory of the Subject*. New York: State University of New York Press.
Pollock, G. (2004) 'Thinking the feminine: aesthetic practice as introduction to Bracha Ettinger and the concepts of matrix and metramorphosis', *Theory, Culture and Society*, 21(1), 5–65.
Pound, M. (2007) *Theology, Psychoanalysis and Trauma*. London: SCM Press.
Pound, M. (2008) *Žižek: A (Very) Critical Introduction*. Grand Rapids, MI: Eerdmans.
Power, L. and Pilgrim, D. (1990) 'The fee in psychotherapy: practitioners' accounts', *Counselling Psychology Quarterly*, 3(2), 153–170.
Proctor, G., Cooper, M., Sanders, P. and Malcolm, B. (eds) (2006) *Politicizing the Person-centred Approach: An Agenda for Social Change*. Hay-on-Wye: PCCS Books.

Pupavac, V. (2005) 'Human security and the rise of global therapeutic governance', *Conflict, Security and Development*, 5(2), 161–181.
Rabaté, J.-M. (ed.) (2000) *Lacan in America*. New York: Other Press.
Ragland, E. and Milovanovic, D. (eds) (2004) *Lacan: Topologically Speaking*. New York: Other Press.
Rajchman, J. (1991) *Truth and Eros: Foucault, Lacan, and the Question of Ethics*. London and New York: Routledge.
Regnault, F. (1999) 'Hegel's master and slave dialectic in the work of Lacan', *Psychoanalytical Notebooks of the London Circle*, 2, 91–106.
Regnault, F. (2009) 'Saintliness and the sainthood', *Lacanian Ink*, 33, 115–125.
Reich, W. (1972) *Sex-Pol: Essays, 1929–1934* (edited by B. Ollman). New York: Random House.
Reinhard, K. and Lupton, J. R. (2003) 'The subject of religion: Lacan and the Ten Commandments', *Diacritics*, 33(2), 71–97.
Renik, O. (1999) 'Playing one's cards face up in analysis: an approach to the problem of self-disclosure', *Psychoanalytic Quarterly*, 64, 521–539.
Renik, O. and Spillius, E. B. (2004) 'Intersubjectivity in psychoanalysis', *International Journal of Psycho-Analysis*, 85, 1053–1056.
Richards, B. (1995) 'Psychotherapy and the injuries of class', *BPS Psychotherapy Section Newsletter*, 17, 21–35.
Richards, G. (2000) 'Britain on the couch: the popularization of psychoanalysis in Britain 1918–1940', *Science in Context*, 13(2), 183–230.
Ricoeur, P. (1965/1970) *Freud and Philosophy: An Essay on Interpretation*. New Haven, CT: Yale University Press.
Riha, R. (2003) 'Seeing the revolution, seeing the subject', *Parallax*, 9(2), 27–41.
Riviere, J. (1929) 'Womanliness as a masquerade', in V. Burgin, J. Donald and C. Kaplan (eds) (1986) *Formations of Fantasy*. London: Methuen.
Roazen, P. (1996) 'Lacan's first disciple', *Journal of Religious Health*, 4, 321–326.
Roberts, J. (2008a) 'The "Returns to religion": Messianism, Christianity and the revolutionary tradition. Part I: "Wakefulness to the future"', *Historical Materialism*, 16(2), 59–84.
Roberts, J. (2008b) 'The "Returns to religion": Messianism, Christianity and the revolutionary tradition. Part II: The Pauline tradition', *Historical Materialism*, 16(3), 77–103.
Robertson, R. (1995) 'Glocalization: time-space and homogeneity-heterogeneity', in M. Featherstone, S. Lash and R. Robertson (eds) *Global Modernities*. London and Thousand Oaks, CA: Sage.
Rodríguez, S. A. and Rodríguez, L. S. (1989) 'On the transference', *Analysis*, 1, 165–185.
Roper, B. (2009) 'Practices, provenances, homologies?', *Annual Review of Critical Psychology*, 7, 91–100.
Rose, N. (1985) *The Psychological Complex: Psychology, Politics and Society in England 1869–1939*. London: Routledge & Kegan Paul.
Rose, N. (1996) *Inventing Ourselves: Psychology, Power and Personhood*. Cambridge: Cambridge University Press.
Rosemont, F. (1978) *André Breton and the First Principles of Surrealism*. London: Pluto Press.

Roudinesco, E. (1990) *Jacques Lacan and Co.: A History of Psychoanalysis in France, 1925–1985*. London: Free Association Books.
Roudinesco, E. (1997) *Jacques Lacan: An Outline of a Life and a History of a System of Thought*. Cambridge: Polity Press.
Roudinesco, E. (2002) 'Homosexualities today: a challenge for psychoanalysis? (Interview)', *Journal of European Psychoanalysis*, 15, http://www.psychomedia.it/jep/number15/roudinesco.htm (accessed 5 September 2009).
Roudinesco, E. (2006) 'The psychotherapist and the state', *European Journal of Psychotherapy and Counselling*, 8(4), 369–374.
Rowan, J. and Dryden, W. (eds) (1988) *Innovative Therapy in Britain*. Buckingham: Open University Press.
Rowbotham, S., Segal, L. and Wainwright, H. (1980) *Beyond the Fragments: Feminism and the Making of Socialism*. London: Merlin.
Rustin, M. (2003) 'Learning about emotions: the Tavistock approach', *European Journal of Psychotherapy, Counselling and Health*, 6(3), 187–208.
Safouan, M. (1983/2000) *Jacques Lacan and the Question of Psychoanalytic Training*. London: Macmillan.
Said, E. (2003) *Orientalism: Western Conceptions of the Orient*. Harmondsworth: Penguin.
Said, E. (2004) *Freud and the Non-European*. London: Verso.
Samuels, A. (1985) *Jung and the Post-Jungians*. London: Routledge & Kegan Paul.
Samuels, A. (1993) *The Political Psyche*. London and New York: Routledge.
Samuels, A. (2009) 'Carnal critiques: promiscuity, politics, imagination, spirituality and hypocrisy', *Psychotherapy and Politics International*, 7(1), 4–17.
Sandler, J., Dare, C. and Holder, A. (1979) *The Patient and the Analyst*. London: Maresfield Reprints.
Sandler, J., Holder, A. and Dare, C. (1970) 'Basic psychoanalytic concepts: II. The treatment alliance', *British Journal of Psychiatry*, 116, 555–558.
Santner, E. (1996) *My Own Private Germany: Daniel Paul Schreber's Secret History of Modernity*. Princeton, NJ: Princeton University Press.
Sato, T. (2002) 'Nihon ni okeru Shinrigaku no Juyo to Tenkai', *Kitaohji Shobo* (English unpublished manuscript, 'Acceptance and development of psychoanalysis in Japan').
Saussure, F. de (1915/1974) *Course in General Linguistics*. Glasgow: Fontana/Collins.
Sauvagnat, F. (2007) 'A few thoughts about the Lacanian movement's position on the gay question', *JCFAR: Journal of the Centre for Freudian Analysis and Research*, 17, 29–37.
Schepeler, E. (1993) 'Jean Piaget's experiences on the couch: some clues to a mystery', *International Journal of Psycho-Analysis*, 74, 255–273.
Schmideberg, M. (1971) 'A contribution to the history of the psycho-analytic movement in Britain', *British Journal of Psychiatry*, 118, 61–68.
Schwarz, J. (1999) *Cassandra's Daughter: A History of Psychoanalysis in Europe and America*. Harmondsworth: Penguin.
Scraton, P. and Davis, H. (2001) *Disaster, Trauma, Aftermath*. London: Lawrence and Wishart.
Sedgwick, P. (1982) *Psychopolitics*. London: Pluto Press.

Seligman, M. E. P. (1998) 'Message from the President of the APA', APA Annual Convention Program. Washington, DC: American Psychological Association.
Seshadri-Crooks, K. (2000) *Desiring Whiteness: A Lacanian Analysis of Race.* London and New York: Routledge.
Sharpe, M. (2006) '"In the Name of the Father . . ." Descartes, psychosis, God and "Reality"', *Journal for Lacanian Studies*, 4(2), 214–232.
Shingu, K. (1995/2004) *Being Irrational: Lacan, the Objet a, and the Golden Mean.* Tokyo: Gakuju Shoin.
Shingu, K. and Funaki, T. (2008) '"Between two deaths": the intersection of psychoanalysis and Japanese Buddhism', *Theory and Psychology*, 18(2), 253–267.
Shotter, J. (1987) 'Cognitive psychology, "Taylorism", and the manufacture of unemployment', in A. Costall and A. Still (eds) *Cognitive Psychology in Question.* Brighton: Harvester.
Showalter, E. (1997) *Hystories: Hysterical Epidemics and Modern Media.* New York: Columbia University Press.
Shuttleworth, A. (2002) 'Turning towards a bio-psycho-social way of thinking', *European Journal of Psychotherapy, Counselling and Health*, 5(3), 205–223.
Singh, G. (1999) *Sikkhism and Postmodern Thought.* Delhi: Ajanta Publications.
Skinner, B. F. (1969) *Contingencies of Reinforcement.* New York: Appleton-Century-Crofts.
Slattery, M. (2002) 'How Françoise Dolto links Lacanian psychoanalysis with the Christian gospels', *Journal of Pastoral Care and Counseling*, 56(4), 363–375.
Smith, D. (2006) 'Inside out: Guattari's *Anti-Oedipus Papers*', *Radical Philosophy*, 140, 35–39.
Smith, D. L. (2002) *Fearfully and Wonderfully Made: The History of the Duquesne University's Graduate Psychology Programs (1959–1999).* Pittsburgh, PA: Simon Silverman Phenomenology Center of Duquesne University.
Sohn-Rethel, A. (1978) *Intellectual and Manual Labour: A Critique of Epistemology.* London: Macmillan.
Solano-Suárez, E. (2007) 'Identification with the symptom at the end of analysis', in V. Voruz, and B. Wolf (eds) *The Later Lacan: An Introduction.* New York: State University of New York Press.
Soler, C. (1994) 'Some remarks on the Love Letter', *JCFAR: Journal of the Centre for Freudian Analysis and Research*, 4, 5–24.
Soler, C. (1995) 'The body in the teaching of Jacques Lacan', *JCFAR: Journal of the Centre for Freudian Analysis and Research*, 6, 6–38.
Soler, C. (1996a) 'Hysteria and obsession', in R. Feldstein, B. Fink and M. Jaanus (eds) *Reading Seminars I and II: Lacan's Return to Freud.* New York: State University of New York Press.
Soler, C. (1996b) 'Transference', in R. Feldstein, B. Fink and M. Jaanus (eds) *Reading Seminars I and II: Lacan's Return to Freud.* New York: State University of New York Press.
Soler, C. (1996c) 'Time and interpretation', in R. Feldstein, B. Fink and M. Jaanus (eds) *Reading Seminars I and II: Lacan's Return to Freud.* New York: State University of New York Press.
Spandler, H. (2006) *Asylum to Action: Paddington Day Hospital, Therapeutic Communities and Beyond.* London and Philadelphia, PA: Jessica Kingsley.
Spence, D. P. (1982) *Narrative Truth and Historical Truth.* New York: Norton.

Spiegel, A. (2005) 'The dictionary of disorder: how one man revolutionized psychiatry', *New Yorker*, 3 January, available at http://www.newyorker.com/fact/content/?050103fa_fact (accessed 27 September 2009).
Spivak, G. C. (1990) *The Post-Colonial Critic*. London and New York: Routledge.
Stavrakakis, Y. (1999) *Lacan and the Political*. London and New York: Routledge.
Stavrakakis, Y. (2007a) 'Wallon, Lacan and the Lacanians: citation practices and repression', *Theory, Culture and Society*, 24(4), 131–138.
Stavrakakis, Y. (2007b) *The Lacanian Left: Psychoanalysis, Theory, Politics*. Edinburgh: Edinburgh University Press.
Stern, D. N. (1985) *The Interpersonal World of the Infant: A View from Psychoanalysis and Developmental Psychology*. New York: Basic Books.
Strachey, J. (1934) 'The nature of the therapeutic action of psycho-analysis', *International Journal of Psycho-Analysis*, 15, 127–159.
Straker, G. (1994) 'The interface between refugee groups and assistance groups: an exploration of dynamics and the design of a treatment programme', *Free Associations*, 4(3), 320–327.
Strathern, M. (2000) 'The tyranny of transparency', *British Educational Research Journal*, 26(3), 309–321.
Sulloway, F. J. (1980) *Freud, Biologist of the Mind: Beyond the Psychoanalytic Legend*. London: Fontana.
Symington, N. (1990) 'Religion and psychoanalysis', *Free Associations*, 19, 105–116.
Szasz, T. (1961) *The Myth of Mental Illness*. New York: Harper & Row.
Szasz, T. (2004) '"Knowing what ain't so": R. D. Laing and Thomas Szasz', *Psychoanalytic Review*, 91(3), 331–346.
Szasz, T. (2009) *Antipsychiatry: Quackery Squared*. New York: Syracuse University Press.
Tamboukou, M. (2003) 'Interrogating the "emotional turn": making connections with Foucault and Deleuze', *European Journal of Psychotherapy, Counselling and Health*, 6(3), 209–223.
Teitelbaum, S. H. (1990) 'Supertransference: the role of the supervisor's blind spots', *Psychoanalytic Psychology*, 7(2), 243–258.
Therborn, G. (1976) *Science, Class, Society: On the Formation of Sociology and Historical Materialism*. London: Verso.
Thomson, M. (2006) *Psychological Subjects: Identity, Culture and Health in Twentieth-Century Britain*. Oxford: Oxford University Press.
Thurston, L. (1998) 'Ineluctable nodalities: on the Borromean Knot', in D. Nobus (ed.) *Key Concepts in Psychoanalysis*. London: Rebus Press.
Thurston, L. (ed.) (2002) *Re-inventing the Symptom: Essays on the Final Lacan*. New York: Other Press.
Timms, E. and Segal, N. (eds) (1988) *Freud in Exile: Psychoanalysis and its Vicissitudes*. New Haven, CT and London: Yale University Press.
Totton, N. (ed.) (2006) *The Politics of Psychotherapy: New Perspectives*. Buckingham: Open University Press.
Townshend, J. (1998) *Possessive Individualism and Democracy: C. B. Macpherson and His Critics*. Edinburgh: Edinburgh University Press.
Trist, E. and Murray, H. (eds) (1990) *The Social Engagement of Social Science: A Tavistock Anthology: Vol. 1, The Socio-Psychological Perspective*. London: Free Association Books.

Trotsky, L. (1936/1973) *The Revolution Betrayed: What Is the Soviet Union and Where Is It Going?* London: New Park.
Tudor, K. and Worrall, M. (2006) *Person-Centred Therapy.* London and New York: Routledge.
Turner, B. S. (1987) *Medical Power and Social Knowledge.* London: Sage.
Ullman, C. (2007) 'Commentary on special issue on "Relational psychoanalysis in Europe": how is this dialogue different?', *European Journal of Psychotherapy and Counselling*, 9(1), 105–116.
Ussher, J. (1991) *Women's Madness: Misogyny or Mental Illness?* Hemel Hempstead: Harvester Wheatsheaf.
Vaillant, G. E. (1971) 'Theoretical hierarchy of adaptive ego mechanisms: a 30-year follow-up of 30 men selected for psychological health', *Archives of General Psychiatry*, 24, 107–118.
Van Haute, P. (1995) 'Fatal attraction: Jean Laplanche on sexuality, subjectivity and singularity in the work of Sigmund Freud', *Radical Philosophy*, 73, 5–12.
Van Haute, P. (2002) *Against Adaptation: Lacan's 'Subversion of the Subject'.* New York: Other Press.
Vanheule, S. (2009) 'Psychotic delusions: pathological products or attempts at recovery? A comparison of the psychiatric and Lacanian psychoanalytic approach to psychosis', International Society for Theoretical Psychology Biennial Conference, Nanjing, May.
Vanheule, S. and Verhaeghe, P. (2009) 'Identity through a psychoanalytic looking glass', *Theory and Psychology*, 19(3), 391–411.
Verhaeghe, P. (1999) *Does the Woman Exist? From Freud's Hysteric to Lacan's Feminine.* London: Rebus Press.
Verhaeghe, P. (2004) *On Being Normal and Other Disorders: A Manual for Clinical Psychodiagnostics.* New York: Other Press.
Vicens, A. (2009) 'Some cases of ordinary psychosis in the CPCT of Barcelona', *Psychoanalytical Notebooks*, 19, 89–98.
Vogt, E. (2006) 'Schmittian traces in Žižek's political theology (and some Derridean spectres)', *Diacritics*, 36(1), 14–29.
Voruz, V. (2007) 'A Lacanian reading of *Dora*', in V. Voruz and B. Wolf (eds) *The Later Lacan: An Introduction.* New York: State University of New York Press.
Voruz, V. and Wolf, B. (eds) (2007) *The Later Lacan: An Introduction.* New York: State University of New York Press.
Wake, N. (2008) 'Sexuality, intimacy and subjectivity in social psychoanalytic thought of the 1920s and 1930s', *Journal of Community and Applied Social Psychology*, 18, 119–130.
Walkerdine, V. (1988) *The Mastery of Reason.* London and New York: Routledge.
Wallerstein, R. (1988) 'One psychoanalysis or many?', *International Journal of Psycho-Analysis*, 69(5), 5–21.
Ware, V. (1982) *Beyond the Pale: White Women, Racism and History.* London: Verso.
Watson, E. (2009) 'Queering psychoanalysis / psychoanalysing queer', *Annual Review of Critical Psychology*, 7, 114–139.
Waugaman, R. M. (1987) 'Falling off the couch', *Journal of the American Psychoanalytic Association*, 35, 861–876.

Webb, R. E. and Sells, M. A. (1995) 'Lacan and Bion: psychoanalysis and the mystical language of "unsaying"', *Theory and Psychology*, 5(2), 195–215.

Went, R. (2000) *Globalization: Neoliberal Challenge, Radical Responses*. London: Pluto Press.

Westen, D., Novotny, C. and Thompson-Brenner, H. (2004) 'The empirical status of empirically supported psychotherapies: assumptions, findings, and reporting in controlled clinical trials', *Psychological Bulletin*, 130(4), 631–663.

White, J. (2006) *Generation: Preoccupations and Conflicts in Contemporary Psychoanalysis*. London and New York: Routledge.

Wilden, A. (1972) *System and Structure: Essays in Communication and Exchange*. London: Tavistock.

Winnicott, D. W. (1957) *The Child and the Family: First Relationships*. London: Tavistock.

Wolf, B. (2007) 'The perception and politics of discourse', in V. Voruz and B. Wolf (eds) *The Later Lacan: An Introduction*. New York: State University of New York Press.

Wolfe, B. (1989) 'Diagnosis and distancing reactions', *Psychoanalytic Psychology*, 6(2), 187–198.

Wolfenstein, E. V. (1993) *Psychoanalytic-Marxism: Groundwork*. London: Free Association Books.

Worthington, A. (2008) 'Freud's young female homosexual: a clinical exemplar of the three essays?', *JCFAR: Journal of the Centre for Freudian Analysis and Research*, 18, 43–68.

Wright, E. (1999) 'Transference: The impossible relation', *Psychoanalytic Studies*, 1(3), 263–267.

Young, R. M. (1992) 'Science, ideology and Donna Haraway', *Science as Culture*, 15(3), 165–207.

Young, R. M. (1999) 'Psychoanalysis and psychotherapy: the grand leading the bland', *Free Associations*, 7(3), 437–458.

Young-Eisendrath, P. and Muramoto, S. (eds) (2002) *Awakening and Insight: Zen Buddhism and Psychotherapy*. Hove, East Sussex: Brunner-Routledge.

Zaretsky, E. (1976) *Capitalism, the Family, and Personal Life*. London: Pluto Press.

Zeitlin, M. (1997) 'The ego psychologists in Lacan's theory', *American Imago*, 54(2), 209–232.

Žižek, S. (1986) 'Pathological Narcissus as a socially mandatory form of subjectivity' (published in the Croatian edition of *The Culture of Narcissism* by Christopher Lasch (Narcisistička kultura, Naprijed, Zagreb, 1986), translation at http://www.manifesta.org/manifesta3/catalogue5.htm (accessed 7 July 2009)).

Žižek, S. (1989) *The Sublime Object of Ideology*. London: Verso.

Žižek, S. (1994) *The Metastases of Enjoyment: Six Essays on Woman and Causality*. London: Verso.

Žižek, S. (ed.) (1995) *Mapping Ideology*. London: Verso.

Žižek, S. (2000a) 'Postface: Georg Lukács as the philosopher of Leninism', in G. Lukács, *A Defence of History and Class Consciousness: Tailism and the Dialectic*. London: Verso.

Žižek, S. (2000b) *Did Somebody Say Totalitarianism? Five Interventions in the (Mis)use of a Notion*. London: Verso.

Žižek, S. (2002) *For They Know Not What They Do: Enjoyment as a Political Factor*. London: Verso.
Žižek, S. (2003) *The Puppet and the Dwarf: The Perverse Core of Christianity*. Cambridge: MA: MIT Press.
Žižek, S. (2006) *The Parallax View*. Cambridge, MA: MIT Press.
Žižek, S. (2008) *Violence: Six Sideways Reflections*. London: Profile Books.
Žižek, S. (2009) *First as Tragedy, Then as Farce*. London: Verso.
Žižek, S. and Milbank, J. (2009) *The Monstrosity of Christ: Paradox or Dialectic?* Cambridge, MA: MIT Press.
Zupančič, A. (2000) *Ethics of the Real: Kant, Lacan*. London: Verso.
Zwart, H. (1998) 'Medicine, symbolization and the "real" body: Lacan's understanding of medical science', *Medicine, Health Care, and Philosophy*, 1(2), 107–117.

Author index

Adorno, T. W., 24, 109
Agamben, G., 40, 162
Ahmed, S., 140
Alexander, F., 111
Althusser, L., 90, 92, 139, 186
Anderson, P., 84
André, S., 48
Ansermet, F., 60
Appignanesi, L., 85
Aquinas, St, 156, 161
Ariès, P., 28
Atkinson, D. R., 113
Augustine, St, 156
Austin, S., 143

Badiou, A., 53, 94, 113, 137, 162, 197
Bailly, L., 127
Bakan, D., 30, 134
Balibar, E., 126
Balint, M., 49, 68, 129
Baraitser, L., 170
Barnard, S., 158
Bassols, M., 165
Bateman, A., 82, 122, 177
Beauvoir, S. de, 196
Beck, A., 67
Beechey, V., 85
Beirnaert, L., 154–155
Beloff, Z., 20
Benjamin, J., 32, 188
Benjamin, L. T., 66
Bennani, J., 165
Bensaïd, D., 113
Benslama, F., 166
Bentall, R. P., 93
Bentham, J., 137
Benvenuto, S., 151
Bernheim, H., 20, 47
Bettelheim, B., 19, 27, 109

Bick, E., 96
Billig, M., 75
Bisson, T., 23
Blass, R. B., 60, 189
Bourdieu, P., 117, 132
Boynton, P., 31
Bracken, P., 171
Braverman, H., 87
Brennan, T., 23, 134, 184
Breuer, J., 19, 48, 71, 85
Britton, H., 36
Brousse, M.-H., 46, 143
Budgen, S., 91
Burgoyne, B., 120, 184
Burman, E., 28, 72, 110, 111, 132, 133, 182
Burston, D., 24
Butler, J., 16, 32, 95, 182, 196

Campling, P., 177
Cantin, L., 144
Carmeli, Z., 60, 189
Casement, P., 68, 69, 137
Certeau, M. de, 154–155
Chakrabarti, A., 30
Charcot, J.-M., 20, 33, 47
Chase, C., 48
Chasseguet-Smirgel, J., 49, 187
Chiesa, L., 20, 34, 35, 52, 56, 101
Clarkson, P., 68
Clemens, J., 25
Clough, P. T., 140
Colletti, L., 116
Coltart, N., 96, 132, 154
Cooper, M., 192
Copjec, J., 30, 114, 163
Corti, L., 42
Cottet, S., 59, 183
Craib, I., 79, 121
Cushman, P., 71

Dallos, R., 138
Dalzell, T., 158, 160, 164
Danto, E. A., 31, 180
Danziger, K., 120
Dare, C., 98, 121, 167
Davis, H., 171
De Shazer, S., 122
De Vos, J., 65, 80, 131, 170
De Zulueta, F., 177
Declercq, F., 54
Deleuze, G., 72, 140
Derrida, J., 32, 159
Descartes, R., 43, 79–80
Descombes, V., 76
Dhar, A., 30, 168
Dolar, M., 43, 81
Dolto, F., 77, 155–156
Dryden, W., 108, 124
Dufour, D.-R., 33, 94, 129
Dunker, C., 59, 71, 75, 179
Duns Scotus, J., 161

Easthope, A., 95
Ecclestone, K., 110, 131
Eisenstein, Z., 85, 130
Ellenberger, H., 20
Ellis, A., 67
Engels, F., 54, 117
Erikson, E., 77
Ernst, S., 194
Esposito, R., 82
Ettinger, B., 32, 34
Evans, C., 135
Evans, J., 67
Evans, K., 68, 69

Fairfield, S., 64, 112, 189
Fanon, F., 29
Fee, D., 115
Feher-Gurewich, J., 64
Ferenczi, S., 48, 187
Fernando, S., 40
Fink, B., 18, 48, 52, 58, 91, 158, 184, 185
Fonagy, P., 122, 125, 189
Forrester, J., 16, 85
Foster, J. B., 116
Foucault, M., 26, 34, 65, 79, 111, 168, 177
Freeman, E., 69
French, T. M., 111
Freud, S., 1, 5, 9, 11, 15–19, 21, 26–28, 31, 33, 35, 39, 41–42, 45–50, 52–54, 57–58, 60, 64, 67, 71, 76–77, 85–86, 89, 91–92, 94–96, 100–102, 107, 109–110, 113, 115–116, 120, 129, 133,
138, 143, 145–146, 152–155, 157, 159, 167, 174, 183–185, 187–190, 197
Friedlander, S., 65
Fromm, E., 187
Frosh, S., 20, 53, 64, 75, 115, 165, 170
Funaki, T., 164, 174
Furedi, F., 110

Gardiner, M., 180
Gay, P., 85, 154
Gellner, E., 167
Georgaca, E., 93, 144
Gergely, G., 189
Gibson-Graham, J. K., 30
Giddens, A., 65
Gilbert, M. C., 68, 69
Gilman, S., 20, 30
Glejzer, R., 156
Glynos, J., 75, 120
Goethe, J. W. von, 43
Golan, R., 164
Goldacre, B., 136
Goldiamond, I., 125
Gómez, C., 19
Gordo-López, A. J., 93, 144
Gramsci, A., 191
Green, A., 154
Greenhalgh, T., 31
Grigg, R., 25, 44, 85
Groarke, S., 72
Grunberger, B., 187
Guattari, F., 35, 72
Guéguen, P.-G., 23, 67, 169
Gutwill, S., 31, 51, 168, 193

Haas, E. T., 137
Hackett, C. D., 158, 160
Haddad, G., 165
Halberstam, J., 174
Halley, J., 140
Halstead, J., 135
Hanly, C., 129
Haraway, D. J., 23
Hardt, J., 19
Hardt, M., 117
Harrington, R., 29
Hartmann, H., 37, 48
Hartnack, C., 184
Hayes, D., 110, 131
Healy, D., 18
Heaton, J., 136
Hecq, D., 85
Hegarty, P., 188
Hegel, G. W. F., 23, 39, 70, 156, 159, 161, 162, 163, 178, 191, 192, 193

Author index

Heimann, P., 47, 130, 167
Hinshelwood, R. D., 63, 167
Hoens, D., 95
Holder, A., 98, 121, 167
Hollander, N. C., 31, 51, 168, 193
Hook, D., 16, 100, 163
Horkheimer, M., 24, 109
House, R., 66, 108, 114, 133, 135
Howarth, D., 120, 189
Hyppolite, J., 28

Ingleby, D., 15, 25

Jacobs, M., 132
Jacoby, R., 64
Jakobson, R., 22
Jerry, P. A., 186
John the Baptist, St, 156
Johnstone, L., 138
Jung, C. G., 154
Jurist, E. L., 189

Kakar, S., 89
Kant, I., 78–79, 111, 137
Kareem, J., 172
Kelly, S. D., 179
Kierkegaard, S., 156
Kirk, S. A., 18
Kirsner, D., 25
Klein, R., 58, 103
Klotz, J.-P., 36, 44, 181
Kojève, A., 23, 39, 71
Kotsko, A., 140
Kouvelakis, S., 91
Kovel, J., 42, 51, 89, 119, 128, 152, 171, 187
Kumar, M., 31
Kutchins, H., 18
Kutter, P., 64

Lacan, J., 1–2, 9, 11–12, 16–18, 20–28, 33, 35–38, 40–46, 48–60, 68, 70–81, 84, 86, 88, 90–91, 93–95, 97–105, 107–108, 110–111, 113, 115, 119–120, 123–124, 127, 128–130, 134, 138, 140, 142–147, 151, 153–170, 178, 181–184, 192–195, 197–198
Laclau, E., 96, 113, 189, 191
Laing, R. D., 17
Lander, R., 154
Laplanche, J., 71, 109, 115, 159, 173
Laqueur, T., 21
Lasch, C., 146
Laurent, É., 87, 144, 186

Layton, L., 31, 51, 112, 168, 189, 193
Leader, D., 82
Lecourt, D., 119
Lefort, C., 117
Leitner, M., 167
Leon, A., 75
Lévi-Strauss, C., 21, 22, 26, 145, 166
Libbrecht, K., 37, 55
Lichtman, R., 60, 179
Lindner, R., 171
Lipsedge, M., 30
Litten, R., 69
Littlewood, R., 30, 172
Llorens, M., 179
Loewenthal, D., 66, 108, 112, 114
Lorde, A., 91
Low, J., 135
Lukács, G., 121, 126
Lupton, J. R., 74, 157, 164–165
Lyotard, J.-F., 113

Mace, C., 134, 135
Macey, D., 18, 26, 41, 46
Machado, D., 51
Magistretti, P., 60
Maguire, M., 194
Malcolm, B., 192
Maleval, J.-C., 89
Malone, K. R., 65, 73, 130, 179
Mandel, E., 54, 87, 97, 102, 115, 119, 122, 123, 124, 126
Mangabeira, W. C., 183
Marcuse, H., 187
Mark, P., 177
Marx, K., 54, 116, 117, 121, 190, 191
Maucade, J., 165
Mazin, V., 24
McCarney, J., 121
McLaughlin, K., 110
Meissner, W. W., 166
Micklethwait, J., 153
Mieli, P., 164, 196
Milbank, J., 156, 160
Mill, J. S., 85
Miller, J.-A., 16, 24, 34–35, 42, 44, 48, 60, 61, 67, 70, 74, 105, 109, 111, 117, 120, 139, 172, 174, 182, 186
Miller, L., 72, 136
Miller, M., 119, 180
Miller, P., 15, 112, 177
Millett, K., 85
Milovanovic, D., 93, 159, 191
Mitchell, J., 20, 31, 58, 90, 168
Mitchell, S., 111, 188

Moènik, R., 139, 189
Moncayo, R., 134
Moscovici, S., 41
Mowbray, R., 135
Muller, J. P., 31, 58, 99
Muramoto, S., 115
Murray, H., 112

Napoli, D. S., 86
Nasio, J.-D., 170
Negri, A., 117
Neill, C., 32, 114, 140, 153
Nichols, C., 129
Nobus, D., 78, 179
Norval, A., 189
Novack, G., 87, 97
Novotny, C., 111

O'Connor, N., 146
Oliver, B., 119
Orbach, S., 187, 188, 192
Owens, C., 65

Palmer, S., 173
Palomera, V., 167
Pappenheim, B., 85
Paré, A., 19
Parker, I., 70, 75, 76, 162, 172
Passeron, J.-C., 117, 132
Pavón Cuéllar, D., 25, 65
Piaget, J., 77
Pilgrim, D., 67, 180
Pluth, E., 163
Pollock, G., 32, 34
Pound, M., 112, 140, 154, 155, 156, 157, 158, 161, 165
Power, L., 180
Proctor, G., 192
Pupavac, V., 129

Quinn, M., 78, 179

Rabaté, J.-M., 64
Ragland, E., 93, 159, 191
Rajchman, J., 40, 86, 138
Regnault, F., 71, 192
Reich, W., 187
Reinhard, K., 74, 157, 164–165
Renik, O., 111
Resnick, S. A., 30
Resnik, A., 186
Revelli, S., 70
Richards, B., 132
Richards, G., 64
Ricoeur, P., 159
Riha, R., 169

Riviere, J., 59
Roazen, P., 77, 154, 158
Roberts, J., 153, 162, 178
Robertson, R., 116
Rodríguez, L. S., 182
Rodríguez, S. A., 182
Rolnik, S., 72
Roper, B., 35
Rose, N., 15, 25, 112, 122, 177
Rosemont, F., 26, 46
Roudinesco, E., 21, 50, 75, 76, 98–99, 154, 156, 165, 166, 192
Roustang, F., 154–155
Rowan, J., 108, 124
Rowbotham, S., 191
Rowland, N., 135
Rustin, M., 72, 136, 140
Ryan, J., 146

Safouan, M., 73, 131
Said, E., 29, 40
Samuels, A., 31, 130, 141, 143, 170
Sanders, P., 192
Sandler, J., 98, 121, 167
Santner, E., 92, 93
Sato, T., 42
Saussure, F. de, 21, 22, 27
Sauvagnat, F., 50
Schepeler, E., 77
Schmideberg, M., 184
Schroder, T., 135
Schwarz, J., 129, 136
Scraton, P., 171
Sedgwick, P., 35
Segal, L., 191
Segal, N., 27
Seligman, M. E. P., 65, 123
Sells, M. A., 195
Seshadri-Crooks, K., 194
Seyan, K., 31
Sharpe, M., 143
Shingu, K., 101, 118, 158, 159, 164, 174
Shotter, J., 87
Showalter, E., 21, 47
Shuttleworth, A., 122
Shuttleworth, J., 72, 136
Singh, G., 114
Skinner, B. F., 86
Slattery, M., 155
Smith, C., 85
Smith, D., 72, 140
Smith, D. L., 160
Snell, R., 112, 114
Sohn-Rethel, A., 42, 121
Solano-Suárez, E., 49

Soler, C., 46, 54, 59, 60, 61, 169, 185
Spandler, H., 34, 177
Spence, D. P., 109
Spiegel, A., 18
Spillius, E. B., 111
Spinoza, B., 156
Spivak, G. C., 141
Stack, C., 112, 189
Stavrakakis, Y., 36, 75, 117, 120, 178, 189, 191
Stern, D. N., 71
Strachey, J., 33, 48–49, 71
Straker, G., 185
Strathern, M., 133
Sullivan, H. S., 188
Sulloway, F. J., 39
Symington, N., 154
Szasz, T., 17, 24

Tamboukou, M., 140
Target, M., 189
Teitelbaum, S. H., 68
Therborn, G., 97
Thompson-Brenner, H., 111
Thomson, M., 66
Thurston, L., 44, 158
Timms, E., 27
Tort, M., 64
Totton, N., 135, 152
Townshend, J., 121
Trist, E., 112
Trotsky, L., 116
Tudor, K., 100
Turner, B. S., 24

Ullman, C., 190
Ussher, J., 89

Vaillant, G. E., 133
Van Haute, P., 20, 71
Vanheule, S., 36, 70

Verhaeghe, P., 70, 85, 100, 112, 115, 190
Vicens, A., 186
Vogt, E., 156, 159, 161, 162
Voruz, V., 45, 61, 170

Wainwright, H., 191
Wake, N., 188
Walkerdine, V., 195
Wallerstein, I., 126
Wallerstein, R., 154
Wampold, B. E., 113
Ware, V., 113
Watson, E., 158, 170, 196
Waugaman, R. M., 184
Webb, R. E., 195
Went, R., 126
Westen, D., 111
White, J., 104, 125, 195
Wilden, A., 22
Winnicott, D. W., 155–156
Wolf, B., 45, 70
Wolfe, B., 172
Wolfenstein, E. V., 187
Wolff, R., 30
Wollstonecraft, M., 85
Wooldridge, A., 153
Worrall, M., 100
Worthington, A., 85, 170
Worthington, R. L., 113
Wright, E., 185

Young, R. M., 23, 25
Young-Eisendrath, P., 115

Zaretsky, E., 56, 89
Zeitlin, M., 74
Žižek, S., 42, 46, 48, 56, 78, 91, 92, 100, 122, 146, 147, 151, 156, 160, 162, 163, 170–171, 178, 186, 192, 194, 197
Zupančič, A., 137, 195
Zwart, H., 57

Subject index

Absences, 3, 4
'Absolute difference', 45–46
Academic institutions, 130–131, 132–133, 134–137
Accountability, 69, 83, 197
'Acts', 162–163, 195
Adaptation, 18–20, 35–36, 79, 106, 115, 164, 176–177
Affect, 133, 139, 140, 141, 148, see also Emotions
Agency, 23, 45, 114, 193–195
Aggression, 99, 101, 190
Alienation, 30, 87–90, 96–97, 121, 139, 151
  class, 148
  Dolto, 155
  escape from, 153
  father figure, 56
  Goethe, 43
  institutional sites, 55
  surplus value, 54
American Psychiatric Association, 18
Anatomy, 57–58
Anthropology, 58
Anti-psychiatry, 24, 26–27, 34–35
Anti-Semitism, 75, 155, 157, 165
Anxiety, analyst's, 146–148, 171
Archetypes, 8
Asymmetry, 179–181
Attachment, 188–189, 190, 191
Autonomy, 118

Behaviourism, 86
Binary operations, 25–26, 190
Biologistic perspective, 60
Biopolitics, 40, 82
Body/mind relationship, 24, 195, 196
Borderline personality disorder, 177

Borromean knot, 44–45, 159, 191, see also 'Knotting'
Boundaries, 4, 168, 171, 187
Buddhism, 164, 166, 174

Capitalism, 7, 12, 13–14, 64, 74, 101
  alienation, 87–88, 89, 97, 139, 151
  biopolitics, 40, 82
  birth of, 30
  Cartesian reasoning, 78, 79–80
  Christianity, 154
  development of, 102
  excess, 54
  failures to overthrow, 125
  feminisation of psychotherapy, 164
  feminist challenge to, 130
  feudal social links, 25
  free market ideology, 106
  hetero-patriarchal, 191
  ideological beliefs, 55–56
  individual rights, 86
  individualisation, 126
  'knotting', 93
  Marxist opposition to, 117, 118–119, 123, 149
  obsessional neurosis, 42, 43
  oppressive social forms, 38
  perverse subject, 94, 95
  'psy complex', 36
  'psychologisation', 65–66, 82
  psychology, 105, 151
  psychotherapy, 107, 127, 147–148
  revolution in subjectivity, 198–199
  science under, 76, 79, 80, 86
  sexual division of labour, 54–55
  technologies of the self, 150
  triumph of, 115, 173, 178
  women's resistance to, 91

Subject index

Cartesian cogito, 43, 79, 80
'Case presentations', 6, 33
Castration, 32, 49, 76, 190
   Christian imagery, 157
   as cut into power, 53, 59, 61, 140
   father figure, 56
   symbolic, 164
CBT, *see* Cognitive behavioural therapy
Child observation, 71–72
Christianity, 153–164, 165, 166
Class, 30–31, 53–54, 148, 194
   academic reproduction of, 132
   feudal relations, 33
   identity politics, 96
   sexualisation of, 32
   silent assumptions about, 38
Clinical practice, 2–6, 50, 55, 171–173
   antagonism structures, 178–179
   asymmetry, 179–181
   Christianity, 166
   content, 181–183
   'correct' speech, 128
   disjunction, 52, 148–149, 183–185
   ethics, 62
   politics of the personal, 196
   presence, 185–186
   'psychologisation', 66
   psychotherapy, 127
Cognitive behavioural therapy (CBT), 8, 66–67, 77, 129
Communication, 12, 69, 98, 125, 189, 197, *see also* Speech
Communism, 162
Compliance, 41
'Conceptual capsules', 37–38, 151, 152, 168
Consciousness, 26, 27, 43, 50
   Cartesian reasoning, 81
   psychosis, 104
   revolutionary, 162
Couch, use of, 2–3, 183–184
Counselling, 8, 135
Countertransference, 111, 129, 130, 138, 167–169
   academic work, 170
   clinical structure, 139–140
   embodiment, 195
   hysteria, 47
   materiality of the signifier, 60
   psychotic clients, 144
   relational psychoanalysis, 188
   supervision, 68
Critical theory, 8
'Cultural baggage', 172
Cultural imperialism, 194

Death drive, 40, 43, 53, 101, 102, 190
Delusion, 92
Democracy, 42, 65, 117, 177–178, 191, 192
Depth psychology, 8
Desire, 35, 49, 54
   object a, 197
   of the Other, 166, 193
   religious, 158
   women, 48
Diagnosis, 5, 24
   psychiatry, 17, 18
   psychoanalysis, 41
   psychosis, 44, 45
Diagnostic and Statistical Manual of Mental Disorders (DSM), 18, 40, 51, 67
Disavowal, 49, 51, 93, 95
Dreams, 47–48, 182, 197
DSM, *see* Diagnostic and Statistical Manual of Mental Disorders

Economic system, 54, 55, 106, 116, *see also* Capitalism
Ego, 26, 27, 37, 80, 82, 96, 98, *see also* Self
Ego psychology, 37, 48, 67, 74, 80, 121, 194
Embodiment, 195, 196
Emotional literacy, 111, 149
Emotions, 133, 143, 148, *see also* Affect
Empathy, 110, 189
Empiricism, 76, 125
'End of analysis', 10, 11, 161–162, 191, 198
Ending of therapeutic session, 4
Enlightenment, 19, 76, 85, 112
   binary operations, 26
   bourgeois ideology, 24
   postmodernism, 114
   rationality, 30
   reason, 78–80
   science, 173
   truth, 109, 110, 111
Epistemology, 38
Ethics, 6–7, 39–41, 53, 61, 62, 94, 190
   academic research, 136–137
   Dolto, 155
   femininity, 195
   individualised, 83
   Kantian, 137–138, 145
   politicised psychoanalysis, 187
   psychology, 84, 86, 106
   psychotherapy, 128, 131, 138
   relativism, 119

rights, 85–86
social change, 176–177
therapist identity, 132
uncertainty, 191
Eucharist, 161
Evidence, 3, 69, 71, 87, 136
Excess, 53–54, 55
Existentialism, 102
Experience, 34
'Extimacy', 70, 74, 126, 147

False consciousness, 42, 43, 95, 98, 105, 106, 121, 168
Family
'complexes', 58
nuclear, 44, 56–57
Fantasy, 52, 54, 55, 101, 136
antagonism structures, 179
child observation, 71–72
perversion, 95, 146
sexual, 181, 182, 187
Father, 31–32, 43
Christian imagery, 157
decline of paternal imago, 33, 56, 57, 157
'family romance', 57
Feedback, 69
Femininity, 141, 158–159, 170, 195–196
feminised therapeutic practice, 143
hysteria, 29, 90, 140, 142
idealisation of, 166, 169
as 'masquerade', 59
pathologisation of, 168
'repudiation of', 190
spirituality, 164, *see also* Gender; Sexual difference; Women
Feminisation, 20, 130, 143, 152, 164, 173–174, 195
Feminism, 9, 10, 11, 164, 169, 173–174, 195
Catholic, 165
emancipation of women, 85
patriarchal triangle, 31
personal as political, 188, 196
political activity, 130
psychotherapy, 152, 168
resistance to capitalism, 13–14, 91
socialist, 190–191
third wave, 170, *see also* Gender; Patriarchy
Fetishism, 95
Feudalism, 23, 25, 28, 30, 33–34
psychiatry, 43–44, 105
recognition, 70–71
transformation into capitalism, 82, 84

Foreclosure, 44, 45, 51, 57, 93
Free association, 2, 3, 35, 106
failure of, 4
Marxism, 121
obsessional neurosis, 41–42
Freedom, 28, 121, 122
Freudian psychoanalysis, 1, 11–12, 15–16, 19, 52–53, 76

Gender, 11, 32, 90–91, 163–164
'deep', 143, 147
hysteria, 20–21, 140–141
obsessional neurosis, 142
sex distinction, 84, 85, 102–103
as signifier, 58, *see also* Men; Patriarchy; Sexual difference; Sexuality; Women
'Generalised transference', 150, 170, 171, 173
'Glocalisation', 115–116, 126
Guilt, 47, 89, 102, 138, 182

Hate, 51–52
Heterosexuality, 85, 93–94, 103
'Hollow transference', 172–173
Holy Trinity, 159
Homosexuality, 49–50, 94, 146, 188
DSM, 51
paranoia as defence against, 46, 143
Human nature, 19, 23, 52–53, 78
Humanism, 8, 19–20, 77, 100
Hydraulic model, 129
Hypnotism, 20, 33
Hysteria, 5, 11, 20–21, 30, 46–49, 51, 91–92
alienation, 87, 89
analysts, 140–141
'conceptual capsules', 168
double-function, 158
femininity, 29, 140
induced through hypnosis, 33
as productive challenge, 39
subjection and revolt, 89–90
unsatisfied desire, 54
'Hystericisation', 35, 40, 46–49, 50, 104–105, 140–141, 195

Idealism, 59–60
Identification, 37, 47–48, 173
Identity, 73, 74–75, 96, 105, 193
language, 93
'psychologisation' of, 139
questioning of, 94
reflexive, 131–132

Ideology, 7, 8, 9, 62, 163, 175, 194
  bourgeois, 24, 25
  capitalist, 55–56
  'end of analysis', 198
  of expertise, 98
  hysteria, 90
  obsessional neurosis, 42
Imagery, religious, 157–159
the Imaginary, 29, 33, 97–99, 130, 144, 197
  analytic communication, 183
  gender, 58
  Holy Trinity, 159
  'knotting', 44, 93
  power relations, 191
  relational psychoanalysis, 189
  social bonds, 178
Imago, paternal, 33, 56, 57, 157
Incest, 49
Individualism, 87, 174
Internalisation, 68, 69, 82, 137
International Psychoanalytical Association (IPA), 60, 64, 72–74, 77, 80, 99, 153–155, 165
'Interpellation', 139, 147
Interpretation, 61, 103–105, 106
  analyst/analysand relationship, 185
  'cut' of, 33–34, 198
  transference, 59, 182–183
Intersubjectivity, 49, 55, 110, 113, 129, 130, 189
Introjection, 82
IPA, see International Psychoanalytical Association
Islam, 165–166

Jews, 20, 74–75, 165, 194, see also Judaism
Jouissance, 42, 47, 52, 53–55, 83, 102
  capitalist ideology, 55–56
  of the Other, 195
  perverse subject, 49, 145
  religious desire, 158
  'training analysis', 74
  women, 48, 142
Judaism, 161, 164, 165

Kantian ethics, 137–138, 145
'Knotting', 44–45, 93, see also Borromean knot
Knowledge, 21–22, 91, 99, 101, 103, 183
  academic institutions, 134, 136
  Cartesian separation, 78
  'end of analysis', 191
  epistemological questions, 38
  ethics, 62
  psychiatry, 23, 24, 117–118

psychology, 65, 72, 120
psychosis, 45
psychotherapeutic, 117, 118, 119, 123–124, 131, 133
scientific, 76, 78, 80, 119
sharing of, 174–175
'training analysts', 73
truth, 109–110
unconscious, 137

Language, 12, 21–22, 27, 30, 34
  'absolute difference', 45–46
  binary operations, 25–26
  failure of representation, 29
  'knotting', 93
  as material force, 29, 60
  supervision, 69
  the unconscious, 108
  wall of, 97, 98, see also Metalanguage; Signifiers
Libido, 53
Life drive, 53
Linguistics, 21–22, 25, 52, see also Language; Signifiers
Loss, 28–29
Love, 48, 51–52, 94, 155

Marxism, 9, 10, 11, 116–117, 118–119, 171
  capitalist rebellion against, 107
  collectivity, 126
  psychoanalytic complicity with, 149
  psychotherapy, 123–124
  relational psychoanalysis, 190
  resistance to capitalism, 13–14, 91
  revolutionary, 178
  Stalinist, 107, 116, 121–122, 123, 126
Masculinity, 43–44, 46, 53, 158–159, 195
  analysts, 169–170
  feminised therapeutic practice, 143
  as 'masquerade', 59
  obsessional, 89, 174, see also Gender; Men; Sexual difference
Master-slave dialectic, 23, 70–71, 100, 192–193
  death drive, 101
  'obsessionalisation', 41
  psychiatry, 39–40
Materialism, 59–60, 87, 108, 119, 178
Meaning, 13, 16, 122
Mediation, 12, 32
Medicine, 17–21, 23–24
Men, 90, 140, 142, 163, see also Masculinity
Mental automatism, 21
Mentalisation, 82

Subject index

Metalanguage, 36, 69–70, 88, 97, 100
Mind/body relationship, 24, 195, 196
Mindfulness, 96
Mirror stage, 99
Monetary exchange, 179–180
Mother, 32, 56
Multiculturalism, 126

Name-of-the-Father, 44, 52, 57, 62, 93, 143, 157
Naming, 57, 120
Narcissism, 94–95, 146
Nationalism, 40–41, 126
Negativity, 178, 190, 191
Neurosis, 5, 11, 51, 104, 146
  diagnosis, 18
  fantasy structures, 94
  sex, 20–21, see also Obsessional neurosis
New Ageism, 164
Normalisation, 112, 115
Nuclear family, 44, 56–57

'Object a', 28, 54, 56, 100, 124–125, 146, 179, 197
Object relations, 34, 37, 82, 129, 186, 187, 188
Objectification, 100, 103
Obsessional neurosis, 5, 11, 39, 41–44, 51, 91–92
  alienation, 87, 88, 90
  analysts, 141–143
  'conceptual capsules', 168
  fantasy, 146
  Freud on, 48
  interpretation, 104
  jouissance, 54
  masculinity, 89, 140
'Obsessionalisation', 40, 41–44, 47, 50
Oedipal relations, 32, 43
Oedipus complex, 31, 33, 43, 51
Other, 13, 35, 36, 47, 101, 159
  analyst as, 147
  capitalist ideology, 55–56
  consistency of the, 109, 120
  desire, 166, 193
  discourse of the, 105, 108, 113
  femininity as, 196
  'hystericisation', 48
  jouissance of the, 54, 195
  perversion, 49, 146
  postmodern psychoanalysis, 113
  psychosis, 144
  relational psychoanalysis, 190
  the symbolic, 100
  veiled women, 166

Parallel processing, 68
Paranoia, 46, 143
Pathology, 15, 83, 115
  focus on, 31
  psychiatry, 39, 50, 57
  reductionism, 16–17, 30
Patriarchy, 31, 32, 58, 84–85, 130, 195
  capitalism, 89, 90, 91
  Name-of-the-Father, 93
  nuclear family, 44
  rebellion against, 168
Penis, 57–58, 95, see also Phallus
Performativity, 16, 182, 183
Perversion, 5, 11, 49–50, 51, 94–95, 104
  alienation, 87
  analysts, 145–148
  diagnosis, 18
  as transgression of bond with others, 39
'Perversionalisation', 40, 49–50, 104
Phallus, 52, 54, 57–58, 101, 179
  castration, 49, 59
  desubstantialisation, 62
  disavowal, 95
Pharmacological remedies, 7
Phenomenology, 23, 52, 76, 102, 129
Phobia, 50
Physical contact, 4
Pleasure, 42, 61, 83, 101–102
Politics, 10, 51–52, 62, 79, 176
  of the personal, 196
  postmodern psychoanalysis, 112
  relational psychoanalysis, 187, see also Marxism
Pop psychology, 7, 8, 108
Positivism, 23–24, 76, 77
Postmodernism, 112–113, 114–115, 160
Power
  language and, 21
  relational psychoanalysis, 190–192, 193
  reproduction of power relations, 95, 103
'Practical psychology', 66
Pragmatism, 76, 125
Presence, 185–186
'Pre-transference', 171–172
'Psy complex', 15, 16, 25, 36, 82
'Psychiatrisation', 40, 105
Psychiatry, 7, 10–11, 15, 37–38, 49, 105, 128
  'case presentations', 33
  'conceptual capsules', 151
  doctor/patient division, 122
  ethics, 39–41
  experience, 34
  knowledge, 23, 24, 117–118
  master signifiers, 120

materialism, 60
as medicine, 17–21
mental hygiene, 51
object a, 124–125
pathology, 16–17, 57
psychiatric frame, 30, 37
psychology relationship, 63–64, 123
psychotherapy relationship, 108
reality, 35
religion, 152
social change, 176–177
social control, 24
structure, 36–37
symptoms, 29
theory of self, 12
Psychodynamic therapy, 194
'Psychologisation', 65–67, 75, 80–82, 83, 87, 110
  Cartesian reasoning, 79
  'generalised' transference, 170
  'glocalisation', 115–116
  of identities, 139
  rise in, 126
  the unconscious, 104, 105
Psychology, 7, 10–11, 63–83, 96, 103, 128
  academic institutions, 131
  capitalism, 105, 151
  democratising impulse, 64–65
  ethics, 84, 86, 106
  knowledge, 120
  mentalisation, 82
  natural science, 75–76
  objects of study, 97, 122–123, 125
  psychiatry relationship, 63–64, 123
  psychotherapy relationship, 108
  social change, 176–177
  supervision, 67–69
  theory of self, 12
Psychosis, 5, 11, 39, 44–46, 51, 92–93
  alienation, 87
  ambiguities, 104
  analysts, 143–145
  Christian imagery, 158
  diagnosis, 18, see also 'Psychoticisation'
Psychotherapeutic capital, 110, 117–118, 120, 122, 126, 127, 130
Psychotherapy, 7, 8, 10–11, 107–127, 149
  class, 194
  clinical structure, 138, 139–140
  cognitive terminology, 133
  'conceptual capsules', 152
  ethics, 128, 131, 138
  feminisation of, 143, 164, 195
  feminist, 168
  hysteria, 141

Marxism, 123–124
object a, 124, 125
obsessional neurosis, 143
perversion, 145–148
postmodern, 114, 115
psychoanalysis distinction, 109, 110, 112, 122, 197–198
psychosis, 144–145
representation, 107–108, 117
resistance to, 129
signifiers, 120–121
social change, 176–177
state regulation, 135
theory of self, 12
training, 68, 69, 130–131, 134
'Psychoticisation', 40, 44–46, 50, 57, 104
Public/private separation, 173–174

Queer theory, 170, 196

Race, 29
Radical orthodoxy, 160
Rationalism, 27, 87
Rationality, 30, 66, 113–114, 133
the Real, 29, 33, 88, 130, 197
  gender, 58
  Holy Trinity, 159
  'knotting', 44, 93
  negativity, 191
  relational psychoanalysis, 189
  social bonds, 178
  'two body' psychology, 129
Reality, 34–36, 52, 136, 178, 197
  alienation, 88
  commonsensical view of, 111
  ego's perception of, 80
  the imaginary, 97, 98
  suffused with fantasy, 112
Reason, 78–80, 159–160
Recognition, 38, 39, 70–71, 100
Reflexive identity, 131–132
Regulation, 105–106, 135
Relational psychoanalysis, 111, 176, 186–190
  agency, 193–195
  dialectics of authority, 192–193
  power, 190–192
Relativism, 119
Religion, 152–153, 168
  Buddhism, 164, 166, 174
  Christianity, 153–164, 165, 166
  Islam, 165–166
  Judaism, 161, 164, 165
Repetition, 59–60, 102

Subject index

Representation, 27, 29, 60, 107–108, 117, 137
Repression, 51, 92, 93, 129
Resistance, 41, 129, 143
 analysts, 100, 115, 175
 to capitalism, 91, 123, 149, 173
 hysteria, 46
Retroactivity, 71, 185
Rights, 85–86
Roman Catholicism, 155–156, 165

Scholastics, 156
Science, 5–6, 19, 86–87
 Enlightenment, 173
 faith, 77, 80
 medical, 23–24
 psychology, 75–76
 signifiers, 174
Stalinism, 119
Secularism, 164, 165, 166, 173–174
Self, 8, 12, 129, 193
 enlightened, 111–112
 object a, 197
 psychotherapy, 108, 127
 technologies of the, 150, *see also* Ego
Self-help programmes, 7, 8, 66
Self-reflection, 6
Semiology, 22–23, *see also* Signifiers
Sex
 class relations, 32
 focus on, 31
 gender distinction, 85, 102–103
 heterosexual intercourse, 58
 jouissance, 53
 neurosis, 20–21
 psychiatry, 17
 reductionism, 15–16, 30
 silent assumptions about, 38
 truth grounded in, 26, *see also* Gender; Sexuality; Sexuation
Sexual difference, 54, 140, 141, 146, 164, 168
 antagonism structures, 179
 gender distinction, 84, 85
 performative account of, 170, *see also* Gender
Sexual division of labour, 54–55
Sexuality, 7, 51, 93–94
 perversion, 50
 psychosis, 46
 women, 48, *see also* Gender; Homosexuality; Sex
Sexuation, 140–141, 142, 146, 158, 163, 164, 165, 168
'Shallow transference', 172

Shame, 89, 102, 182
Signifiers, 22–23, 25, 27, 101, 108, 119–120
 'absolute difference', 45
 alienation, 96–97
 antagonism structures, 179
 chains of, 92
 connections between, 77–78
 eroticised signification, 58–59
 family structure, 56, 57
 formalisation of speech, 52
 the imaginary, 98
 psychotherapy, 112, 120–121
 reduction to nonsense, 179, 183
 re-enactment of, 95
 relational psychoanalysis, 189
 religious, 174
 repetition, 59, 60
 representation, 60
 'training analysts', 73
 transference, 169–170
Signs, 21, 22
Social change, 6, 10, 11, 66, 176–177, 187, 188
Social control, 24
Social practices, 171–173
Social relations, 62, 198
 capitalism, 55
 power, 190–192
 sexualisation of, 52
 transformation of, 116
Social theory, 9, 10, 79, 170, 178
Socialism, 116, 126, 188
Speech, 3, 4–5, 13, 41, 98
 asymmetry, 180–181
 content, 181–182
 'correct', 128
 disjunction, 183
 existence of the Other, 101
 interpretation, 61
 psychoanalytic training, 30
 psychotic, 93
 temporality, 184
Spirituality, 7, 10–11, 12, 150, 152–153, 196
 femininity, 164
 'generalised transference', 173
 renewed engagement with, 178
 signifiers, 174
Stalinism, 107, 116, 119, 121–122, 123, 126
State regulation, 105–106, 135
Structural linguistics, 21–22, 25, 52
Structuralism, 25, 58, 76
Structure, 22, 34, 36–37, 38
 family, 56, 57
 subjectivity, 176

'Subject of the enunciation', 81–82, 162
'Subject of the statement', 81–82
Subjectivity, 9, 13, 87, 164
  analytic relationship, 139
  clinical structures, 171
  DSM categories, 67
  feminisation of, 152
  ideological prescriptions, 174
  'individual' aspect of, 151
  master-slave dialectic, 192
  mindfulness, 96
  politicisation of, 187
  'psy complex', 25
  'psychologisation', 65, 66
  psychotherapy, 107, 130
  relational aspect of, 193
  revolution in, 10, 55, 123, 149, 176, 198–199
  theological conceptions of, 150
Super-ego, 91, 138
Supervision, 67–69
Surplus value, 54, 94
Surrealism, 26–27
the Symbolic, 29, 33, 92, 98, 99–101, 197
  analytic communication, 183–184
  gender, 58
  Holy Trinity, 159
  'knotting', 44, 93
  perversion, 145
  power relations, 191
  psychosis, 144
  relational psychoanalysis, 189
  sexual difference, 146
  sexuation, 163
  social bonds, 178
  'two body' psychology, 129

Theory, 2, 6, 133
'Therapeutic alliance', 177, 178–179
'Therapeutic community', 177
'Therapeutisation', 110, 129, 130, 141
'Third term', 31–32
Time, 134, 184–185
Training, 30–31, 32, 69–70, 72–74
  'medical psychology', 63–64
  psychotherapy, 130–131, 132, 134, 135
  reflexive identity, 132
  supervision, 67–69
  transference, 173

Transference, 3, 52, 130, 167–169
  analytic speech, 181
  'generalised', 150, 170, 171, 173
  'hollow', 172–173
  hysteria, 46
  interpretation, 182–183
  monetary exchange, 180
  object relations, 37
  perversion, 95
  pop psychology, 7
  presence, 185–186
  psychoanalytic materialism, 60–61
  psychotic clients, 144
  relational psychoanalysis, 188–189
  repetition, 59
  'shallow', 172
  of signification, 169–170
  social practices, 171–173
  supervision, 68–69
  'transferential derivatives', 166–167
Trauma, 28–29, 71, 115, 124, 171
Trinity, 159
Truth, 12, 26, 109–110, 112, 162
  language and, 27–28
  scientific, 75, 76, 86–87
'Two body' psychology, 129, 138

the Unconscious, 12, 26–28, 81, 82, 114
  Cartesian cogito, 43
  as discourse of the Other, 105, 108, 113
  interpretation, 33, 104–105
  perversion, 104
  psychoanalytic materialism, 60–61
  psychosis, 45, 143–144
  psychotherapy, 133
  temporal space of analysis, 184, 185

Veil, 166
Voice, 34

Women, 46, 84–85, 90–91, 163
  diagram of sexuation, 142
  hysteria, 47, 48, 140–141
  idealisation of, 173–174
  jouissance, 54
  psychosis, 143
  veiled, 166, see also Femininity; Gender; Sexual difference